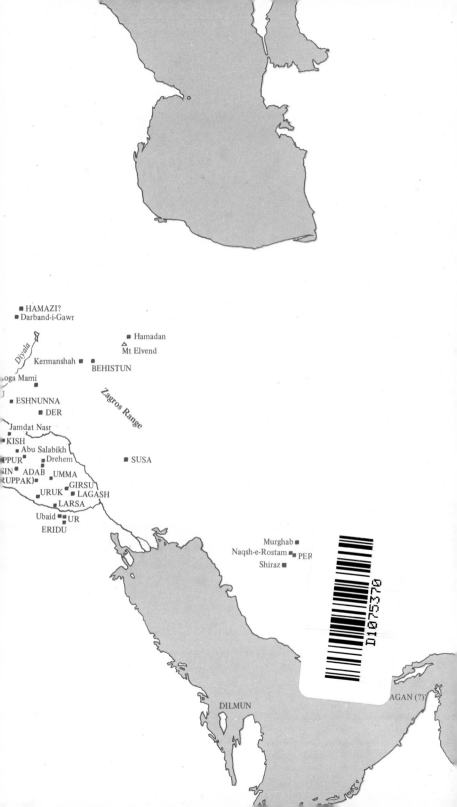

HAMAZI?
Darband-i-Gawr

Hamadan
Mt Elvend

Diyala

Kermanshah
BEHISTUN

oga Mami
J

Zagros Range

ESHNUNNA
DER

Jamdat Nasr
KISH
Abu Salabikh
PPUR
Drehem
SUSA
SIN
ADAB
UMMA
(RUPPAK)
GIRSU
URUK
LAGASH
LARSA
Ubaid
UR
ERIDU

Murghab
Naqsh-e-Rostam
PER
Shiraz

DILMUN

AGAN (?)

EBLA

EBLA

AN ARCHAEOLOGICAL ENIGMA

CHAIM BERMANT AND MICHAEL WEITZMAN

WEIDENFELD AND NICOLSON
LONDON

Contents

Illustrations

Acknowledgements

In preparing this book we have had cause to be grateful to more people than we can name; in fact, anyone in whose company either of us was seen during 1977 was, in all likelihood, being pressed for assistance of one sort or another. But there are some whose names it would be utterly wrong not to mention. Many of our queries were answered, and valuable suggestions made, by Professor M. Boyce, Dr R. J. Coggins, Miss T. J. Firbank, Professor D. N. Freedman, Mr A. Garcia, Professor I. J. Gelb, Dr M. J. Geller, Mr J. D. Hawkins, Amélie Kuhrt, Mr T. C. Mitchell, Dr R. Saville, Dr E. Sollberger and Professor D. J. Wiseman. These scholars are not of course responsible for any shortcomings in the book, and it should perhaps go on record that no help was received, nor indeed solicited, from any of them in respect of Chapter 1. Mr E. Hughes supplied us with some of the most recent literature, which might otherwise have escaped us, and Miss F. Qalaji checked some of our translations from Arabic. During our visits to Rome we were shown every courtesy by Professor G. Pettinato, and by his charming assistant Vanna Biga; the extent of our indebtedness to Professor Pettinato, and also to Professor Matthiae, the Director of Excavations, can best be judged from the book itself. Every possible help was extended to us at the British Library, Dr Williams's Library, and at many libraries within the University of London: the Institute of Archaeology, the Institute of Historical Research, King's College, the School of Oriental and African Studies, Senate House, and University College. Mrs Sharon Ross remained her efficient and unruffled self, even with the intrusions of cuneiform upon our sufficiently illegible script. Mr J. Ramsay Homa, an inveterate traveller and archaeology enthusiast, who visited the Tell Mardikh site, has been kind enough to let us reproduce some of his photographs in this book, and finally we are indebted – though there were moments when our feeling towards him amounted to one of less than gratitude – to Mr Peter Crookston of the London *Observer*, who commissioned the article which gave rise to this book.

CHAIM BERMANT
MICHAEL WEITZMAN
London 1978

Preface

The discovery of a vast palace archive at Tell Mardikh/Ebla in 1975 caused a stir which reverberated well beyond the academic community and which reverberates still. It revealed a civilization which had remained lost and almost forgotten for nearly four thousand years, pushed back the frontiers of recorded history and promised to contribute to the understanding of the cultural development of the human race. Moreover, its very location in northern Syria, by the road to Damascus, aroused hopes that it might (which in some minds were converted to certainties that it did) throw new light on the world of the Bible.

Sharing the excitement engendered by Ebla we (singly or together) visited Syria, spoke to Professor Paulo Matthiae, the head of the expedition, Professor Giovanni Pettinato, its epigrapher, the Director General of Syria's Antiquities and Museums, and others principally concerned both in the excavations and in the evaluation of the discoveries, and have studied all the texts available to date on the subject, with the aim of describing the Ebla discoveries and assessing their significance, not least in regard to the Bible. To this end we have included an introduction to cuneiform, the script in which the Ebla archive was written, and a chapter on the uses and limitations of archaeology as a guide in Bible studies. And finally, we have attempted to outline the early history of the Near East so that the story of Ebla may be read in the context of surrounding events.

CHAPTER 1

What's in a Name?

They were both Italian, both professors, both short and a trifle stocky, and there the similarities ended. Professor Pettinato's glasses shone with the glint of revelation. Professor Matthiae's pale blue eyes looked almost apprehensive and he stood at the back of the hall with his hand to his mouth as if afraid that he might emit an involuntary cry. Both had come upon a momentous discovery. Matthiae seemed shaken by it. Pettinato revelled in it as, with chalk in hand, and talking rapidly in broken English, he filled the half acre of blackboard with some of his more controversial findings.

It was a hot day – 'hotter than in Syria', said Pettinato later – but the large and distinguished audience attending the 1976 Assyriological Congress in Birmingham sat on the edge of their seats and craned forward as name after name came into view – spelt out in staccato syllables as in ancient cuneiform – Mi-kà-ià, Ish-mà-il, and, most enigmatic of all, Ish-ra-il. This followed the announcement in an American paper of the incidence of names like Ab-ra-mu and Da-u-dum. Did they correspond to the biblical names of Micah, Ishmael, Israel, Abraham and David? One biblical scholar and archaeologist, Professor David Noel Freedman of the University of Michigan, was convinced that they did: 'Many, if not most, of the important names in the Bible have already been identified and very often in almost identical form,' he said. 'If the patriarchs and their descendants did not actually live in Ebla, they clearly belonged to the same cultural tradition and came from an area in which that tradition survived and exerted a powerful influence.'[1]

It was this factor which had taken the work of Matthiae and Pettinato out of the learned journals and into the daily

press, and found them blinking uneasily in front of television
and cine-cameras. It was this factor too, which had introduced
differences between them, threatening to disrupt what was beginning to look like an historic partnership. Throughout 1976,
when the full news of their discovery was first made public,
they were inseparable. By the summer of 1977 they were hardly
on speaking terms.

Publicity is often necessary to the success of an archaeological expedition, which almost inevitably involves the use of
public funds, but Matthiae, at least, was troubled by the direction it was taking and the sort of headlines which his work
was attracting – 'Tablets Shed New Light on the Bible'[2] –
'Clay Tablet Names Sodom and Gomorrah'[3] – 'Hebrew
Patriarch Link Discovered'[4] – 'The Abraham Connection'.[5]

Professor Matthiae was at pains to point out that nothing
brought up in the course of his excavations warranted such
stories:

The tablets cover a period a thousand years before Abraham, and
a thousand years, even in the fourth millennium before Christ, was
a very, very long time. They tell us much, but what they don't tell
us – what they *can't* tell us – is whether the Bible is true or not. They
have nothing to do with the Bible, at least not directly, and what
we have here is not a biblical expedition. If we have tablets with
legends similar to those of the Bible it means only that such legends
existed round here long before the Bible.[6]

But nothing he could say could staunch the flow of speculation. One paper picked up the story from another, adding its
own touch of elaboration and it was not long before it was
picked up by the fundamentalists – who believe that the Bible,
being the word of God, is wholly free from error – and who,
in America at least, are not an obscure handful of crackpots,
but a growing and influential section of the church. The Ebla
discoveries, declared a booklet sponsored by the *Christian
Beacon*, 'shatter the whole liberal-modernist approach to the
Scriptures, their views of the structure and making of the Bible
and their views concerning the development of the religion of
Israel.' It went on: 'Everywhere the Bible is being discussed
as never before concerning its authority, reliability and in-
errancy. Numerous translations have appeared which are

questioned pro and con. Now the stones are crying out as the Lord said they would.'[7]

Such euphoria is easy to explain. The Bible intrigues even where it no longer convinces. Many believe in it as the word of God. Others would like to believe in it and, while doubting its divine origin, are unable to regard it as myth. Others still cherish it as part of their heritage and any discovery which suggests that the Bible touched upon actual events and real people must catch the headlines. And here there were both, for Ebla had not only come up with Abrahams and Ishmaels, but with Hazor and Meggido and Ashdod and Gaza and Jerusalem (some five centuries or more before it is mentioned elsewhere), and even the cities of the vale of Sidim in the order that they are listed in Genesis 14:2: Sodom and Gomorrah and Admah and Zeboim and Zoar. 'The similarity of the city names', wrote Professor Freedman, 'and the duplication of the order in which they occur cannot be coincidence.'[8] Few believers were disposed to think it was. Ebla had made the word flesh.

Before 1974 few had heard of Ebla and it was less than a household word even among scholars Matthiae knew of it, but it can hardly be said that he was particularly concerned to find it. Indeed when he started on his excavations in Syria he was a little like Columbus, for he did not have too clear an idea where he was or what he was looking for and he was at first uncertain as to what he discovered. His basic aim was to put Syria on the archaeological – and cultural – map. While scholars elbowed one another among the ruins of ancient Egypt, Mesopotamia and Palestine, Syria felt neglected and, indeed, was neglected. The landscape was blistered with tells – mounds covering the ruins of ancient settlements – crying out for a spade and he felt, after a tour of the country in 1963, that northern Syria, in particular, harboured numerous examples of ancient urban civilization.[9] He had alighted on Tell Mardikh because its massive proportions, the potsherds scattered about the surface and, as we shall see, a major archaeological find just below the surface, held out the richest prospects, but he had no idea he was standing on top of Ebla. He began digging in 1964. It was 1968 before he established his location and 1974 before he achieved his breakthrough, since when it has been almost impossible to open an archaeological publication without encountering a reference to Ebla.

Working in the remains of what had been the royal palace, he stumbled upon an archive of thousand upon thousand of clay tablets, some neatly stacked on their edges for easy retrieval, some cracked, some crumbling into dust, but together comprising one of the most remarkable archaeological finds of modern times. The gold, the bronze, the statues, the very stones of the city which he had uncovered hitherto, sank into insignificance. There is nothing more important to the archaeologist than the written word, and here was a vast library. The tablets, of baked clay, vary in size – the smallest are roundish and under two inches across while the largest are about thirteen inches square – and look like overdone pastry, with little notches on them like one might find on the back of a digestive biscuit. These notches are cuneiform, a mode of writing current in the ancient Near East for three thousand years.

It was at this point that Giovanni Pettinato entered the story. Pettinato who was trained at the Biblical Institute of the University of Naples and Heidelberg University (where he specialized in Assyriology), had already helped Matthiae to decipher a cuneiform inscription found on a basalt statue, and he was now invited to decipher the tablets. It was a daunting task, not merely because of their number, but because two languages were used in writing them, one of them Sumerian, the other completely unknown. Pettinato found the key when he established that this unknown language was related to Hebrew and other Semitic languages common to the area; he first called it Palaeo-Canaanite and then simply Eblaite.

Nearly twenty thousand tablets or fragments (not all of them substantial) have been found, and though few have yet been translated, they readily confirmed Matthiae's belief that Syria was not 'merely a crossroads, but rather an original great cultural centre of the ancient world'.[10] It is perhaps not an exaggeration to suggest that, as a result of his discoveries, much of the history of the ancient Near East may have to be re-written.

Pettinato at first only scanned the tablets. As he began to translate them in detail, differences developed between him and Matthiae on the chronology of the city and its rulers, the sort of differences which can, and frequently do develop between sensitive scholars working in the same field and which would no doubt have been amicably resolved, but added to them came the trouble over what the London *Observer* has called 'the Abraham connection'.[11] Whether such a connection exists at all is yet to be proved, and existing evidence suggests that it is unlikely, but the fact that it has been mooted at all has occasioned the trouble.

All excavations in the Near and Middle East take place in what are called 'politically sensitive areas', and there are few areas more sensitive than Syria. Excavations, moreover, are expensive and those at Ebla are particularly so, for they involve a large site, employ a large work-force and call upon many skills, and the expedition could hardly have got off the ground without the ready support of the Italian Foreign Ministry and, in particular, the backing of Italy's Ambassador to Damascus, Signor Carlo Perrone Capano, who was determined, as Matthiae put it, 'that Italian archaeology in Syria should no longer be silent'.[12] The Syrians, too, were eager to help and the Director General of Antiquities, and the Director of Museums, the Muhafiz of the Muhafazah of Idlib, and the Mudir of the Nahiya of Saraqib (the district and sub-district in which Ebla was situated), put all their facilities at the disposal of the expedition. Public servants, military and civilian, came and went to ease their path. Red tape was cut. Restrictions were eased. Matthiae and his colleagues must have felt that they were heading a goodwill mission – which in a sense they were – rather than an archaeological expedition. It must, therefore, have been something of a shock that when, after twelve years of silent digging, their work finally reached the public eye, it was through the discovery that the early Syrians may have been Jews, or vice versa.

One might have thought that events which may – or may not – have taken place some four and a half thousand years ago could reasonably be assigned to the past, but not in the Near or Middle East, where utterances which may – or may not – have been made millennia ago are still flourished as title-deeds, and when some of the stories circulating in the American press reached Damascus, they caused disquiet and displeasure. Nor did they do anything to improve the relationship between Matthiae and Pettinato. The former is a retiring, donnish figure of German origin, given to few words and long silences. The latter is a bouncy Sicilian, inclined to rush in where Matthiae certainly feared to tread.

Pettinato is in no sense a biblical fundamentalist, but once he discovered that Eblaite belonged to the North-West Semitic group of languages (of which Hebrew is one) it was natural for his eye to alight on those names and other features which might be echoed in the Old Testament. He did not insist that there was a direct connection, but they did, as he put it, 'illustrate the relationship of the Eblaite world to the biblical ambience of a later period'.[13] This was not all that distant from Matthiae's appraisal of the findings, but Pettinato gave them a stress which Matthiae did not, and what is perhaps more to the point, Matthiae has to live with the Syrians and Pettinato does not. As the story snowballed and fundamentalists waved it as proof of the literal accuracy of the Bible, Pettinato found that the flow of photographs, from which he deciphered the tablets, began to dry up. About 1,630 tablets were discovered and photographed in the 1976 season, but no photographs were sent to him. Then, without prior warning or consultation, he was informed that a decision had been taken to form an international committee of 'qualified scholars' to work on the tablets.

Pettinato was at first inclined to dismiss it with an ironic shrug. There was, as far as he knew, only one person qualified in this field – himself. 'Any scholar called in will have to go back to school and learn the new language which I have called Palaeo-Canaanite,' he said. 'It would take about four years and I maintain that they should come and study with me in Rome.'[14] Matthiae, however, persisted with the scheme, and Pettinato, feeling his life's work threatened, circulated an anguished plea for support to other scholars in the same field:

Dear Colleague,
... Since 1974 I have been dealing with the decipherment and study of the royal archive of Ebla, an archive which is revealing data of the greatest interest to our disciplines. Whilst I was engaged, then, in these studies, ... a letter of July 15th 1977, from the Directorate of

the Mission, informed me of the decision to set up an international committee 'for the systematic study of the Ebla texts'...

Such a decision, taken – as appears from the letter – at the proposal of the General Directorate of Antiquities of Syria was, despite my inclusion in that very committee, made without my knowledge.

Neither my activities as an Assyriologist, nor my work on the decipherment of the Ebla texts explain, in my opinion, the absence of consultations, which strikes at my dignity and independence as a scholar. This initiative, moreover, is the culmination of an uninterrupted series of difficulties which for a long time have prevented me from pursuing my researches in peace.

I appeal, therefore, to you, in the knowledge that you will want, in these circumstances, to give me the comfort of your guidance and solidarity.

Alas, he was to receive neither. Scholars do not care to get caught up in political or personal quarrels and this carried every indication of both, even to those who had so lost touch with the academic grapevine as to be unaware that things between Pettinato and Matthiae were not all they should be. The turn of events could not have taken Pettinato by surprise, because some days before he had received the letter, various team members had expressed their fears that the Syrians might expel the expedition if it came up with proof of an early Hebrew presence.[15] It now seemed as if Matthiae and Pettinato would have to go their different ways, but then events once again took a new turn.

In September 1977, the Damascus daily *Tishrin* carried a long article on the expedition under the heading: 'The Ebla Discoveries Arouse Disagreement in International Scientific and Archaeological Circles' and included an interview with Dr Afif Bahnasi, Director General of Antiquities and Museums, in which he spoke of 'the antiquity of the Arab nation and the deep-rootedness of its civilization' as revealed by the Ebla tablets. Asked about rumours 'of the fabrication of scientific and historical evidence in relation to Ebla', Dr Bahnasi replied: 'It is unfortunate that there are people, forgers and perverters of knowledge, who have tried for political motives serving the furtherance of Zionism to reverse the order of events and assert that the antiquities of Ebla and its writings came later than the Old Testament ... One scholar,

called Freedman, started to copy wrong information in the
name of members of the Italian archaeological delegation and
the American press resorted to Freedman's misinforma-
tion.'[16] One paper, he added, suggested that the discoveries
had confirmed the existence of the Jewish patriarchs, 'and this
sensational and false information had various effects':

Firstly: the western reader who based his historical culture
on his knowledge of the Old Testament became very eager to find
out about Ebla, but only in terms of the Old Testament. Secondly:
The Zionists wanted to exploit this misinterpretation in order to
carry through an aim which had long attracted them: to establish
their existence through historical confirmation. In fact, Ebla has
given and will continue to give historical truths and facts, not the
forged or misinterpreted 'proofs' that the Zionists would like to
make of it.

The Old Testament, he went on, was a tissue of legends written
by the Jewish elders from about 537 BC[17] during the Babylonian exile, who drew on the folklore of the surrounding
peoples, and this was now clearly attested by the Ebla tablets.
     He also took pains to point out that 'some of the pro-Zionist
American papers had attributed to Pettinato erroneous statements which might have suggested that he had fallen into the
net of Zionist lies', and that Pettinato had assured him that
statements based on supposed relationships between the
proper names mentioned in the Bible and Ebla 'had been
wished on him'.
     To this end *Tishrin* printed the replica of a declaration (in
French) which Professor Pettinato had sent to Dr Bahnasi,
along with an Arabic version:

The documents which were brought to light in Tell Mardikh-Ebla
during the excavation campaigns from 1974 to 1976, and which I
had the honour of studying and deciphering, bear ever greater testimony to the central role played by Syria in the third millennium
BC, both in terms of the outstanding and fully authentic historical
materials which these documents present, and in terms of the existence of a new Semitic language, the oldest of the Semitic languages
vouchsafed us until now.
     As for the so-called relationships with the texts of the Old Testa-
ment, I feel it my duty to make it clear, once for all, that the news

put out by the press and the interference of our colleagues across the ocean, have exaggerated matters to the point of tendentiousness and danger, for which I wish not only to disclaim any responsibility whatsoever, but also to put other scholars on their guard.

Even if it were true that the study of proper names at Ebla left room for possible comparisons with the proper names in the Old Testament, at times subsequent to those of Ebla, there is no justification for regarding the Eblaites as ancestors of Israel. That the North-West Semitic proper names of Ebla should bear inherent characteristics which render them comparable to the proper names of all other North-West Semitic civilizations is too obvious to occasion any surprise or wonder. It would be a mistake, repeating the tendentious interpretations made in the past, for us to try to re-study the ancient world specifically in the light of Ebla.

I have previously emphasised my viewpoint many times through my lectures, reports to international conferences and in my articles.

The Freedman referred to by Dr Bahnasi, was, of course, Professor Freedman, who, it is safe to presume, was also one of 'our colleagues across the ocean', who, according to Pettinato, 'interfered' with and 'exaggerated to the point of tendentiousness and danger' his innocent observations on Eblaite onomastics.

Professor Freedman, Director of the Program of Studies in Religion at the University of Michigan, and Editor of the *Biblical Archaeologist*, is unabashed by these charges and says quite simply that he has been singled out as a scapegoat. He is of Jewish origin, but not a Jew, or a Zionist, but a Presbyterian who, while believing in the divinity of Christ, is not a fundamentalist in his approach to the Bible. He was almost instinctively alive to the importance of the Ebla tablets as soon as he heard of them. He called on Pettinato and Matthiae in Rome at the first opportunity and visited the excavations in Syria and it was while in Syria that Pettinato told him of a discovery which, says Freedman, 'has changed my whole life'.[18] It was the reference to Sodom and Gomorrah which we have noted before and which bore so many similarities to Genesis 14:2 that it made him feel that here at last was real proof of historicity in the biblical account of Abraham. If there was independent evidence – and the Ebla tablets could not be regarded as anything less – that Sodom and Gomorrah were actual places, then it was more than likely that the Abraham who had sought to save them was an actual person, and if he was, then he must have lived, not during the eighteenth or nineteenth century BC (the period generally ascribed to him by biblical scholars), but around five hundred years earlier, during the heyday of Ebla.

He admits that the information he received from Pettinato and Matthiae in their Rome meetings was given to him in confidence, but orientalists, archaeologists, historians, scholars in different fields, had all heard of the Ebla discoveries, were excited by them and were pressing him for details, and he felt that he would not be in breach of confidence if he prepared a brief memorandum for private circulation. A copy was leaked to the *Los Angeles Times* in June 1976 and the rest is hysteria.

Professor Freedman regretted the leak, but felt that people had a right to know, especially in an area which touched upon issues fundamental to their very being and if, in making the disclosures, he had been guilty of a breach of etiquette, he felt he had acted in the best interests of scholarship. He denies absolutely having 'interfered' with or 'exaggerated' the information he has received and claims that all his utterances on the subject are amply borne out by the available facts, but he is, as a result of his disclosures, *persona non grata* in Syria and doesn't know how warmly he would be received in Rome.

The trouble began, he believes, when Pettinato chanced upon the name 'Ish-ra-il'. It at once set the alarm bells ringing, but before the Syrians could do anything about it, it was out and they have never quite forgiven Pettinato for letting it out. Freedman may have been responsible for giving the utterances wider currency than they might otherwise have received, but Pettinato himself has been less than taciturn on the subject, as one can see from the May 1976 issue of the *Biblical Archaeologist* in which he lists some of the names he found in the tablets and comments: 'These few examples suffice to illustrate the relationship of the Eblaite world to the biblical ambience of a later period. In fact, many of these names occur in the same form in the Old Testament, so that a certain interdependence between the culture of Ebla and that of the Old Testament must be granted.'[19]

He has also drawn attention to the striking resemblance between the name of Ebr(i)um, one of the kings of Ebla, and Eber, mentioned in Genesis 10:21 as the father of the Hebrews and great-great-great-great-grandfather of Abraham, which also does not quite tally with his insistence that 'there is no justification for regarding the Eblaites as ancestors of Israel'. (To which in fairness it must be added that he described his observations in the *Biblical Archaeologist* as 'tentative'.)[20]

It is true that Professor Matthiae has been more reticent in the matter and he was prompt to dismiss as 'silly' recurrent press reports that the Ebla tablets in some way support parts of the Old Testament. They may have similarities in language and names, he said, but that in itself was certainly no proof that the Eblaites could have been the ancestors of the Hebrews. The tablets, he said 'only help to know better the very lively cultural background which existed when the Jews appeared on the scene in Palestine one thousand years later',[21] which is indeed the case, but given the evidence, Professor Pettinato's remarks, if perhaps embarrassing, were not out of place.

It might perhaps be more difficult to justify Professor Freedman's remarks on purely scientific grounds, yet they are not wholly devoid of substance and represent the sort of speculations which all major archaeological finds provoke and which help to give archaeology its peculiar drama. He may have been a victim of what we have called the 'seek-and-ye-shall-find' syndrome, but his observations hardly amount to evidence of a Zionist plot, for if, as he believes, the Ebla tablets establish the historicity of Abraham, then he says something also for the truth of Arab tradition. Moreover, if he has been taken seriously at all, it is by Christian fundamentalists and not Zionists. No reputable Jewish scholar (or indeed Jewish politician) within Israel or without, has drawn on the Ebla findings to show that Jews have a claim on Syria, though the evidence – such as it is – could be equally used to show that the Syrians have a claim on Israel. An article by Cyrus Gordon, Professor of Hebraic Studies at New York University, in the American Zionist monthly *Midstream* was wary of any suggestion that the Ebla discoveries added to the credibility of the Bible. He was rather more interested in the similarities between Hebrew and the Palaeo-Canaanite of Ebla and the most he would say was 'that we are dealing with the same cultural background from which the Hebrews later emerged'.[22]

It is possible, perhaps even likely, that some Jewish individuals or groups might be tempted to use the Ebla tablets to further their belief that Israel was once an empire and must be an empire again, and some Christian fundamentalists have pointed with quivering fingers to Genesis 15:18 and the promise: 'Unto thy seed have I given this land from the river of Egypt unto the great river, the river Euphrates.'[23] But no responsible Jew has suggested they establish a Jewish claim to Syria. Any politics which have been introduced into this matter, therefore, is entirely the work of the Syrians. Bahnasi has, for example, claimed that the Ebla discoveries were 'important for Syria as well as for all the Arabs', because they reveal 'the antiquity of the Arab nation and the deep-rootedness of its civilization', and he continued: 'This kingdom, which goes back 4,500 years, is an Arabian kingdom situated between two important regions: the area enclosed by the two rivers (Akkad) and the region of the Canaanite coast. And all these kingdoms are of one civilization. It is the ancient Arabian civilization.'[24] To which one can only say it is nothing of the sort. The antiquity of the Arabs, and the richness of Arab culture, are well attested, but one does not hear of them until about the ninth century BC, some 1,500 years after the period covered by the Ebla tablets. Eblaite is not Arabic and cannot by any stretch of the imagination be regarded as an ancestor of Arabic. The word Arab appears nowhere in the many papers published by Matthiae and Pettinato and the most charitable construction one can put upon Dr Bahnasi's utterances is that he used the terms Syrian and Arabic interchangeably.

What is rather more disquieting is that since Dr Bahnasi's intervention, references to any Hebraic or biblical connection in the works of both Matthiae and Pettinato have been noticeably fewer. Thus, for example, writing in *Archaeology* in 1977 Matthiae speaks of the 'important analogies' between Eblaite and 'Ugaritic and Phoenician',[25] but not of the equally important analogies to Hebrew. Similarly Pettinato writes about Eblaite's 'very close relationship with Ugaritic and Phoenician',[26] but, again, not with Hebrew, and when he mentions the Old Testament he quickly pulls in a reference to the Koran, as if to give Jews and Arabs equal time.[27] Finally, in his book on Ebla published at the end of 1977 (Einaudi, Turin), Professor Matthiae hardly refers to the Bible at all and makes no mention whatsoever of any of its characters – not even to dismiss the suggestion that there could be any connection between them and the Ebla discoveries.

It had been argued, and not only by the Syrian authorities, that Pettinato was perhaps a trifle too eager to establish connections – if only at a remove of five or six generations – between his tablets and the Bible, and the Syrian *démarche* may therefore prove to be nothing more than a necessary corrective, but it all goes to show that there is more to archaeology than the tranquil turning of soil and the untrammelled contemplation of sherds, especially in a part of the world where people are rather more concerned about their past than their future.

The Ebla excavations, though already fourteen years old, are only in their infancy, for only a small part of the 140 acre site has been uncovered and given the present rate of progress the work – barring untoward political incidents – could continue for generations, especially as the thought that one is working upon a civilization more than four thousand years old in itself induces a certain feeling of timelessness. Moreover, the tablets uncovered to date have only been scanned and not studied in detail. Here too there is work to occupy generations and Professor Pettinato is busy training his own school of epigraphers. In Ebla, Matthiae and his colleagues have not only revealed a new civilization, they have developed a new industry. Nearly all archaeology is a lucky dip (though careful research can help to shorten the odds) and it can hardly be hoped that their efforts in future years will be as richly rewarded as those in the recent past, but even if they should not discover another tablet their work will be the subject of controversy and debate for years to come.

CHAPTER 2

Setting the Scene

Anyone attempting to offer a picture of the early history of the Near East soon discovers that the gaps in his knowledge are far larger than his certainties, and that even the so-called certainties, on which previous generations of scholars may have constructed rococo hypotheses, may be demolished overnight by new excavations or some chance discovery.

Thus, for example, Dame Kathleen Kenyon's discovery of a massive defensive stone wall, dating back to the eighth millennium BC, in her 1950s Jericho excavations, showed that urban development had a far earlier history than was previously thought.[1] Similarly Mellaart's excavation of part of a large, thirty-two acre site at Catal Hüyük in South-West Turkey, dating to the period 6200–5500 BC, revealed the existence of a sophisticated town settlement in an area hitherto regarded as a cultural backwater.[2] Or, to come a little nearer our times, the discovery in the inter-war years of an archive of 25,000 cuneiform tablets at Tell Hariri (the ancient Mari), on the Euphrates, indicated that contrary to what was previously thought, northern Syria had an established pattern of city-states replete with an intricate trading system between c. 1820 and 1750 BC, and that the area, for much of that time, was under Assyrian domination.[3]

Then there is the problem of chronology. Only a few absolute dates exist for Mesopotamia and Egypt and these, on closer examination, are not all that absolute. All of them are derived from astronomical data. In the case of Mesopotamia, for example, we have lists of Assyrian state officials who gave their names to the years in the first half of the first millennium BC. In one such list there is a reference to a solar eclipse which we know took place about 763 BC, during the year of one Bur-

Sagale, from which it is possible to calculate with fair precision when the other officials and their contemporaries lived.[4] Similarly we have Egyptian lists giving the names of various kings and how long they reigned, and we also have a text which records that on a particular date during the seventh year of the reign of Sesostris III (of the twelfth Egyptian dynasty) the star Sirius rose at the same time as the sun. Now the Egyptian civil year consisted invariably of three hundred and sixty-five days, and, as there were no leap years, it steadily fell behind the progress of the seasons. Because of this lag, the occurrence of that astronomical event on the given date is rare, but the year in which it took place has been identified by calculation as (most probably) 1872 BC. Hence it is possible to date the reign of Sesostris, as well, of course, as his successors and predecessors.[5] These dates also provide fixed points to which other data are tethered and which in turn are used to calculate the chronology of other data still, so that anyone writing on the ancient Near East is like an Alpinist tethered to a whole line of climbers at the head of which (he hopes) there is one with his pick firmly anchored in rock. Unhappily the fixed points provided even by astronomy are not all that firm and from time to time whole chains of carefully calculated data slither into oblivion.

Another difficulty is that in the absence of corroborative evidence from external sources one cannot always separate history from myth. In the case of Mesopotamia, for example, much speculation which was built on a list of kings which purported to have been drawn up in order of succession, had to be drastically revised when many of the kings were found to be contemporaries.[6] All facts are tentative, but none are quite as tentative as those divulged by archaeology, and the further one goes back the more tentative they become.

Students of the prehistoric Near East speak of a 'Neolithic Revolution'[7] in or before the eighth millennium[8] which witnessed the settlement of nomads in permanent communities and the change from hunting and food-collecting to farming. 'Revolution' is perhaps a misnomer for it was a painfully gradual process. Neither was it all-embracing and the nomad has lived side by side with the farmer (and sometimes on him) until modern times, but it seems fairly clear that animals were

domesticated and animal husbandry and agriculture were
practised in the Middle East long before they were known elsewhere in the globe.[9] Why the change came about is obscure,
but why it should have come about in the Middle East is more
easily explained. The area was less profoundly affected than
other parts of the globe by the climatic changes which followed
the end of the Ice Age about 10,000 BC. Moreover, the wild
wheat and barley, which were eventually to be cultivated, and
the wild sheep, goats, cattle and pigs which were eventually
to be tamed, were indigenous to the area, and there was
adequate rainfall in the foothills of the mountain ranges. By
the end of the seventh millennium there were stable farming
communities in North-West Iran, in South-West Anatolia, in
North Syria and in Palestine, and that these were not mere
isolated settlements is indicated by the size of some of the
towns that served them (like Jericho) and by commercial networks, the existence of which has been strikingly illustrated
by the widespread trade in obsidian (natural glass).[10]

Until we come to about 3000 BC, when written texts first
appear in Mesopotamia and Egypt, we have no sure basis from
which to infer the ethnic, linguistic, social and economic
character of such settlements, and must content ourselves with
whatever clues the dumb archaeological remains, notably the
ceramics, may suggest. For example, over a period thought
to extend from about 5200 to 4200 BC, we find throughout
northern Syria, northern Iraq and eastern Turkey a range of
distinctive artefacts – such as hard thin pottery on which various designs were painted in black, red and white – which are
taken as evidence of a particular culture. It is called the Halaf
culture, after the site (just east of the Khabur river and south
of the Syrian–Turkish border) where it was first identified, and
many believe it to indicate the advent of new peoples to the
area. The Halaf culture yields convincing evidence of craft
specialization in pottery and of the limited use of metals,
especially copper.[11]

At the same period we find the earliest definite evidence of
artificial irrigation at the sites of Choga Mami and Tell es-
Sawwan in eastern Iraq.[12] The invention of irrigation was
once generally considered the principal factor leading to the
development of the first large-scale political organizations –

the city-states of southern Iraq, and the kingdom of Egypt.[13] But as these organizations do not appear until about 3000 BC, they can no longer be simply regarded as the outcome of artificial irrigation, now attested as far back as the sixth millennium. The impetus for the formation of cities in southern Iraq may in fact have come not from the very invention of irrigation but from the ongoing battle which it necessitated against the forces of nature. There is a fall of only about a hundred feet between the point where the Euphrates and Tigris enter the great alluvial plain of Iraq, and the sea, two hundred miles to the south, and they thus follow their course slowly and majestically, but in the spring, when the snows in the northern mountains begin to melt, the waters suddenly swell and are liable to burst their banks as they enter the plain. The floods often resulted in silting of the irrigation channels, and farmers therefore had to make common cause to deal now with the niggardliness and now with the excess of nature, and out of their efforts there probably evolved the first government. True, the sites of numerous ancient towns such as Eridu, Ur, Nippur and Kish are now well away from the rivers, but the course of the latter has changed over the centuries, so that these cities too were once much closer to or even directly on their banks. In Egypt, on the other hand, the Nile flood waters were less difficult to control; a canal network could thus be constructed on a national scale, and the whole land came to be organized as one cohesive political unit.

The first known settlements in the great alluvial plain date back to about the year 5000 BC and the name given to their culture is Ubaid, again after the site (near Ur) where it was first recognized.[14] The irrigation techniques led to the apportionment of distinct fields each owned by different family units. As some fields produced better harvests than others, and as the owners of the least productive fields were often left compelled to sell them, an ever-widening gap developed between rich and poor, and we may perhaps trace here the beginnings of class divisions in society. It has also been surmised[15] that specialization in different skills was encouraged by the variety of sources of food in the area: wild fowl and fish in the lagoons and marshes, as well as dates and, of course, cereal crops. The Ubaid culture also offers (at Eridu) the first evidence of a mud-brick building in southern Iraq;[16] it was a shrine, rebuilt and enlarged and elaborated by succeeding generations up to about 3000 BC, and – to judge from the remains of fish found at several levels – it may have been devoted to Enki, the Sumerian god of fresh-water, generally depicted, on third millennium cylinder seals, with a fish-filled stream of water gushing from his shoulders.[17] Perhaps both here and in other cities the temple provided a nucleus round which the city grew.

Pottery and mud-brick building techniques of the Ubaid type also occur in the Zagros area, northern Syria and even Saudi Arabia. Perhaps these Ubaid features were spread by trade links between these areas and the Ubaid heartland in southern Mesopotamia; trade was certainly important to the latter, which lacked such essential resources as stone, metal and timber. What it had to offer in exchange is uncertain, but may well have consisted of reed-mats and other reed products, and even of reeds themselves, which could readily be used for thatching, cattle-pens, and much else.[18]

We have rather more information about the Uruk period (which covers approximately the fourth millennium) – so called because most of the discoveries throwing light on the times were found at Uruk in southern Mesopotamia. The technological developments suggest continuity[19] rather than dramatic departures, but towards the end of this period, which is to say about the year 3000 BC, we begin to notice the great ceremonial edifices, together with the numerous ritual appurtenances which indicate the beginning of the large-scale, politically complex city-state. The distribution of artefacts and architecture of the Uruk type is remarkably wide, and the recent discovery of Uruk material as far away as Habuba Kabira[20] in northern Syria on the west bank of the Euphrates caught many scholars by surprise.

It is, however, in Mesopotamia alone that we now meet the invention which divides pre-history from history, namely picture-writing, from which cuneiform was to develop. Although the earliest texts are still undeciphered, the first texts that we can read – from perhaps 2900 BC – are in the Sumerian language, which has left a copious literature. Here is the first point at which we can confidently put a name to the people dwelling in southern Mesopotamia, and read what they said of themselves.

The origin of the Sumerians is a celebrated problem.[21] No etymology has been found in the Sumerian language for such great Sumerian cities as Uruk, Ur and Lagash, which suggests that the first Sumerians may have been immigrants to Iraq. Again, many Sumerian words relating to such activities as farming, fishing, building and handicraft consist of two or more syllables and are often thought to be alien to the Sumerian language (which is built up predominantly of units of one syllable) and therefore to have been borrowed from the language of another people who supposedly inhabited the area before the advent of the Sumerians.[22] The myths of the Sumerians are also adduced – for example, that they first learnt the arts of civilization from amphibious creatures who emerged from the sea,[23] that they had once ruled over Aratta (which was perhaps located near the Caspian Sea),[24] and that they located the paradise of the gods in Dilmun (which is probably Bahrein).[25] As to the date of their migration, some consider that the rapid advances of the Uruk period can only be due to the advent of a new people, whom they equate with the Sumerians.[26] Others think the Sumerians arrived much earlier, and were the progenitors of the Ubaid culture.[27] Nor is there any consensus on their former homeland. Some think of southern Iran, others look to the Caspian Sea, while one scholar suggests that they came from the direction of the Upper Euphrates, and that such settlements as that at Habuba Kabira, now submerged by a lake that was recently enlarged, were founded by other members of that population movement, who stopped off en route.[28] But many scholars are content to believe that the Sumerians were indigenous to Sumer (that is, southern Mesopotamia). We do not yet know Sumerian well enough to be at all certain about the linguistic arguments on city names and other words; one may, for example, imagine a future scholar of English failing to recognize that Preston and Sheffield derive from the Old English forms of 'Priests' Town' and 'Sheep Field', and attributing these names to an earlier population. Nor do the arguments based on myths or on archaeological remains, amount to proof; and one is tempted to agree with Georges Roux that the Sumerians 'may have "always" been in Iraq, and this is all we can say'.[29]

Another people whose presence in Iraq in the third millennium is attested by their own inscriptions are the Akkadians, who were Semites, in that they spoke a language belonging to the Semitic family, which includes Hebrew and Arabic.[30] To account for the resemblance between the Semitic languages, a mother-tongue, called Proto-Semitic, must be posited; and it is generally deduced that the Semites were originally one people speaking that one language, and dwelling in a common home. How they came to be in Iraq is variously explained. Most seek the original home of the Semites in and around the Syrian desert, where they supposedly led a nomadic life.[31] The migration of the Akkadians – and of other Semitic peoples at different times – might then be explained by either the 'wave theory' or the 'infiltration theory'. The former supposes that from time to time – most recently in the seventh century AD – the population of the homeland outgrew its natural resources, and that an almost irresistible wave of migrants surged forth to establish themselves elsewhere. On the latter view the Semites, in their search for pastures, would move about the fertile periphery of their homeland where it abutted on the areas occupied by settled populations, whom they would regularly meet, if only to trade, and with whom many of them eventually opted for a settled life. But it has also been maintained that the true homeland of the Semites is not the Syrian Desert but rather 'the Fertile Crescent and possibly parts of the outskirts of the Arabian peninsula',[32] in which case the Akkadians too might 'always' have been in Iraq.

Southern Mesopotamia, then, possibly because of its unique environment, was the centre of the first literate urban civilization. But at the same time the adjacent areas – northern Mesopotamia, Syria, and south-west Iran, called Elam – were developing along parallel lines, though with variations which may be attributed to their different geography and climate and earlier cultural history. Just how much in this development they owed to Sumer is a vexed question. In Palestine this period witnessed the development of a number of city-states – Jericho, Megiddo, Beth Shan, Ai, and Khirbet Kerak, on the western shore of Lake Tiberias – but the archaeological remains tell us little more than that the cities were prosperous and enjoyed trade links with Egypt.[33] Egypt herself was evolving a civilization that was very much her own. By about 3100 BC the land was united under one king, and for many centuries enjoyed a degree of political stability and of centralized administrative efficiency unknown in Mesopotamia. Here too writing was in use as early as about 3000 BC – perhaps under Sumerian influence,[34] since both systems utilize the same principle of phonetization (see p. 119) – and the centuries that followed brought prosperity and great cultural advances, notably in mathematics and astronomy; but Egypt was separated by desert from western Asia, with which her relations were – during the third millennium, at least – largely restricted to commerce.

Perhaps the most valuable source for the history of Mesopotamia is the so-called Sumerian king-list,[35] though one must approach it with caution; first because among a great deal of factual material there are many myths, and it is not always easy to disentangle the one from the other (though, of course, even myths can throw light on their times) and secondly because it was compiled about 2120 BC, long after the events it describes, and human memories were fallible even then. And finally, it clearly had a purpose, which was to show that the lands of Sumer and Akkad (i.e. the area south of Baghdad and bounded by the Tigris, the Euphrates and the Persian Gulf) were always united under one king, though at most times it was in fact a patchwork of minor and major principalities which were sometimes brought together by one dominating force, but which were not infrequently at war with one another.

After the first eight kings, who were said to have ruled for 241,200 years altogether,[36] the king-list states that 'the Flood then swept over (the land)'. Mythological texts describe it in detail, and its striking resemblances to the biblical Flood are common knowledge. The gods are angry with mankind and are determined to destroy the earth and all therein, save for a pious, god-fearing king called Ziusudra, who builds (presumably, for the details are missing) a giant boat to save himself from extinction. The waters descend for seven days and seven

nights, after which the sun-god Utu warms up the earth. Ziusudra prostrates himself before Utu and offers up sacrifices of
oxen and sheep, and is later himself deified and transported
to Dilmun 'the place where the sun rises'.[37]

The first post-diluvian city to be mentioned in the king-list
was Kish, later to become the capital of Akkad, most of
whose rulers have Semitic Akkadian names. Curiously, many
rulers hundreds and even thousands of years later use the title
'King of Kish' as if it meant 'King of the universe', and so
it is possible that Kish gained control over the whole of Sumer
and even beyond. It is at Kish, incidentally, that the earliest
building which may be described as a palace has been found.[38]

The archaeological evidence suggests that by the middle of
the third millennium some of the Sumerian city-states included
not only a walled city dominated by its temple precinct (hous-
ing the tutelary deity of the city), but also a surrounding tract
of countryside, and numerous smaller settlements. Such exten-
sions were not necessarily due to conquest but may have arisen
out of the need for smaller cities to align themselves with the
larger ones equipped with weapons and chariots, in case of
war. In the king-list there is a reference to Enmerkar, second
ruler of Uruk's first dynasty, as the builder of Uruk. As the
city had two main sanctuaries, devoted, apparently, to two different tutelary deities – An, the deified Heaven, and Inanna,
goddess of fertility – it may have been amalgamated from two
separate settlements, and Enmerkar's achievement might have
been the linking of the two temples and the erection of a wall
encircling the whole of Uruk. The warlike, heroic spirit of the
kings of Uruk was later celebrated in epic cycles, the best
known of which concerned Gilgamesh, grandson of
Enmerkar, who was himself the subject of more than one epic.
One story relates how Aka, son of Mebaragesi of Kish,
besieged Uruk and was repulsed by Gilgamesh. The council
of elders had urged submission presumably in the face of impossible odds, but Gilgamesh ignored them, gathered a small
band of warriors about him and led them to victory.[39]
Whether the story is true or not, is less important to the historian than the surrounding detail, such as the fact that at this
period city-states had their own councils. Two royal inscriptions of Mebaragesi have been recovered,[40] largely dispelling

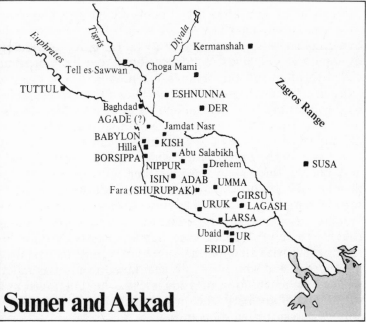

Sumer and Akkad

the doubts once entertained as to whether Gilgamesh was an historical figure at all. He is best known on account of the Akkadian Epic of Gilgamesh, a masterly and highly original work which welded together various Sumerian legends,[41] and which includes an account of the Flood referred to above.

The title assumed by the rulers of the various city-states varied. In Lagash, for example, the ruler was called *Ensi*, in Uruk he was called *En*. Elsewhere one finds the title *Lugal*. All three are generally rendered in English as king. The literal meaning of *Lugal* is 'big man', and may have represented the simple realities of the situation where a military leader, first called forth at a time of emergency, declined to surrender power. *Ensi* in later centuries meant governor rather than king, and possibly the title suggested that the holder was merely viceroy, the true king being the tutelary deity of the city.[42] Finally, the title *En* of the hero-kings of Uruk later denoted the spiritual head of the temple of a city (who had, incidentally, to be of the opposite sex to the city's tutelary deity);[43] perhaps, then, at least in Uruk, the ruler originally belonged to the temple hierarchy, and his office became secularized only later

(though never completely so). Divinity did hedge a king more
then than at any later period and some of the figures in the
Sumerian king-list were deified.[44] By far the most outstanding
example was Gilgamesh's predecessor, whom the Sumerians
called Dumuzi and the Semites Tammuz, and who lingered
as a deity into much later times. Ezekiel in 592 BC was troubled
by the following he excited among the Israelites: 'He said also
unto me, Turn thee yet again, and thou shalt see greater
abominations that they do. Then he brought me to the door
of the gate of the Lord's house which was toward the north;
and, behold, there sat women weeping for Tammuz.'[45] The
memory of Tammuz was not, however, eradicated altogether,
for the Jews later – unwittingly, borrowing from the Babylonians – used his name for a Hebrew month (corresponding
roughly to July). Various later Sumerian texts describe his
relationship with Inanna, the Sumerian Venus, to whom he
was married and who eventually sent him down to the under-
world. The lamentation rites suggest that he functioned as a
sort of god of greenery who died each summer and (presumably) was resurrected each spring.

In spite of the different developments in the individual city-
states, they were linked by a similar culture and a common
religion. The types of monumental architecture, the building
materials and techniques, and ornamental motifs make it possible to speak in general terms of Sumerian art. Again, various
lists were used in the training of scribes – lists of cuneiform
signs, of gods, professions, and so on – and the same text
often crops up at many different locations within Sumer, the
earliest copy sometimes dating as far back as the beginning
of the third millennium; thus the Sumerians held a long tradition of scholarship in common.

The Sumerians believed that the universe and all it contained were created and organized by four deities, the heaven-
god An, the air-god Enlil, the water-god Enki, and the mother-
goddess Ninhursag. These were the chief gods with Enlil perhaps cast in the role of *primus inter pares*, while Enki appears
to have functioned as his executive arm so that where Enlil
proposed, Enki disposed. They all, of course, possessed divine
power. The Sumerian faith was characterized by a dark fatal-
ism. They cherished the accepted virtues, yet reconciled them-

selves to the belief that sin and evil, pain and misfortune, were all part of the divine plan, that a descent into the dark nether world was the ultimate fate of all, and that nothing happened or failed to happen without the intervention of the gods, and in particular *the* god, Enlil, as may be seen from the following extract from a hymn composed in his honour:

> Without Enlil, the great mountain,
> No cities would be built, no settlements founded,
> No stalls would be built, no sheepfolds established,
> No king would be raised, no high priest born ...
> Workers would have neither controller nor supervisor ...
> The birds of heaven would not build nests on the wide earth,
> In heaven the drifting clouds would not yield their moisture,
> Plants and herbs, the glory of the plain, would fail to grow,
> In field and meadow the rich grain would fail to flower,
> The trees planted in the mountain forest would not yield their
>   fruit.[46]

The chief gods gave birth to a host of puisne deities, some of whom functioned as the patron gods of the different cities. Thus, for example, the moon-god Nanna (who was also known as Sin) was the patron god of Ur, while his daughter Inanna, goddess of fertility (who was identified by the Akkadians with the Semitic deity Ishtar) was patroness of Uruk. Enlil, on the other hand, had his chief shrine at Nippur, which seems to have functioned as the Canterbury of Sumer and a sort of federal capital. No ruler is ascribed in the king-list to Nippur and it is suggested that whoever claimed hegemony over the others had his claim validated by a meeting of them all at Nippur and that he stood to the other rulers as Enlil to the other gods.[47]

Historically, the best-documented city-state is Lagash, which stood to the north-east of Uruk on a tributary of the Tigris, and a large mass of material has been dug up throwing light on the middle years of the third millennium,[48] though it is perhaps ironic that the one Sumerian city-state whose life and times can be studied in some detail is not mentioned in the king-list at all. Yet one of its rulers, Eannatum, claimed the title 'King of Kish', and asserted that the political dominion of Lagash extended to Kish in the north, Mari in the west, Uruk in the south and Elam in the east. The incidence at Uruk and Ur of inscriptions commemorating Eannatum tends to support these claims, and clearly the title which Eannatum gave himself, as 'He who subjects the lands' was not an empty one.[49]

One event which dominated the history of Lagash was a long running frontier dispute with the neighbouring state of Umma and concerned the use of a canal and an area of grazing land called Edin. Much survives of a stele celebrating, both in writing and pictorially, the victory won by Eannatum over Enakalle of Umma, with vultures carrying away the heads of the slain. The victory could not have been decisive for the struggle was continued by Eannatum's second successor Entemena, who finally overcame Umma after enlisting the help of Lugalkinishedudu, king of Uruk and Ur.[50]

The most memorable ruler of Lagash was perhaps the last one, Urukagina, probably a usurper, who became king about 2378 BC. Texts found at Lagash suggest that the people were plundered by an all-powerful bureaucracy and a whole host of abuses had grown up so that there was hardly an activity untouched by impositions. Divorce meant a payment of five shekels to the governor, and one to his vizier, and a perfumer paid the same on every oil preparation, and even funerals involved the bereaved in the payment of barley, bread and wine. The governor treated the temple as his private property and, to quote an inscription: 'The oxen of the gods ploughed the *ensi*'s onion patches; the onion and the cucumber patches of the *ensi* were located in the gods' best fields.'[51] The rich grew richer, the poor, poorer and corruption was everywhere. It was at this low point in the fortunes of Lagash, we are told, that Ningirsu, the tutelary deity of the city, chose Urukagina to re-establish 'divine laws' and restore justice to Lagash. He immediately brought to an end the abuse practised by his predecessors. He declared an amnesty for citizens imprisoned for the non-payment of debts or taxes, gave food to the needy and 'made a covenant with the god Ningirsu that a man of power must not commit an injustice against them'. He also brought to an end the depredations of the bureaucrats and bailiffs so that by the time he was finished 'there were no tax-collectors', an idyllic state, but perhaps too idyllic for a city with a relentless enemy at its door. Umma, now ruled by the redoubtable

Lugalzagesi, attacked again, routed Urukagina, and sacked Lagash and its temples. Urukagina himself appears to have survived the catastrophe and retreated to Girsu, a town within his kingdom which had not fallen to Umma. The sad event is commemorated in one of the Lagash tablets: 'Because the Ummaite destroyed the bricks of Lagash, he committed a sin against the god Ningirsu; he [Ningirsu] will cut off the hands lifted against him. It is not the sin of Urukagina, the king of Girsu. May Nidaba the goddess of Lugalzagesi, the *ensi* of Umma, carry this sin on her neck.'[52]

Thereafter Urukagina vanishes from history.

One scholar has suggested that Urukagina launched his reforms not out of kindness of heart but out of the need to mobilize popular support for the war against Umma,[53] but even after all these centuries the Lagash tablets still echo with a certain benignity of intent especially as contained in the word *amargi*, whose literal meaning is 'return to mother', but is translated to mean 'freedom' – the very first instance in which the expression appears in a human document.[54]

After the destruction of Lagash Lugalzagesi went on to conquer Uruk and Ur (which by then formed a condominium), and in an inscription claims to have brought all the foreign lands under his rule so that there was nothing but bliss, peace and prosperity throughout his dominions which, he claims, stretched 'from the Lower Sea along the Tigris and Euphrates Rivers to the Upper Sea', a claim which foreshadowed the imperial conquests of the Akkadian period (*c.* 2371–2230 BC).[55]

The Akkadian period is named after the city of Agade (biblical Akkad – Genesis 10:10), whose founder, Sargon the Great, made it the capital of an empire embracing most of the then known world. It was probably located somewhere near Kish, but its exact whereabouts are still unknown. The reason that 'Akkadian' has also come to denote the earliest Semitic inhabitants of Iraq, and their language, is that inscriptions in that language first appear in quantity under Sargon (Sumerian having previously enjoyed almost exclusive use),[56] who himself stemmed from a predominantly Akkadian-speaking area. The rulers of Agade were far better remembered than any of their predecessors, and their history was successively embroidered by later generations – some of whom saw Sargon as the archetypal emperor, and projected their own aspirations for conquest back to him – which makes it a delicate task to identify the historical kernel within the traditions. Sargon's name (Sharru-kēn(u) in Akkadian) means 'legitimate king', as if to assert a claim which may have been questioned, and it is unlikely that he received it at birth. The legends surrounding his birth and upbringing confirm this impression. His origins were mysterious: 'my mother was a priestess (or changeling), my father I knew not'.[57] His mother, the legend continues, cast him at birth into the Euphrates, having set him in a basket of rushes sealed with pitch. He was found by a water-drawer who brought him up as his own son and appointed him his gardener. The goddess Ishtar (or Inanna) then adopted him as her protégé and he rose to become cup-bearer to Ur-Zababa, the Sumerian king of Kish.

There is an obvious resemblance between Sargon's story and that of Moses but some conservative scholars have sought to identify him with a very different biblical figure, namely Nimrod (Genesis 10:8) the 'mighty hunter', the mainstays of whose kingdom were 'Babylon, Erech (Uruk) and Accad, all of them in the land of Shinar', but of whom no historical record exists outside the Bible.[58] It is conceivable that Nimrod was another name of Sargon, but apart from the desire to establish the biblical Nimrod as historical, there is no reason to suppose so.

According to legend Ur-Zababa incurred the displeasure of Enlil as a result of some cultic offence and the kingship went to Sargon. The Sumerian king-list, however, tells another story and attributes to Ur-Zababa four or five successors before the dynasty expired. It in fact seems likely that Sargon moved from Kish to build up his own kingdom at Agade and that Ur-Zababa's fall may have been due less to the gods than to the fact that he stood in the way of the all-conquering Lugalzagesi. Sargon went on to establish a far-flung empire, but in what order he achieved his conquests is not clear. Many suppose that he began with the cities of Sumer and worked outwards, in which case his well-remembered conflict with Lugalzagesi came early in his career: he is recorded to have attacked Uruk and razed its walls and destroyed most of its forces and eventually brought Lugalzagesi in chains to the gates of Nippur. On that view, he then turned south, attacked Ur and advanced to the shores of the Persian Gulf, where, in the tradition of victors, he ceremonially washed his weapons in the water. Then with southern Sumer in his grasp, he turned northwards, acquiring the area later to become Assyria, and then westwards, where he conquered Mari, Iarmuti and Ebla – its first appearance in recorded history – to the 'Cedar Forest', in the Amanus range, and the 'Silver Mountains' in the Taurus.[59] Finally he marched eastwards across the Tigris into Iran and subjected Elam and Barakhshi. Much inconsistency, however, exists between the various historical traditions, and some scholars interpret the evidence differently. Sargon, they suppose, began his conquests not in Sumer but in Syria, and extended them into Assyria and Elam, establishing his power in a great ring about southern Iraq; Sumer he left unmolested until, towards the end of his reign, the Sumerian cities themselves challenged his authority, and paid the penalty.[60] But whenever it was that Sumer came under Sargon's control, we know that he proceeded to enhance his authority there by appointing his daughter Enheduanna to serve as chief priestess of the moon-god at Ur, and also (apparently) as a ritual representation of Inanna at Uruk – a shrewd move which gave Sargon a family connection with two of the principal Sumerian deities. Enheduanna composed two large cycles of hymns, which have been preserved, and is the first author whose name is known to history.[61]

Tradition credited Sargon with yet more distant conquests, accomplished with astonishing mobility. According to one later text, when a colony of Akkadian traders was being harassed in Purushkhanda, high up in Anatolia, he led an expedition to protect them.[62] One scholar has even interpreted another such text as a claim that Sargon's armies reached as far as Egypt, Ethiopia and India.[63] But his list of well documented conquests is impressive enough. Just how firm a grip he maintained even on these, once his armies (as they soon must have done) moved on, is not clear; although he well deserves the title of emperor, he can hardly have welded them into any such tight political organization as, say, the later empire of Assyria (p. 39). The matter might be clarified if we knew more about relations in earlier periods between

Mesopotamia and the other lands conquered by Sargon. In Syria, for example, much has been discovered that is characteristic of and betokens close contact with Mesopotamia. Some of the finest examples of Sumerian art of about 2600 BC (inlay-work and statues of worshippers) were found at Mari; typically Mesopotamian architecture appears about the same time at Tell Chuera,[64] and artefacts of the Uruk type (fourth millennium) occur at Habuba Kabira and elsewhere. Again, right back in the fifth millennium, the pottery and the mud-brick building techniques typical of the Ubaid culture of southern Iraq appear also in the north of Iraq, North Syria, and the Zagros area. All this implies some cultural continuity linking Mesopotamia and its neighbours, which in turn suggests that the political unification which Sargon achieved between them might not have been wholly without precedent.

Not unexpectedly, Sargon's death was the occasion for widespread rebellions, which his son Rimush, upon his accession, had to confront in Ur, Umma, Adab, Lagash, Der and Kazallu within Sumer itself, and in Elam and Barakhshi to the east. Yet according to one inscription they did not pose a lasting threat:[65] 'Rimush, king of Kish, to (whom Enlil) has given (the entire country): he holds the Upper Sea and the Lower Sea and all the mountains for Enlil.'

Rimush remained on the throne for nine years and was succeeded by his older brother (according to some authorities, his twin) Manishtushu, who had to cope with new outbreaks, but again, according to an inscription, he appears to have defeated them all: 'When he [Manishtushu] had crossed the Lower Sea in ships, thirty-two kings gathered against him, but he defeated them and smote their cities and prostrated their lords and destroyed (the whole countryside?) as far as the silver mines.'[66] There is evidence to suggest that this was not mere bombast. An inscription in Ashur acknowledges his hold over that city, and another, by Shamshi–Adad I of Assyria (c. 1813–1781 BC) recalls that he was the first builder of the Temple of Ishtar at Nineveh, which suggests that Nineveh too was under his control.[67]

Manishtushu ruled for fifteen years (c. 2306–2292 BC), and was succeeded by Naram-Sin, a grandson of Sargon and as tireless and forceful a figure as his grandfather. He has left more inscriptions than Sargon, and become the subject of almost as many traditions, some of them contradictory, and well embellished with legend. We may accept the traditions (though the order of events is not clear) that, like Sargon, he routed a rebellious coalition in Sumer, and pushed southwards to the Persian Gulf, eastwards beyond the Tigris to the Zagros mountains and perhaps also into Armenia, and north-westwards as far as the Mediterranean and the Taurus and the Amanus mountains.[68] Among the kings he conquered was Manium, of a land called Magan. In later ages Magan denoted Egypt, whence the suggestion that Manium was none other than Menes, traditionally the first king of all Egypt[69] – who is however usually dated about 3100 BC. More probably Magan, at this period, meant the mountainous part of Oman. At all events, it was with good reason that Naram-Sin described himself as 'king of the four quarters', which evidently meant lord of the then known world; and not satisfied with that he appointed himself 'the god of Agade'.[70] Physical evidence of the extent of his dominions is provided by the monuments which have been found as far afield as Darband-i-Gawr in South-East Kurdistan, and Pir Hussein in South-East Turkey (both rock-reliefs), all dedicated to the power and glory of the all-victorious 'strong male god' (as the inscriptions put it)[71] Naram-Sin, and, in one case, depicting him literally as a giant among men.[72]

At home, Naram-Sin continued Sargon's policy of appointing daughters to the temple priesthood, but carried it further by making one of his daughters a high priestess in the temple of the moon-god Sin at Ur, while another served as a priestess to the sun-god at Mari, and two of his sons were appointed governors of cities.[73] He built temples at Lagash, Nippur and Adab, and established garrisons at Lagash, Susa, Nineveh and Tell Brak, on the banks of the Khabur river in North Syria, where the remains of one of his fortified outposts have been found.[74]

But resistance to the Akkadian dynasty's claims to world domination did not abate. Apart from the many revolts which Naram-Sin's own inscriptions relate, a telling piece of evidence is a rock-relief discovered near Sar-i-Pul, about seventy miles west of Kermanshah. Shortly after Naram-Sin's reign it was erected by Annubanini, king of the Lullubi, a people dwelling in south-western Persia, who had been subdued by Naram-Sin; and it defiantly imitates, in language and design, the very rock-relief at Darband-i-Gawr in which Annubanini's own earlier defeat had been commemorated by Naram-Sin.[75]

One widespread tradition asserts that Nemesis overtook Naram-Sin himself. The cause, it was said, was sacrilege against Nippur and its god Enlil. As a result Enlil 'the raging flood which has no rival, because of his beloved house which had been attacked, what destruction wrought', and brought down upon Agade 'a people which brooks no controls ... The herald could not proceed on his journey, the sea-rider could not sail his boat ...; brigands dwelt on the roads; the doors of the gates of the land turned to clay ... The great fields and meadows produced no grain; the fisheries, no fish; the watered gardens neither honey nor wine.' Tradition identified the 'people which brooks no controls' as the Gutians.[76]

The end of Akkad is very differently related and explained by modern scholarship.[77] First, it is far from certain that Naram-Sin's own reign ended in disaster; the disintegration of the empire is rather to be set in the reign of his son Shar-kali-sharri, whose inscriptions show him constantly struggling to ward off the Lullubi and the Amorites (of whom more below), as well as the Gutians, and who survived twenty-five years on the throne before Akkad lapsed into anarchy. Secondly, the role of the Gutians seems much exaggerated. Although tradition singled them out as the tool of divine retribution, archaeology has yielded little that can be characterized as 'Gutian'. It is true, as Shar-kali-sharri's own inscriptions report, that the Gutians entered Iraq at this time (perhaps moving from the north or north-west into the Diyala region), but it seems unlikely that they posed a more serious threat to Akkad than the other peoples also known to have been present – the Lullubi, the Amorites, and the Hurrians,[78] of whom the last may have come from the general area of Lake Van and seem to have been contesting the power of Akkad in North Syria also.[79] Thirdly, internal conflicts and the continual difficulty involved in administering so large and un-wieldy an empire probably contributed at least as much to the downfall of Akkad as all these external pressures. And so, in the words of the king-list, 'Agade was smitten and its king-ship carried to Uruk.'

Some centuries elapse before anything so formidable as the Akkadian dynasty is encountered in the Near East again, which at this point – about 2200 BC – presents a prospect of widespread decline. Mesopotamia fell into anarchy, and into general decadence. The development of the city-states of Palestine had been abruptly halted in the late twenty-fourth century BC, and we instead find houses of inferior construction in unwalled settlements, and other changes too (in pottery, weaponry, and the practice of individual instead of multiple burials) mark a clean cultural break. In Egypt the Old Kingdom collapsed and was succeeded by a period of internal strife which (though the chronology is doubtful) seems to have lasted through much if not all of the twenty-second century BC. Many scholars[80] lay the blame for much of this on the Amorites – a people whose language (reflected in their names) is Semitic, but quite distinct from Akkadian, and from about 2000 BC onward and well into the second millennium we find throughout Mesopotamia, Syria and Palestine a profusion of names characteristic of the Amorites. Appealing to the 'wave' theory of Semitic migration, we may suppose that about 2200 BC hordes of Amorites erupted from the Syrian desert, and threw the whole Near East into confusion, eventually settling in those areas – Mesopotamia, Syria, Palestine – where Amorite names later abound.

Others wonder whether the explanation can be so straight-forward. Syria, where Amorites were present as early as Shar-kali-sharri's time, and which later shows as great a concentra-tion of Amorites as anywhere else, seems to have suffered no general disruption or massive invasion. Gudea of Lagash (second half of the twenty-second century?) travelled back and forth to northern Syria without let or hindrance (see p. 41), and the archaeological evidence – such as it is – shows no general pattern of destruction or decline until the third mil-lennium is over. It has been argued, then, that the Amorites immigrated mainly by peaceful 'infiltration', and that one should seek elsewhere the primary causes of the eclipse of Egypt (where, towards the end of the Old Kingdom, the central administration seems to have been losing its hold),[81] and the city-states of Palestine (natural disasters, perhaps, or inter-city warfare).[82]

In southern Mesopotamia, Utuhengal of Uruk (c. 2120–2114 BC) managed in the course of his short reign, to establish a semblance of unity among the small city-states, and the effort was carried further by Ur-Nammu (possibly his son)[83] who made Ur his capital, and established a new dynasty which lasted over a century. Although the major spoken language of the area was probably Akkadian, all texts – administrative and literary – were composed in Sumerian and the period witnessed the production of some of the major Sumerian epic cycles. At the same time a new type of Sumerian literary genre was created, the royal hymn, and some scholars even speak of a 'Sumerian renaissance'. The period is richly documented and indicates a political organization reminiscent of the Akkadian dynasty rather than the city-state system which preceded it. There are tablets dealing with trade in textiles and metals and the supply of sacrificial animals for the temples of Nippur, Uruk and Ur, and as they are derived from the state archives of cities like Umma, Nippur and Lagash, one eminent scholar has felt justified in describing the entire system as a 'bureaucratic national state'.[84] One does get the impression that the state not only controlled trade, but intervened in many aspects of day to day life. Ur-Nammu, for example, initiated a large building programme, which included the erection of the ziggurat of Nanna which dominated the central area of the city, and of other religious edifices at Nippur, Uruk, Eridu, Larsa, Kish and Umma, and provided for the maintenance of canals, which were, of course, of crucial importance to an area so heavily dependent on irrigation.[85] His example appears to have been followed by his son Shulgi, who reigned for forty-eight years, and his grandsons, Amar-Sin and Shu-Sin. Both Shulgi and his sons were deified and temples were dedicated to the worship of Shu-Sin at Ur, Lagash, Adab and Eshnunna,[86] in his own lifetime, and the sort of devotion they inspired may be seen from the following poem addressed to Shu-Sin by a priestess selected as his bride:

Bridegroom, dear to my heart,
Goodly is your beauty, honeysweet,
Lion, dear to my heart,
Goodly is your beauty, honeysweet ...

Bridegroom, you have taken your pleasure of me,
Tell my mother, she will give you delicacies,
My father, he will give you gifts.

Your spirit, I know where to cheer your spirit,
Bridegroom, sleep in our house until dawn,
Your heart, I know where to gladden your heart,
Lion, sleep in our house until dawn.

You, because you love me,
Give me pray of your caresses,
My lord god, my lord protector,
My Shu-Sin, who gladdens Enlil's heart,
Give me pray of your caresses ...[87]

Deification clearly had its compensations.

It is not easy to establish the areas dominated by Shulgi and his sons, though the reference in their texts to places as distant from Ur as Urshu, Arman, Ebla and Mukish, suggests at least far-flung trading interests, if not imperial dominion.

One of the interesting features of the texts of this period is the increasing incidence of Amorite[88] and Hurrian[89] names, and it appears that some Hurrians were settled within Sumer and Akkad and others employed as emissaries from more distant parts, such as Urshu and Urkish, in North Syria, and Karahar, in the Zagros mountains. One also finds Amorites, or at least people with Amorite names, as sheep and goat traders in Drehem, buying finished leather goods at Isin, and hiring themselves out as labourers in Lagash and Umma. Others seem to be permanent residents in Ur and its surroundings, leading lives substantially like those around them. By no means all of the Amorites, however, had given up nomadic life, and there is evidence that some who had not came into conflict with the Ur authorities possibly because they were inclined to use pasture land which was not theirs, or even to raid passing caravans. Both Shulgi and Shu-Sin had to lead

punitive expeditions to keep them in check, and the latter even
built a wall stretching from the Tigris to the Euphrates, probably not far north-west of Baghdad.[90] Even so communica-
tions between Sumer and Syria were not infrequently dis-
rupted to a degree which on occasion resulted in economic
difficulties both in the north and the south, and which threatened the hegemony of Ur. The final blow, however, came
from the Elamites who destroyed both the city and its temples,
and, as the king-list notes laconically, 'kingship was carried off
to Isin'.

At Isin, Ishbi-Erra tried to establish himself as legal successor to the Ur dynasty, but without lasting effect, and in fact
until the beginning of the eighteenth century BC there
was no one state with any overwhelming claim to hegemony,
though smaller states formed alliances round the larger ones.
To judge from the names, many of the rulers in Syria, Iraq
and Palestine, were Amorite. The archives discovered at Mari
on the Euphrates in eastern Syria, indicate close trading relationships and diplomatic contacts between Syria, Assyria and
southern Mesopotamia. The Assyrians in particular were
highly organized traders and one finds them in places as
distant as Kültepe (ancient Kanesh) in Anatolia.[91] The domi-
nant kingdom in Syria was Yamhad, centred on Aleppo, about
which, in archaeological terms, we know practically nothing,
for Aleppo has been in continuous occupation since the third
millennium and is unlikely to be dug up to satisfy the curiosity
of scholars.

The best-known figure of this period is surely the Amorite
Hammurapi, who brought together numerous small Mesopotamian states into an empire centred on his own city, Babylon.
He reigned for forty-two years (1792–1750 BC) and in the
course of that time vanquished Zimri-Lim and seized Mari,
overcame the power of Rim-Sin at Larsa, and conquered
Assyria as well as various city-states east of the Tigris,
though an attempt to expand further west beyond Mari was
halted by the strength of Yamhad. Hammurapi, however, is
best remembered not so much for his short-lived empire as
for his Law Code, which led some scholars to speak of him
as the Moses of Babylon, for his code does show remarkable
similarities both in content and character and even termino-

logy to the Old Testament, although it in turn stands in a legal tradition which goes back at least as far as the law code promulgated by Ur-Nammu.[92] Hammurapi's immediate successors were of lesser significance and his dynasty was brought to a violent end about 1595 BC by an incursion of the Hittites under Murshilis I.

The Hittites, who spoke an Indo-European language, had established a kingdom at Hattusas (modern Boghazköy) in northern Anatolia about 1650 BC and may have been forced by economic need to expand beyond the Anatolian plateau. They pushed into Cilicia and Syria and vanquished Yamhad; it was probably in the course of their Syrian campaign that they raided Babylon, whose destruction marked the end of the first phase of their expansion.

It is this period too which saw the emergence of the Hurrians as a major force and one finds large numbers of them in Syria and Palestine. In the middle of the sixteenth century BC there was formed in the Khabur region of North Syria the Hurrian kingdom of Mitanni which included Alalakh (south of Aleppo) and Nuzi (east of the Tigris in Iraq), and which dominated Assyria as a vassal state.

The Hittites did not tarry in Babylon, and the fall of Hammurapi's dynasty was followed by the rise of the Kassites, who had been infiltrating into Mesopotamia from the north-east at least as early as 1700 BC. The Kassites differed culturally and linguistically from the other inhabitants of Babylonia. They also had a rather different social structure, largely because they were – together with the Hurrians – the first people to use the horse-drawn two-wheeled chariot, the swiftest vehicle of its day, and treated the owners of horses and chariots as an elite group. Nevertheless, they soon adapted themselves to their surroundings, and it was under their rule that many of the literary works which had long circulated in Babylonia were edited into a canonical form which remained virtually unchanged until the cuneiform tradition finally died out. Probably in the fourteenth century they founded a new city called Dur Kurigalzu (near modern Baghdad), though Babylon continued throughout to retain much of its earlier importance.

Egypt at this time witnessed the emergence of the New

Kingdom (c. 1567 BC), the conquest of large areas of Palestine (which she was to retain for nearly three hundred years), and the reign of some of her most famous Pharaohs, including Queen Hatshepsut, Akhenaten and Ramses II. This period may have provided the background for the biblical story of Joseph and his brethren. The northward thrust of Egypt brought her into conflict first with the kingdom of Mitanni and later with the Hittites, who about 1380 BC, under their king Suppiluliumash, overran Mitanni and extended their dominion over Syria, with Aleppo and Carchemish as their main seats of government. The period is brilliantly illuminated by a cuneiform archive found at El-Amarna, a village about 190 miles south of Cairo, and consisting of the correspondence of the Pharaoh Amenophis III (1417–1379 BC) and of his successor not only with their vassal kings in Syria and Palestine but also with the rulers of the other great powers of the time – including Mitanni and Babylonia. The Hittite advance to the south made war with Egypt inevitable, and in 1300 BC the battle of Kadesh was fought, with the former led by Muwatallish and the latter by Ramses II, as a result of which Syria–Palestine was partitioned between the two.

The elimination of Mitanni by the Hittites encouraged the emergence of Assyria as a major force which threatened the might of the Hittites themselves, but the whole power structure was dislocated by the movements of peoples who surged forth, possibly as a result of severe famines, from (as is usually supposed) Anatolia and the Aegean, and substantial groups of these so-called 'Sea Peoples' swept through Syria and Palestine. At the same time the Hittite empire disintegrated, while the power of Egypt also entered upon a steady decline, the Pharaohs gradually losing control of their realm. One group among the 'Sea Peoples', the Philistines, now settled along the coast of Palestine, initially perhaps as Egyptian garrison troops. Further north, the Phoenicians (who belonged to the native Semitic population, or at least spoke a Semitic language) established extensive international trade networks using primarily sea but also land routes, while at the same time a people known as Israelites made their homes first in the hill-country of Palestine and eventually in some of the older Canaanite cities. A little later another Semitic people, the Ara-

maeans, enter the stage of history, though their origins, and
the question of whether they spread by a 'wave' or 'infiltration'
process, remain obscure. Some of them seem to have merged
peacefully with the existing population, especially in Babylonia. Others established city-states of their own, particularly
in North Syria, where the rise of Aramaean power can be
traced at Sam'al, Hamath, Arpad and (as the Old Testament
records) Damascus. There were yet other Aramaeans who
long retained their semi-nomadic way of life, and periodically
raided settled populations, especially in Assyria. Because of
this wide distribution of Aramaeans, the Aramaic language
spread over much of the Near East. It was later to become
a potent factor in holding together, successively, the great
empires of Assyria, Babylonia and Persia. The last adopted
it as the official *lingua franca*, and it remained current throughout the Near East until the Arab conquests of the seventh century; it also served as the language of a great ecclesiastical
literature (in which context it is usually called Syriac) and of
the Talmud.

Tiglath-Pileser I (1115–1077 BC), king of Ashur, checked the
spread of Aramaean power with a series of campaigns in the
west, and under Ashurnasirpal II (883–859 BC) Assyria grew
into an extensive empire. His son, Shalmaneser III, successfully confronted a formidable federation in the west led by
Damascus and including the kingdom of Israel under Jehu.
After a temporary decline, when Assyria was threatened by
the kingdom of Urartu (north of Lake Van) and lost much
of her empire, Tiglath-Pileser III ascended the throne of
Assyria in 745 BC and re-asserted Assyria's imperial might.
His policies, continued by his successors, included the estab-
lishment of a system of provinces, each under the control of
a governor directly responsible to the king, and the deporta-
tion of subject peoples, such as the 'Ten Tribes' of Israel, conquered by his successor in 722 BC. He also set out to reduce
to vassalage the states beyond his borders, including the
kingdom of Judah. The Assyrians, however, were finally over-
whelmed by a coalition between the Medes (from North-West
Iran) and a resurgent Babylonia in 612 BC, and fifteen years
later their vassal Judah also succumbed to the Babylonians.

The reader will have gathered that Ebla was not exactly the

centre about which the whole history of the ancient Near East revolved – at least as written hitherto. Among the hundreds of thousands of cuneiform tablets available,[93] it is mentioned about sixty times, and mostly in routine delivery notes and receipts.[94] It first[95] appears in Sargon's account – preserved in a carefully executed copy from the Old Babylonian period (early second millennium) – of his campaign in Syria:[96]

... Sargon, king of Kish,[97] was victorious in thirty-four campaigns and dismantled all the cities, as far as the shore of the sea ... Sargon, the king, prostrated himself in prayer before the god Dagan in Tuttul [modern Hit] and he gave him the Upper Region – Mari, Iarmuti and Ibla as far as the Cedar Forest and the Silver Mountain. Enlil did not let anybody oppose Sargon ...

In a list written about two thousand years later of Sargon's conquests, it was still remembered that they included the region 'from Ebla to Bitnadib (in) the land of Arman'.[98] Ebla is next heard of in an inscription on a stone mace offered to Naram-Sin by a loyal subject who hails him:[99] 'O divine Naram-Sin, king of the four regions, conqueror of Arman, Ebla and Elam'. Naram-Sin's own account of his conquest of Ebla survives in an Old Babylonian copy. It will be noted, incidentally, that the scholars responsible for the translations on this page speak of Ibla rather than Ebla. Cuneiform signs can often be read in more than one way (see p. 99), and the name of the city is almost always spelt with just two signs, of which the second is certainly to be read *la* but both *eb* and *ib* are possible values for the first. Hence the rival form Ibla, which some scholars continue to prefer:[100]

In all time, (since) the creation of men, no king among kings had ravaged the land of Armanum and Ibla. Henceforth (?) the god Nergal, having opened the way for the valiant Naram-Sin, has delivered Armanum and Ibla into his hands and made him a grant also of the Amanus, Mountain of Cedars, and of the upper sea. So it is that, by the arm of Dagan, who has made his royalty prevail, the valiant Naram-Sin conquered Armanum and Ibla: from the bank of the Euphrates as far as Ulisum, he having subdued the peoples of whom Dagan had lately made him a grant, they have become liable to do service to his god Aba, and he has conquered Amanus, Mountain of Cedars.

When Dagan, having decided in favour of the valiant Naram-Sin,

delivered Rish-Adad, king of Arman into his hands, and he had
bound him to the uprights of the entrance gate, he made himself
a statue of dolerite and dedicated it to Sin in these terms: 'Thus [says]
the valiant Naram-Sin, king of the four regions. When, Dagan having delivered Armanum and Ibla into my hands, I had bound up
Rish-Adad, the king of Armanum, it was then that I made my image
[which is here] ...[101]

Sargon's successes had evidently been short-lived; indeed the
opening sentence by implication denies them altogether. So
too, of course, were those of Naram-Sin.

At Lagash, under king Kaku probably less than a century
later, a piece of linen about twenty-five yards (forty-five cubits)
long is mentioned as having come from Ebla. Gudea, who
ruled Lagash during the second half of the twenty-second century BC, turned to Ebla for wood when he was commanded
in a dream to build a temple for Ningirsu, the tutelary deity
of his city. 'From the town of Urshu in the mountain (i.e.
upland plain) of Ebla, Gudea brought logs of pine, great fir-
trees, trunks of plane-trees and trees of the mountain; he made
them into roof beams in the temple.'[102]

The Third Dynasty of Ur has yielded more than half of the
extant references to Ebla; the majority come from Drehem
(ancient Puzrish-Dagan), the great centre established by Shulgi
for the maintenance and disposal of livestock. In one we read
that the 'man of Ebla' and others receive one goat each 'for
their house'.[103] In several other tablets the 'man of Ebla' (usually alongside 'men' of other cities, notably Mari) receives one
(or more) sheep, and more rarely an ox, ram, pig or even 'weak
beer and strong beer'.[104] No doubt these 'men of Ebla' were
visiting merchants (in fact the term 'merchant of Ebla' is once
substituted).[105] It is not clear whether the state felt obliged
to provide these victuals gratis for the emissaries of distant
cities such as Ebla, or whether the recipients had to pay for
them.[106] The latter must have been true of other consignments
received by various 'men of Ebla' – 'asses trained for riding',
a 'pig for pasturing', and quantities of copper and lead.[107] The
names of some 'men of Ebla' survive and should reflect the
town's ethnic composition; the verdict of I.J. Gelb was that
they were either Semitic and more precisely Akkadian (e.g.
Ili-Dagan) or 'of unknown background' (e.g. Kurbilag).[108]

Ebla's political status at this period is indicated by a few texts in which the 'man of Ebla' does not receive from the Ur authorities but gives, and not, it would seem, out of sheer generosity. One tablet, dated to the day during the forty-sixth year of Shulgi (2050 BC?),[109] records 'tribute' received from the 'man of Ebla' and consisting of five hundred wooden artefacts of some sort, variously explained as spindles[110] or throwing sticks.[111] Others mention offerings, mostly sheep, to the gods of Sumer.[112] In the reign of Shu-Sin (2038–2030 BC), Ebla features in a geographical list; since such lists generally enumerated conquests and dependencies (real or pretended), Ebla's inclusion tends to confirm that she was now an outpost of the Ur empire.[113] An added glimpse of her economic life is afforded by the commendation of her wood in a Sumerian myth, usually dated to this period, of a journey of the moon-god Nanna-Sin to Nippur. The god's advent, probably acted out in a ritual procession of divine images or emblems, would bring prosperity to the city; but to carry him a boat had to be built, and 'from Ebla its planking was brought'.[114] There are also a few references to a 'canal of Ebla' from which – or possibly to which – thirteen date-palms were once delivered,[115] but its connection with the town of Ebla is doubtful.

References to Ebla tail off as we enter the second millennium. Probably in the nineteenth century BC, we find Eblaite merchants at Kanesh,[116] near modern Kayseri, Turkey, where they upset the market by selling silver in exchange for copper at something like half the normal price.[117] One merchant, who has somehow acquired a quantity of copper, writes with obvious excitement to his partner: 'Many Eblaites have come here. The palace authorities have been giving them copper and getting silver in return at a rate of 1:26. In ten days at the most they will have exhausted all the copper in the palace and then I shall have a chance to buy some silver and deliver it to you.' Thereafter, tablets from the petty kingdom of Alalakh (south-west of modern Antakya in Turkey), from the seventeenth century BC, record that one king of Alalakh chose as his son's bride the daughter of the governor of Ebla and that he and one of his officials once travelled there; we also hear of a merchant of Alalakh who acquired the house – together with the maidservants – of a certain native of Ebla. From the fourteenth century layer at Alalakh, another tablet mentions a 'man of Ebla' in a list of soldiers.[118] Meanwhile the Pharaoh Tuthmosis III (1504–1450?) had included Ebla in a long list of his short-lived Syrian conquests.[119] The record to date peters out finally with a 'man of Ebla', tentatively dated between 1310 and 1187 BC, reported from Emar[120] (about sixty miles south-east of Aleppo), where the French began excavations in 1972.

The inadequacy of these references in fixing the site of Ebla is plain from the variety of locations suggested.[121] Most of these lay not in Syria but in Turkey, along a great arc extending from Mardin (about 250 miles north-east of Tell Mardikh) through the area of Gaziantep (about 100 miles north) as far as the Taurus Mountains (over 150 miles north-west). Of those scholars who did think of Syria, one located Ebla near modern Raqqah[122] (about 120 miles east-north-east) and another 'between Byblos and Alexandretta, near the coast'[123] (60 miles west at the nearest point). The most accurate guess was that of A. Goetze, who placed Ebla 'close to Aleppo'.[124] Gudea's reference to the 'mountain' or 'upland plain' of Ebla, whereas the terrain around Tell Mardikh is quite flat, was enough to put anyone off the scent.

All this documentation, it must be admitted, hardly amounts to very much. But the discovery of the fundamental importance of the Sumerians, whose very name had been erased from memory for thousands of years, suffices to show how rash it would be, on the basis of the paucity of outside references, to belittle the significance of Ebla.

CHAPTER 3

The Things That You're Liable to Read ...

What most people really want to know about any archaeological excavation anywhere between the Nile and the Tigris is: how does it relate to the Bible? Many investigators of the ancient Near East are rather tired of preoccupation with the Bible, and justifiably so. The civilizations that they bring back to life which pre-date on any reckoning the earliest writings in the Bible are of major importance in their own right and much of their legacy – witness, for example, the beginnings of medical science in Egypt or of astronomy in Mesopotamia – has come down to us through channels that have nothing to do with the Bible. To look at them with one eye alone while the other remains fixed on the Bible is to induce an astigmatism that distorts one's view both of these ancient civilizations and of the Bible itself. And yet public interest in the bearing of archaeology on the Bible is not to be ignored, and before going any further it may be useful to explain some of the fundamental issues.

The subject, to the layman, is a trifle perplexing. On the one hand he is assured that archaeological discoveries have dispelled the scepticism of past generations and confirmed the Bible as history[1] – 'as if the words of the Psalmist, "Truth shall spring out of the earth," had become literally fulfilled'.[2] On the other, he is told that archaeology has shown the Bible to be 'quite simply wrong';[3] and he is advised by Professor J.B.Pritchard, an eminent Biblical scholar, 'to face candidly some of the hard questions that have for so long perplexed scholars as they have tried to reconcile what has been handed down in the Bible with the artefacts which have come up from archaeological excavations in the lands of the Bible'.[4] Something is obviously wrong somewhere.

The first point that must be made is that the archaeological evidence is merely one of the factors which have to be considered in examining the historical realities which underlie the Bible. What matters just as much is one's assessment of the relevant biblical texts – when they were written, what they are based on, their authors' motives, their convictions as to the meaning of history – in short, the questions which fall under the heading of biblical criticism. The text of the Bible and the artefacts revealed by archaeology are, ideally at least, objective facts on which all agree; but very different views of the Bible can be and are reached by fitting these facts into different theoretical frameworks. Biblical criticism is less photogenic than archaeology, which may be why so few popular books on archaeology and the Bible give it attention. Conservatives tend to confine themselves to occasional sneers at 'long-outdated philosophical and literary theories (especially of the nineteenth-century stamp)'[5], even though it is no less true now than it was in the past that the vast majority of scholars rely on the separation of sources and on other bible-critical techniques as an indispensable tool of research. A more sceptical work might quote results which depend on various bible-critical theories without giving direct information as to the nature of and justification for the theories involved. Our first tack, then, must be to set out the problems which called biblical criticism into being, and to indicate briefly how it can work. For the purposes of the present book, which deals by and large with the most ancient periods, we may confine ourselves to the Pentateuch.[6]

Although the Pentateuch itself does not explicitly name Moses as the author of more than a few sections,[7] the belief that he wrote the whole appears in later books of the Old Testament (e.g. Malachi 3:22, Nehemiah 8:1), and is attributed to Christ himself in the New (e.g. Luke 24:44), and it thus became binding both in Judaism (in which it was stressed that the true author was God and Moses merely his scribe)[8] and in Christianity. But doubts soon arose. The Talmud records an argument between two rabbis of the second century AD[9] as to whether Moses could have written the last eight verses of the Pentateuch (which begin 'And Moses died there ...'). One Rabbi ascribed them to Joshua, but the other insisted that Moses, in tears, wrote even these last verses.[10] The

Gnostic teacher Ptolemaeus, during the same century,[11] divided the Pentateuch into three parts – the work of Moses, of the elders, and of God himself – on doctrinal grounds. It could not, he argued, have emanated from God alone, for much of it (e.g. the law of divorce in Deuteronomy 24) was rejected by the Saviour.[12] In the Clementine Homilies (early third century?), rational and doctrinal considerations together[13] lead to the conclusion that the Pentateuch is a corrupt form of a transcript derived by the Elders of Israel from Moses' oral teachings.[14]

Among the Jews of medieval Spain, Isaac ibn Yashush (died 1056) concluded that the account in Genesis 36:31ff. of kings who reigned over Edom 'before there reigned any king over the children of Israel' was written after the foundation of Israel's monarchy, and he assigned it to the reign of Jehoshapat. Abraham ibn Ezra (1089–1164), through whom alone ibn Yashush's suggestion has reached us,[15] dismissed it scornfully and declared that his book should be burnt. Yet he himself hinted that parts of the Pentateuch were post-Mosaic. On Genesis 12:6 ('and the Canaanites were then in the land'), he remarks: 'It appears that Canaan had captured the "land of Canaan" from others. But if it is not so, there is a secret to it, and the prudent will keep silent.' The 'secret' is that the verse seems to imply that the Canaanites had ceased to be a distinctive part of the population, which did not however take place before Solomon's time (1 Kings 9:16). Elsewhere he calls attention to such phrases as 'And Moses wrote'[16] and 'the other side of the Jordan' (Deuteronomy 1:1, applying to the eastern side and therefore written on the western, to which Moses never crossed), and advises the reader: 'If you will understand the secret of them, you will recognize the truth.' Some commentators were alarmed by such asides, and the great Nachmanides (1194–1270 AD), urged that 'molten gold be poured into his mouth'.[17]

Later scholars alighted on such passages as 'The Horites lived in Seir at one time, but the descendants of Esau occupied their territory . . . and then settled in the land instead of them, just as Israel did in their own territory which the Lord gave them' (Deuteronomy 2:12) or 'But to this day no one knows his [Moses'] burial-place,' seemingly written long after Moses' time.[18] Comparison of the Pentateuch with the other books of the Hebrew Bible pointed in the same direction. True, the latter refer to many of the enactments of the former. For example, Moses' command (Deuteronomy 11:29 ff.) to pronounce blessings and curses on Mount Gerizim and Mount Ebal was fulfilled by Joshua (Joshua 8:30 ff.), and it is stated of Amaziah (2 Kings 14:6) that he spared the sons of his father's murderers 'in obedience to the Lord's command written in the law of Moses', that children should not be put to death for their fathers (Deuteronomy 24:16). But at many points the remaining books seem surprisingly unaware of what the Pentateuch said. When Solomon dedicated the Temple he feasted fourteen days (1 Kings 8:65), and the following day was the twenty-third of the seventh month (2 Chronicles 7:10). But the Day of Atonement falls on the tenth of the seventh month (Leviticus 23:27); it would follow that Solomon and all Israel feasted through the Day of Atonement. Again, the Pentateuch stresses that sacrifice may be offered only in the one place 'which the Lord your God will choose as a dwelling for his Name' (Deuteronomy 12:11), by priests of Aaron's line (Numbers 18, etc.). Yet we find sacrifices by Gideon, Samuel and – most surprisingly – Elijah on Mount Carmel. The Pentateuch commands that fruit trees be spared in war (Deuteronomy 20:19), yet Elisha commands the Israelites 'to fell every good tree' in Moab (2 Kings 3:19). Most paradoxical of all are Ezekiel's enactments for the restored Temple (Ezekiel chapters 40–48). Sacrifices are to be slaughtered on tables (Ezekiel 40:41), while the Pentateuch speaks throughout of altars. He prescribes an atonement ceremony (Ezekiel 45:20) for the seventh day of the first month, of which the Pentateuch knows nothing. The New Moon offering enjoined by him quite differs from that of the Pentateuch. Numbers 28:11 f. has 'two bullocks, one ram, seven lambs, three tenths (of an ephah) of fine flour mingled with oil for each bullock ...' Ezekiel 46:6 f. specifies 'one bullock, one ram, six lambs, one ephah as grain-offering with the bullock ...' Most scholars, therefore, concluded that the Pentateuch was the work not of Moses but of a far later age.

At the same time scholars had long been labouring to reconcile the Pentateuch not with archaeology but with itself, and many concluded from the difficulties thus raised that the Pentateuch was not the work of any single author. Thus at Genesis 17:17 Sarah is ninety years old, yet in chapter 20 she is the target of King Abimelech's advances. The interval between the sale of Joseph and the arrival of his brethren in Egypt is twenty-two years,[19] yet within that period his brother Judah marries and has two sons who grow to manhood (and die), is subsequently seduced by his daughter-in-law (in disguise), who bears him twin sons (Genesis 38), one of whom (Perez) has two sons of his own (46:12).[20] Could three generations have been accommodated in so short a span? The Ark was made according to Deuteronomy 10:3 by Moses, and according to Exodus 37:1 ff. by Bezalel. It was installed in the Tent of Meeting (Exodus 40:21), which always according to Numbers 2:17 remained fast in the centre of Israel's camp, yet according to Numbers 10:33 it travelled three days' journey before them. Was the sending of spies the bidding of God (Numbers 13:2), or the people (Deuteronomy 1:22)? Did Aaron die on Mount Hor (Numbers 33:31 ff.) or at Moserah (Deuteronomy 10:6)?

Again, a number of duplicate accounts of the same event, with apparent discrepancies, have been identified – relating say to the creation,[21] or to the naming of places (e.g. Beersheba)[22] or people (e.g. Jacob).[23] Somewhat differently, what purport to be two (or more) different events are recounted in such terms as to suggest that we are in fact dealing with two (or more) accounts of the same occasion. Hagar is twice expelled by her mistress (Genesis 16 and 21:9 ff.), and an angel comes to her aid near a well in the wilderness. Sarah is twice passed off as Abraham's sister, and taken to the house or harem of the local king, but released after divine intervention (Genesis 12:10 ff. and 20); much the same befalls Isaac's wife Rebecca (26:7 ff.). The line of descendants of Cain (Genesis 4:17 ff.) and Kenan (Genesis 5:12 ff.) look like variants with a common origin:

```
                                                      /Jabal
        /Cain — Enoch — Irad — Mehujael — Methushael — Lamech—Jubal
  Adam                                                 Tubal-cain
       \ Seth
          \ Enosh                                          Shem
             \Kenan–Mahalalel–Jared–Enoch–Methuselah–Lamech–Noah–Ham
                                                             \Japheth
```

The examples may be multiplied endlessly and were all seen as evidence that the Pentateuch had more than one source.

Moreover, some narratives seem heavy with repetitions and, on occasion, discrepancies. Thus there is one flood story, but Genesis 6:5–8 (which describes the wickedness of mankind whose punishment Noah alone deserves to escape) is paralleled in the next four verses; Genesis 6:18–20 (the command that Noah and the animals should enter the ark) is virtually repeated in 7:1–3, except that the former always requires just one pair and the latter sometimes seven; and so on. Again, the sale of Joseph to Egypt is recounted but once, yet it raises the same sort of questions: What did happen to Joseph between the Ishmaelites (Genesis 37:25, 27, 28; 39:1), Midianites (37:28) and Medanites (37:36)? Why does Judah urge his brothers not to commit murder (Genesis 37:26) when Reuben has already dissuaded them (v. 22)? Why is Reuben unaware (v. 29) of what had happened to Joseph? Many deduced that in such cases two alternative accounts, from two different sources, had been reworked by an editor to yield a single, composite version.

It is one thing to find the Pentateuch to be composite but quite another to unscramble it. The latter endeavour has produced a vast literature, and there is room here for only the barest sketch. In 1753 Jean Astruc set out to distinguish what he called 'the original documents which Moses appears to have used to compose the book of Genesis'.[24] Noting that the deity was sometimes (e.g. throughout chapter 1) called 'God' (Hebrew *Elohim*) and sometimes 'the Lord' (Hebrew *Yhwh*, which had commonly but wrongly been read Jehovah by Christian scholars), he supposed that two main documents were present, each characterized by one of these names – apart from a residue of some 130 verses, which he distributed among ten minor sources. He was thus able to attribute, say, the story of Hagar's expulsion in Genesis 16 to the 'Jehovistic' source and that in Genesis 21 to the 'Elohistic' source, and treat similarly the two accounts of Sarah's abduction in Genesis 12 and Genesis 20. In 1805 De Wette drew attention to the distinctive style and thought of Deuteronomy and maintained that it must have had a separate author.[25] Then in 1853, Hupfeld found[26] that the Elohistic portions of Genesis varied in diction, some parts being especially formal and precise[27] and others relatively vivid and brisk.[28] He pointed to the two Elohistic accounts of the naming of Bethel[29] and of the re-naming of Jacob as Israel[30] and inferred the existence of not one but two Elohistic writers, which brought the number of sources up to four: J, who used the name Yhwh throughout; D, the author of Deuteronomy; and the two employers of Elo-him – the most formal of whom came to be called P (because of his supposedly priestly character) and the other E.

In some sections of the Pentateuch, identification of these sources seemed straightforward. Genesis 24, for example, could be assigned to J, Genesis 21:5–21 to E, Genesis 23 to P. But others (e.g. the flood) required extensive surgery; for example Genesis 7:16 has Elohim in its first half and Yhwh in its second, and was therefore divided between P and J. The separation of E from P, despite the fact that both used the same divine name, was nevertheless found to be feasible on account of the striking differences in style. The attempt to con-tinue this analysis beyond Genesis was impeded by the phasing out of Elohim after the first few chapters of Exodus. Before Exodus 6 the name appears about twice per chapter, after it appears about one chapter in five.[31] But through detailed study[32] of the content and style of the passages attributable to each source (J, E, P) in Genesis, scholars were not only con-vinced that all three continued into Exodus–Numbers, but even identified, for much if not all of the time,[33] the contribu-tion of each right down to the end of Numbers (Deuteronomy, of course, belonged to the fourth source, D).

The attempt to date these four sources began with D. In 2 Kings 22 f. we read that, in the eighteenth year of King Josiah (622/1 BC), 'the book of the law' was found in the Temple and it moved the king to carry out a great reform. He swept away idolatry including the worship of the 'host of heaven' and sup-pressed the many 'high places' where people had worshipped in Judah. These measures suggest that the book was Deu-teronomy, which emphatically confines sacrifice to a single site (Deuteronomy 12) and which is the only book of the Penta-teuch to proscribe explicitly[34] the worship of the 'host of heaven'. The date of composition of D was thought to be no more than a generation or two earlier, partly because the worship of the 'host of heaven' seems to have been first introduced by King Manasseh (686–642 BC) and partly because of the similarities in style between D and the seventh-century prophet Jeremiah. The dating of the other sources was much more difficult, but the work of Julius Wellhausen[35] led to a scheme that has won widespread acceptance. Space permits us to touch on the arguments based on just one of his criteria, namely the place of worship. He showed that in both J and E the patriarchs set up altars wherever they abide, at what later appear as famous sacred places (e.g. Hebron, Bethel). Yet the accounts of their foundation contain no hint that these are, as in D's day, illicit cult-centres. On the contrary, Bethel 'is none other than the house of God, and ... the gate of heaven'. Thus he assigned J and E to a period before Josiah, when – as the historical books show – sacrifice was offered by prophets, kings and others in a multiplicity of holy places.[36] The relative priority of the two was much debated, but the impression grew that E was more advanced[37] and therefore later. J is now generally ascribed to the tenth century and E to the eighth.

Before Wellhausen, P was believed to be the oldest source in view of its many numbers, names and other details.[38] Wellhausen pointed out, however, that P throughout envisages a single centre of sacrifice – the Israelites worship at the Tabernacle during their wilderness days, and this is to be 'an everlasting statute throughout their generations' – and thus presupposes that very centralization which D was striving to introduce; hence P was to be dated later than D. Moreover, the discrepancies between the ceremonial enjoined in Ezekiel chapters 40–48 and in P imply that Ezekiel (in the early sixth century BC) was unaware of, and therefore wrote earlier than, P; P was then a product of the sixth or fifth century. As for P's numbers, names, etc., Wellhausen held that 'they are not drawn from contemporary records, but are the fruit solely of late Jewish fancy, a fancy, which, it is well known, does not design or sketch, but counts and constructs, and produces nothing more than barren plans.' The complete Pentateuch, in which all these documents had been combined by a series of editors, was first promulgated by Ezra c. 444 BC at the assembly reported in Nehemiah 8.[39]

Such a reconstruction of course drastically affects the

inferences which can be drawn from the texts. Wellhausen regarded his sources as written documents, each of which came into existence at a particular point in time. Each would then reflect the life of the period in which it was written, rather than that which it purported to record. For example, the story of the Golden Calf was assigned to J and E, and thus to the eighth century BC or thereabouts. If we look to that period for the origin of the story, we could suppose that it arose from an attempt to discredit the worship of golden calves then practised in the northern kingdom.[40] Again, P is considered the source of the story in Numbers 16 in which Moses faced a rebellion of Levites, led by Korah, who complained to Moses and Aaron: 'You take too much upon yourselves. Every member of the community is holy ... Why do you set yourselves up above the assembly of the Lord?' Now in D the priests are called Levites, or sons of Levi, with no hint of any distinction among the Levitical families; but in P (especially Numbers 3–4) the priests are called sons of Aaron, and the Levites are strictly separated from them and limited to menial duties in the sanctuary. We may suppose that in D's time all Levites could officiate as priests, but that by P's time only one family, which traced its ancestry back to Aaron, had secured the priesthood for itself.[41] The Korah rebellion might then reflect the resentment the Levites may have felt at that period – not in Moses' time. Similarly, 'we attain to no historical knowledge of the patriarchs, but only of the time when the stories about them arose in the Israelite people; this later age is here unconsciously projected, in its inner and its outward features, into hoar antiquity, and is reflected there like a glorified mirage'.[42]

The division of the Pentateuch between the four sources J, E, D and P has won at least qualified acceptance from the vast majority of biblical scholars, but there are many variations on the theme. Some discrepancies and duplications were soon seen within the four sources themselves. For example J twice recounts the abduction of a patriarch's wife, in Genesis 12 (Sarah) and Genesis 26 (Rebecca); E sometimes retains the use of Elohim after Exodus 3 (e.g. in Exodus 13 f., 18 f., Numbers 22 ff.) but usually prefers Yhwh (in Exodus 32 etc.); D addresses Israel now in the singular, now in the plural, with

1 The palace ruins at Persepolis, the ancient capital of the Persian kings

2 The Darius inscription carved into the rock at Behistun

3 An artist's impression of Ebla before it was sacked in the third millennium BC (*from* Science Year, The World Book Science Annual. © *1977 Field Enterprises Educational Corporation*)

4 The village, Tell Mardikh today

5 The Ebla acropolis as seen from the lower town

6 A shepherd sets out with his flock as dawn rises over Tell Mardikh

7 Part of the Ebla excavations showing, in the foreground, the squares into which the sectors are divided

8 The remains of private dwellings in the lower city. The surrounding city ramparts may be seen in the distance.

9 Reconstructed pottery in
Professor Matthiae's office

10 Panniers of pot-sherds
awaiting classification in the
outer courtyard of the Tell
Mardikh base camp

11 Professor Matthiae (with book in hand) and Professor Fronzaroli (with glasses) taking an early morning roll-call of Arab labourers

12 Professor Matthiae with one of his assistants in his Tell Mardikh office

13 Living quarters at the Tell Mardikh base camp

14 Some of the younger members of the Ebla expedition relaxing over
Turkish coffee after their day's work. Chaim Bermant is in the foreground

15 Close-up of one of the trenches at Ebla

16 Ebla – the remains of a temple

some duplication (contrast 6:6ff. with 11:18ff.); P seems inconsistent in naming Esau's wives.[43] Some reacted by adding to the number of sources, suggesting,[44] for example, J^1 and J^2, and – in an extreme case[45] – seven sub-sources for P, each with one or more revisers plus various redactors. Since these additional documents were assigned to much the same age (tenth to fifth centuries BC), they required little change in the estimate which Wellhausen had ascribed to them. Most scholars, however, were wary of excessive fragmentation, if only because it would leave the basic unity of purpose of the Pentateuch unexplained. Instead, a new view arose of the function of the writers J E D P: they were not primarily authors but compilers, and each transmitted material of varying origins, within which discrepancies were only to be expected. The material reached J E D P largely in oral form for which many possible origins have been proposed – the popular circulation of folk-lore, the recitation of epic poetry, the liturgy of some festival at which the nation recounted its history,[46] the scholarly tradition of a particular (e.g. priestly) school over many generations – and the possible role of written documents (e.g. laws, genealogical lists) is not ruled out. At all events, the very principle of attaching a single date to any source was largely abandoned[47] and it was suggested that all four sources embodied elements ranging over a considerable time-scale (though not all periods were equally represented in all the sources).[48]

All this, however, meant that the J E D P documents raised almost as many problems as they solved – if, indeed, they solved any at all. One now had to identify the constituent literary units of each document and then investigate the prehistory of each unit. Many began to wonder whether it was still justifiable to divide the Pentateuch into as many as four separate documents if discrepancies could be tolerated in one and the same document, and so we find proposals to reduce their number. Some suggested that the E sections in fact consisted of supplements to J, and never constituted a separate document. In Sweden, Ivan Engnell[49] proposed a prehistory of the Pentateuch which involved no documents at all. One circle of scholars edited into written form various oral traditions that had long been current in Israel, and combined them

with elements from their own traditional lore; in extent th
latter correspond roughly to the P, and the former to th
J and E together, of earlier critics. This work (called the 'l
work' by Engnell) was completed in the fifth century; it com
prised Genesis–Numbers, ending with Moses' death. Abou
the same time, the material which now stands in the book
Deuteronomy–Kings was similarly compiled from ancien
traditions by another circle, with rather different interests an
outlook. They began their work (which he called the D work
with speeches attributed to Moses which roughly correspon
to the present book of Deuteronomy. That material was late
detached and inserted just before the last item in the P work
the death of Moses. Thus the authors D and P become circle
or schools, and the authors J and E disappear altogether. I
is the elimination of J which moves most scholars to protes
for they claim to see in the material ascribed to J the unifyin
stamp of an individual of genius. But this is a subjective im
pression, which Engnell evidently did not share.

Analysis, then, moved on from the documents to the variou
units – such as poems, codes of law, narrative – embedde
in each. Thus much of the Pentateuch came to be considere
far more ancient than earlier critics would have conceded, bu
not necessarily more trustworthy as history. Two example
from the work of Gunkel, the pioneer in this area, will be in
structive. The story of Jacob and Esau in Genesis chapters 25
28 originated as a popular tale which contrasts two differen
occupations, represented by two brothers – shepherd an
hunter. The tale commends the shepherd: he always has foo
to eat, and thus he has the advantage over the hunter, wh
has to find his living day by day. Only later was this tale recas
and referred to Jacob and Esau, in the light of the very dif
ferent competition between Israel and Esau's supposed de
scendants, the Edomites.[50] Again the historical meaning o
Genesis 38 is that the tribe of Judah once had three clans, Er
Onan and Shela. The first two died out, but two new clan
(Perez and Zerah) emerged. Hence a tale which represente
each clan or tribe as an individual, and which is held togethe
by the purely fictional motif – familiar also from the book o
Ruth – of the widow (Tamar) who requires issue from her lat
husband's kin.[51]

Many conservative scholars have stressed[52] that, for all the discrepancies, the overall correspondence in content (regarding the narrative passages at least) between the different 'documents' is impressively close. They have inferred that the channels of oral prehistory that lead back from each 'document' meet ultimately in a single main stream of living tradition which continued unbroken from the days of Moses or even of Abraham. On that basis, one may resort to any part of the Pentateuch for an historical reconstruction, because all spring from the same source. Through such treatment of biblical passages, in combination with archaeological evidence, scholars such as W.F. Albright have maintained, for example, the historicity of the three Patriarchs.

Yet two of the most recent studies, by T.L. Thompson and J. van Seters,[53] though concerned primarily with the accounts of the Patriarchs, have pleaded for a return to something like Wellhausen's view of the character of the documents and argue that the only sort of oral traditions on which the documents need be supposed to have drawn[54] are the folklore motifs of the (first millennium) Canaanite/Israelite world –motifs which had not originally had anything to do with the Patriarchs. This judgment on the literary background, together with their own reassessment of the archaeological evidence, has led them to doubt whether the Patriarchs ever lived at all.

The countless generations of devout Jews and Christians who accepted – and still accept – the Bible as the word of God were not unaware of the discrepancies, inconsistencies and duplications. How did they explain them?

The classical Jewish commentators ingeniously explained away some of the indications of post-Mosaic date within the Pentateuch. Ibn Ezra for example, took 'king (of Israel)' at Genesis 36:31 to refer to Moses. Sforno (c. 1500) explained 'Israel's territory which the Lord gave to them' (Deuteronomy 2:12) as the lands of the kings Sihon and Og, which Israel had already conquered.[55] One could in any case appeal to Moses' prophetic power, which enabled him to speak from the standpoint of a later generation.[56] Some Christian fundamentalists have conceded the presence of post-Mosaic additions and amendments,[57] but this would have been (and remains) unacceptable to traditional Judaism.[58]

Such passages as those assembled on p. 47 from outside the Pentateuch, suggesting that many of its enactments had not been promulgated even by the time of Ezekiel, were very differently expounded in the Jewish sources. Amid the celebrations surrounding the dedication of the Temple, Solomon forgot the Day of Atonement, and was much distressed, until the Holy Spirit reassured him: 'Go, eat thy bread with joy ...'[59] Elijah did not break the law restricting sacrifice to priests, for he was none other than Phineas[60] and the command that Mount Carmel be the site of his sacrifice established the principle that temporary enactments may supersede in times of dire emergency.[61] The atonement rite which Ezekiel (45:20) enjoined: 'And so shall you do on the seventh of the month' was re-interpreted to read: 'And so shall you do if seven (of the Twelve Tribes) make a new (and false enactment which leads the community to sin).'[62] Other parts of Ezekiel which seemed to contradict the Pentateuch, would, said the Rabbis, be explained in the fulness of time by Elijah,[63] but it was axiomatic that an explanation, however elusive, did exist

Duplication in itself has not greatly worried conservatives. R.K. Harrison points to the duplicate dreams of both Joseph (Genesis 37) and Pharaoh (Genesis 41),[64] and to the frequent repetitions elsewhere in New Eastern literature, and concludes that duplication is only to be expected.[65] The Rabbis even added their own duplications to explain inconsistencies. Since Numbers 10:33 states that the ark kept three days' journey ahead of the people, while in Numbers 2 the ark was at the centre of the camp, they deduced that there were two arks[66] and from the different tithe laws in Numbers 18:21 ff. and Deuteronomy 14:22 ff., they inferred that two tithes were demanded.[67] Other inconsistencies involved the Rabbis in complex hypotheses, as the problem of the Midianites and Ishmaelites in Genesis 37 will illustrate.[68] Nachmanides (born 1194) declared that a *caravan of Ishmaelites* (37:25), which Judah thought to be manned by Ishmaelites alone (v. 27) had in fact been hired to *Midianite traders* (v. 28). Joseph's brethren sold him to the latter, who handed him over to the *Ishmaelite* caravaneers, who *brought* everyone (and therefore *Joseph*) down *to Egypt* (v. 28; 39:1), and then handed Joseph back to the *Midianites* to be *sold* (37:36). In many such cases, conservative Christian scholarship today prefers to ascribe the apparent conflict to an imperfect understanding of the ancient Near Eastern background of the Old Testament. Thus, K.A. Kitchen finds nothing uncommon in the use of different names for one group within a short compass and points to 'the Egyptian stele of Sebekkhu (*c.* 1850 BC), who refers to the one general foe of his pharaoh's Palestinian campaign as "Asiatic bedouin", "vile Syrians" and "Asiatics" '.[69] Again to stray for a moment outside the Pentateuch, the reason for the discrepancies between numbers in Chronicles and in Kings[70] is that 'oriental peoples of antiquity frequently assigned symbolic and schematic categories to numbers ... If other evidence from Near Eastern sources concerning numbers generally is of any value in this connection, it would imply that the Old Testament numerical computations rest upon some basis of reality which was quite familiar to the ancients, but which is unknown to modern scholars.'[71]

On the variation in the use of 'the Lord'/'God', taken as the first clue in source analysis, conservatives point out that much the same occurs in other works whose literary unity is not in question, both within the Bible (e.g. the Book of Jonah) and outside (cf. the alternation of Baal and Haddu in Ugaritic myths). Many suppose that the two names had different associations, and that the choice between them was determined by the context, but just what these associations were is not agreed. G.T. Manley supposed that 'God' retains an 'abstract and conceptual quality', while 'the Lord' in contrast 'presents God as a Person, and so brings Him into relationship with other, human, personalities'.[72] To the Rabbis, 'the Lord' indicated the attribute of mercy and 'God' that of justice. Such verses as 'And the *Lord* said : I will destroy man' (Genesis 6 : 7), or 'And *God* heard their groaning' (Exodus 2 : 24) – led them not to abandon that belief but to declare : 'Woe to the wicked who turn the attribute of Mercy into the attribute of Judgment' – and vice versa.[73]

Conservatives today have devoted their energies not only to resolving problems within the Bible but also to direct attacks on critical theories. Some passages, for example, best fit Moses' time, such as Deuteronomy 11 : 10 : 'For the land which you are entering to occupy it is not like the land of Egypt

from which you have come, where, after sowing your seed
you irrigated it *by foot like a vegetable garden*' – a detail natura
in the mouth of Moses, but unexpected in a document origi
nating centuries after the conquest.[74] The redactor(s) responsible for combining the sources must have been, to judge from
the many duplications and inconsistencies that critics dis
cover, remarkably dim-witted; to this one could reply tha
each source was held sacred, and that editorial authority to
amend them was exercised with the greatest circumspection.[75]
P too emerges as a puzzle in purely psychological terms, e.g
in devising elaborate rules and procedures for the Levites
carrying the Tabernacle (Numbers 4) – a situation which (if
its reality is granted at all) lay in the distant past. Again, relations between Samaritans and Jews were – or so it was once
thought – bitterly hostile in Ezra's day, and ended in schism;
if the Pentateuch was not complete until Ezra's day, how could
its acceptance by the Samaritans be explained? And here the
reply might be that to judge from the evidence now available,
the estrangement between Samaritans and Jews was a far
slower process than was previously imagined, with close relations between the two persisting well into the Christian era,
and the Samaritans took over their Pentateuch in the Has-
monean period.[76]

All that having been said one must add that the overwhelming majority of biblical scholars employ some sort of distinction between older and younger material in the Pentateuch
but – barring some such unlikely event as the excavation of, say,
a ninth-century BC copy of the J document – debate will long
continue as to what is really meant, in historical terms, by the
Bible. One question, more than any other is likely to bring
out the variety of views current today. Have the artefacts and
texts revealed through archaeology proved that the Old Testament in any instance is in error?

We may begin with the problem of the camel. The Bible
tells us that the wealth of Abraham and Jacob included camels
– and, in particular, that Jacob had thirty camels to spare as
a gift for Esau (Genesis 32:16). Yet there is very little evidence
of the effective domestication of the camel (at least beyond
Arabia) before the very end of the second or the beginning
of the first millennium,[77] and so the mention of camels here

is widely regarded as an anachronism.[78] Conservatives may reply that sporadic cases of limited domestication, of which archaeological traces would not necessarily have been found, must have preceded the general use of camels attested in the first millennium, and cannot be ruled out even as early as the patriarchal age;[79] and they marshal whatever meagre evidence exists (e.g. early remains of camel bones, possible written allusions) in support.[80] More serious problems are posed by the mention of a Philistine kingdom in Palestine, in the days of Abraham (Genesis 21:22 ff.) and Isaac (Genesis 26), for we first hear of the Philistines in the fifth year of Ramses III (c. 1190 BC), as one of the 'Sea Peoples' who were migrating from the Aegean shores and isles and tried to invade Egypt. Against this it is argued that objects of Aegean manufacture, dating from a much earlier period (c. 1900–1700 BC) and suggesting major expansion of Aegean trade at that time, have been discovered at Palestinian sites such as Hazor and Lachish; it would thus not be impossible to imagine, in the second millennium, one or more colonies of Aegean traders, among whom Philistines (though not mentioned outside the Bible until later) might have been present and even predominant.[81] Also problematic is the name 'Ur of the Chaldees' (Genesis 11:31). Cuneiform documents from Ur never associate it with the Chaldeans,[82] who indeed did not appear as an ethnic element in Babylonia before the eleventh century BC. A conservative might regard 'of the Chaldees' as an addition by a later scribe (or a prescient Moses) to identify the city more readily in a period when it was under Chaldean control.

At Jericho, John Garstang excavated what he thought to be the great walls that fell in Joshua's day.[83] The conclusion, however, which Dame Kathleen Kenyon reached from her own excavations, and which has won general acceptance, is that the walls in fact date from the third millennium BC.[84] She also found that Jericho was abandoned shortly after 1350 BC,[85] and this conflicts with the thirteenth-century date posited for Joshua by most scholars today.[86] Dame Kathleen considers the possibility that Jericho may have been reoccupied in the thirteenth century, and that natural erosion in the centuries that followed swept away all trace of it, but adds: 'all that can be said is that there is no evidence at all of it in stray finds or in tombs'.[87] Not surprisingly, however, some conservatives take the possibility seriously.[88] There is also the case of Ai (also destroyed by Joshua) which the Bible tells us, was a city of twelve thousand inhabitants (Joshua 8:25). Excavation, however, revealed a third-millennium city which was destroyed c. 2400 BC with hardly a trace of later occupation.[89] One could still suppose with R.K. Harrison,[90] that the inhabitants of nearby Bethel occupied Ai as an advance defensive base (though this turns the Bible's 'king of Ai' into a military commander from Bethel), or, with Kitchen,[91] that the levels of Joshua's day may have been eroded away, or that Ai has been wrongly located. Most archaeologists, however, feel that Ai raises the problem of conflict between Bible and archaeology in an acute form, and that attempts to harmonize the two are nothing more than special pleading.[92]

In Jonah 3:3 we read that Nineveh was 'a vast city, three days' journey across', yet excavation has demonstrated that 'at the height of its prosperity Nineveh was enclosed by an inner wall of about seven and three quarter miles circuit'.[93] In explanation, A.L. Oppenheim suggested that 'the green reaches of the outer city' beyond the walls, containing houses and farms which provided the city with food and raw materials, were included.[94]

The Book of Daniel states that, on the fall of Babylon 'Darius the Mede took the kingdom' (Daniel 6:1); his father is named as Ahasuerus, equivalent to Xerxes (Daniel 9:1, cf. p. 77); and in Daniel 6:26f. this King Darius writes 'to all peoples and nations of every language throughout the whole world', informing them: 'I have issued a decree that in all my royal domains men shall fear and reverence the God of Daniel.' That he reigned before Cyrus is implied by Daniel 6:29, as usually translated: 'So this Daniel prospered in the reign of Darius, and in the reign of Cyrus the Persian.' But contemporary inscriptions tell us that it was Cyrus who conquered Babylon, adding it to his great empire, and they give no hint of his having been preceded by any Darius.[95] This Median kingdom under Darius is therefore dismissed by most scholars as fiction. D.J. Wiseman, however, proposes to identify

Darius with Cyrus himself,[96] translating Daniel 6:29 anew:
'... in the reign of Darius, even the reign of Cyrus the Persian'.[97] True, the inscriptions never call Cyrus by the name
Darius; moreover, Cyrus' father is always called Cambyses,
never Xerxes; but as Wiseman points out, kings in the ancient
Near East often bore more than one name. Again Cyrus was
of Persian lineage, not Median; but Wiseman reminds us that
Cyrus had been king of the Medes since he overcame the
Median monarch Astyages, his maternal grandfather,[98] in 550
BC. Worse still, Daniel elsewhere refers to Cyrus not as 'Darius
the Mede' but by his usual name and title 'Cyrus king of Persia'
(10:1; compare 1:21); Wiseman hopes that further research
may explain this peculiarity'.[99]

Much briefer consideration needs to be given to the more
precarious arguments from silence that are sometimes directed
against the historicity of the Bible. For example, the biblical
accounts of Joseph, the plagues or the Exodus have been
questioned on the ground that they are not mentioned in contemporary Egyptian records. However, details of officials
other than the pharaohs themselves are scanty, particularly
in the period of the foreign Hyksos dynasty (c. 1684–1567 BC),
to which Joseph is often dated;[100] and the Egyptians' reluc-
tance to record reverses would explain the silence as to the
Exodus. Again, the Bible gives frequent details of settlement
which are not always confirmed by excavations on site, but
archaeology is not and has never claimed to be an exact
science, and a chance probe with a spade can overturn conclusions built up by several generations of scholars. It is not
unusual for a gap in the archaeological record, from which
a break in occupation was once inferred, to be filled in by subsequent excavations.[101] An example is Gezer, which appeared
after the expedition of R.A.S. Macalister in the first decade
of this century to have lain abandoned between the ninth and
seventh centuries BC, yet the findings of the American expedition over the past decade point to continuous occupation.[102]
What has not been excavated to date is not automatically ficti-
tious and as Professor William Dever once observed: 'I sometimes get to think that the worst way to find anything is to
go looking for it.'

Let us now turn to the earliest periods, for which one may

speak more properly of geology than of archaeology. The findings of science have of course compelled the all but universal abandonment of literal interpretation of the biblical creation stories and the faithful now argue that the Bible expressed itself in figurative terms which could be readily understood in every age, and that an account which conformed with the conclusions of modern science would have been unintelligible before the nineteenth century and, no doubt, long obsolete by the twenty-ninth. There are, however, still Rabbis of whom Rabbi Menachem M. Schneerson is the most eminent, who insist that Genesis 1 is literally true and that the world is some 5,738 years old.[103]

The Flood is placed by the biblical chronology in the late third millennium BC,[104] but excavations at many sites outside Mesopotamia have reached down to a much earlier age (estimated, for example, as 8000 BC at Jericho or 6000 BC at Mersin in southern Turkey) without finding any trace of a universal deluge. At Ur in 1929, Sir Leonard Woolley made his famous discovery of a stratum of mud some ten feet thick at a level dating to the Ubaid period (usually dated to the last centuries of the fifth millennium – see p. 17), and many saw this as proof of Noah's Flood. Excavations elsewhere, however, have offered little confirmation. At Ur itself Woolley apparently dug five pits down through the early levels of occupation and found 'flood deposits' in only two,[105] though a level of mud and river sand some six feet thick found at Nineveh may belong to the same period. But at other sites, though 'flood layers' have occasionally been found, these prove to belong to a different age and most sites (including Ubaid, only four miles from Ur, and excavated down to the level of the Ur 'flood layer' by Woolley himself) have yielded none at all. All these 'floods' must have been more or less localized, requiring no more dramatic explanation than that the Euphrates had burst its banks.[106]

Where does all this leave the historicity of the biblical Flood?[107] That it is pure myth is certainly one conclusion which the archaeological evidence admits (though, incidentally, it does little to explain the remarkably widespread currency of flood stories).[108] Others have posited a cataclysm far back in the Stone Age,[109] without venturing, in view of the lack of archaeological data, to speculate as to its precise nature and scope,[110] but this sacrifices the biblical chronology if nothing else. Another view is that the Flood was purely local and that one or more of the Mesopotamian mud-layers might even relate to it.[111] The biblical text, however, cannot be so construed.[112] Perhaps one way of accepting the literal truth of all that the Bible has to say about the time and scope of the Flood is to dwell on the statements (Genesis 8:13 f.) that the earth dried out, and argue that there is no knowing *a priori* what sort of archaeological traces (if any) the Flood might have left, though of course, if one is bent on defending the literal truth of the Flood, the lack of archaeological support is the least of one's problems.[113]

The biblical creation and flood stories are, it is well known, paralleled by accounts in cuneiform and so they raise another, more general, question: do the parallels that can be drawn between the Bible and more ancient writings discredit the Bible? The question reaches at least as far back as the second century AD, when Trypho the Jew assailed Justin Martyr's belief in the virgin birth by pointing to the Greek legend of Perseus 'born of Danae, still a virgin, by him that they entitle Zeus flowing down upon her in the form of gold'.[114]

Three points may be made here. First, not all parallels are equally significant, and some are not significant at all. Friedrich Delitzsch, for example, called attention to such similarities as that between David's claim that he had slain lions[115] and the reliefs showing the Assyrian monarch Ashurbanipal hunting lions.[116] To collect parallels such as these is certainly possible and some may even find it interesting, but it is hard to see what point there is in the exercise; it seems rather to be a symptom of a morbid condition which has been termed parallelomania,[117] in which the patient pays excessive attention to the similarities while all but oblivious to the differences between the products of two distinct cultures, and imagines all manner of genetic connections between the two. We may imagine a scholar four thousand years hence, whose knowledge of the second millennium AD was about as good as our knowledge of the second millennium BC, coming up with something like:

A persistent tradition, which is not at all in keeping with the

general picture established for the political history of Europe in the
eighteenth and nineteenth centuries, asserts that around 1800 AD
France produced a leader called Napoleon, who greatly extended
her dominion. Various sources reckon Holland, Poland and Spain
among the conquests of this Napoleon. That the tradition is devoid
of historical worth has now been demonstrated by the discovery of
two maps of Europe, bearing the dates 1775 and 1825 respectively,
and both assigning to France a far more modest territory than is
claimed in the Napoleonic tales. As to the origin of the myth, an
easy explanation suggests itself. Among the Greeks of the first pre-
Christian millennium, whose influence on later European thought
and culture has been so well documented, we find the worship of
a sun-god Apollon (whence Latin 'Apollo') who was also conceived
of as an archer-god who shot from afar the arrows of destruction.
The Napoleon myth is simply an account of the sun-god Apollon's
career, transposed to the period c. 1800 AD. Evidently the devotees
of Apollon, calling upon his name again and again in their religious
frenzy, had come to run the n which ended one invocation into the
beginning of the next, whence Napollon, which had developed to
Napoleon. The arrows of Apollon are of course replaced by the guns
and other weaponry of the age in which 'Napoleon' was set. He is
related to have been born in Corsica, east of the centre of his supposed empire, and to have died in St Helena, well away to the west.
His face, naturally enough, is depicted as round. Often he is portrayed with an emblem consisting of three strips, coloured blue,
white and red; these must represent in sequence, the early morning
twilight, the blaze of noonday, and the dying hues of sunset. The
primitive imagination saw his rays as arms, and, as a token that the
higher he climbed the nearer he was to setting, often represented
him with one arm withdrawn into his clothing ...

Secondly, it is generally agreed that extensive and well-
founded parallels between a biblical narrative and a pre-biblical
myth – as in the case of the long lives of the earliest men,
or the Flood – are cogent evidence that the former derives
either from the latter or from a yet earlier source common to
both, and is not historically true. Few today would adopt Justin's alternative explanation, that the extra-biblical accounts
are corrupted versions of events of which the Bible alone preserves the true record[118] – though we have encountered one
writer who comes within sight of it.[119]

Thirdly, even sound parallels which suggest that a given
biblical work was influenced by an earlier non-biblical work,

or that the two go back to a common source earlier than either, do not in themselves prove that the two are of equal value.

In 1933, Professor William Albright stated that through archaeological research 'the uniqueness of the Bible, both as a masterpiece of literature and as a religious document, has not been lessened, and nothing tending to disturb the religious faith of Jew or Christian has been discovered.'[120] And in 1956, Professor Nelson Glueck, reviewing W. Keller's book *The Bible as History*, wrote: 'The reviewer has spent many years in biblical archaeology, and, in company with his colleagues, has made discoveries confirming in outline or in detail historical statements in the Bible. He is prepared to go further and say that no archaeological discovery has ever been made that contradicts or controverts historical statements in Scripture.'[121]

Can these judgments be sustained? Fundamentalists troubled by what they may have read so far might prefer to adopt a 'neither thy sting nor thy honey' attitude to archaeology. They could argue that, as regards uninscribed material, its discovery is a fact but its supposed date and place in history rest on theories of cross-dating and the like which are open to human error and hence far from irrefutable. For example, the culture of Vinča (just outside Belgrade), in which the casting of copper was known, was once confidently dated to *c.* 2700 BC but many now assign it on the basis of radio-carbon to between 5300 and 4000 BC.[122] As for written documents, even the reports of eye-witnesses are not always reliable, as is shown by the three accounts we have of the Battle of Der (modern Badra), where Sargon II met the combined forces of Humban-nikash of Elam, and Merodach-Baladan of Babylon. Sargon claims: 'in the neighbourhood of Der I inflicted a defeat on him'[123] while the Babylonian Chronicle states: 'Humban-nikash, king of Elam, did battle against Sargon, king of Assyria, in the district of Der, effected an Assyrian retreat, [and] inflicted a major defeat upon them. Merodach-Baladan and his army, who had gone to the aid of the king of Elam, did not reach the battle [in time so] he withdrew,'[124] and Merodach-Baladan hits back at both: 'The great [Lord] Marduk ... looked upon Merodach-Baladan king of Babylon

... With the power of the great lord Marduk ... he swore [to] overthrow the widespread host of Subartu [i.e. Assyria] and smashed their weapons, he made expulsion of them, and banished their tread from the soil of Akkad.'[125] We have met fundamentalists who dismiss the testimony of archaeology altogether,[126] but most of their conservative brethren would deplore such an attitude for, they argue, there the honey is plentiful, and the sting, while causing occasional discomfort, has never yet proved fatal.

What then, of the reports so often heard, that archaeological evidence is increasingly confirming the accuracy of the Bible? No one could deny that the instances in which the Bible is confirmed by archaeology are numerous. In the mid-nineteenth century, for example, cuneiform inscriptions established that Sargon, Sennacherib, Esarhaddon, and kings of Israel like Menahem and Jehu the son of Omri, all of whom figure fairly prominently in the Bible, were palpable historical personages. The fortifications which Solomon is said to have built at Hazor, Megiddo and Gezer (1 Kings 9:15) have been uncovered;[127] while pieces of ivory recovered from Samaria illuminate Amos' condemnation of 'you who loll on beds inlaid with ivory' (Amos 6:4).[128] The Aramaic papyri discovered in 1907/8 at Elephantine (located on a small island in the Nile, near modern Aswan) confirmed, despite widespread scepticism, that Aramaic was used for state correspondence in the Persian Empire, as exemplified in Ezra 4–7.

Such discoveries may be multiplied a hundredfold, but much, including much that is central to the narratives, remains without archaeological confirmation. We may illustrate the point through a narrative virtually free of the complexities of source criticism: the book of Esther. Though the events it relates are still celebrated annually by the Jews in their Feast of Purim, its value as history has long been suspect. The feast which took six months (Esther 1:4), the beauty treatment lasting a whole year (2:12) and the enormous payment (3:9) offered to the king by Haman of ten thousand silver talents (valued at £3.6 m or $18 m in 1908),[129] strain our credulity, as does much else. The decree of extermination is published eleven months in advance (3:13); Haman never suspects that Esther might be a Jewess, even though all the Jews of Shushan

know it (4:16), and even though he himself knows that Morde-
cai, who visits Esther regularly and openly (2:11), is a Jew.
Many devout Jews and Christians still adhere to the literal
truth of the book. Others see it as an account, overlaid with
much legend and exaggeration, of some real episode in which
the Jews of the Persian Empire were saved from disaster
through the good offices of a Jewess in the royal harem; others
still suppose the book to be pure fiction, written in order to
enrich the Jewish calendar with a new occasion for revelry.

What is the testimony of archaeology?[130] The decipherment of Old Persian cuneiform showed the Hebrew Ahash-
werosh (Ahasuerus) to be a fair transcription of the name
Khshayarsha (which became Xerxes in Greek),[131] and also
confirmed that, as stated in Esther 1:1 his kingdom extended
to India and Ethiopia.[132] The word *pur* said in Esther 3:7 to
mean 'lot', has been identified with just that meaning in Akkadian,[133] and the excavations of Dieulafoy at Susa recovered a
small quadrangular prism, of which each face was engraved
with a number, and which must have served as a die.[134]
Within the acropolis Dieulafoy located the harem (consisting
roughly of the north-east quarter), the throne-room with an
open space which he believed to have contained a garden
(north-west), an 'outer court' (south-west', and, in the south-
east quarter, an inner court flanked by the 'house of the king'
to the north and the 'house of the kingdom' to the south; in the
south of this last was the 'royal gate', which gave access to
the whole enclave.[135] Dieulafoy showed that the details of the
movements of Esther (5:1 f.), Haman (6:4) and Ahasuerus
(7:7) accorded with the layout of Susa as verified by his
excavations.

But all this does not prove that the book is historically true.
It does confirm the authenticity of the background, but that
is no more guarantee here than, say, in the case of the *Arabian
Nights* that the story as a whole is historical. The archaeological evidence in no way precludes, for example, the suggestion
that the author lived between 150 and 100 BC, among Persians
whose traditions preserved details of the palace of Xerxes.[136]
And in general we find archaeology confirming many details
(though rarely as amply as in the book of Esther) while admit-
ting the gravest doubts as to the substance. There is room,

at one end of the spectrum, for the fundamentalist who finds no contradiction between archaeology and the Bible, on whose literal truth he insists; and there is room for a hard-bitten sceptic who refuses to accept anything not borne out by direct archaeological proof. Since Wellhausen's day views have shifted, on balance, in a conservative direction, but this trend is all too often exaggerated. A fair example is the historicity of the Patriarchs, whom Wellhausen considered 'a glorified mirage' from the first millennium. Now more recent scholarship has come upon evidence which has persuaded many that the Patriarchs were real people after all, and lived in the period indicated by the Bible, namely the second millennium BC.[137] Names have been identified in second-millennium documents which seem to correspond to the names of principal figures in the patriarchal narratives – such as the personal names *Abamrama* and *Abiramu* (cf. Abraham), *Ya'qub-el* (cf. Jacob), the tribal name *Banu-yamina* (cf. Benjamin) which appears in the Mari texts. Many patriarchal customs were found to be paralleled in second-millennium texts, notably from the fifteenth- to fourteenth-century levels at Nuzi (near Kirkuk in Iraq). One contract for example, which records a marriage (along with much else), obliges the wife, if childless, to provide a substitute, which reminds one strongly of Hagar (Genesis 16) and Bilhah (Genesis 30). Nearly every town mentioned in the patriarchal narratives, such as Shechem, Bethel and Dothan (but with the notable exception of the five cities of the plain), has been found to have been occupied in the first half of the second millennium.[138] These considerations, and many others, have led to widespread acceptance of the historicity of the Patriarchs, but not necessarily the acceptance of what the Bible says of them; and the suggestion that is so often heard that biblical scholars are steadily drawing closer to accepting the Bible as history is, therefore, grossly misleading.

Archaeology neither proves nor disproves the Bible in conclusive terms, but it has other functions, of considerable importance.[139] It recovers in some degree the material world presupposed by the Bible. To know, say, the material of which a house was built, or what a 'high place' looked like, much enhances our understanding of the text. Secondly, it fills out the historical record. The Moabite Stone, for example, gives the other side of the story treated in 2 Kings 3:4ff.; the Assyrian annals record (what the Bible does not) that Ahab was one of the leaders of a coalition which opposed Assyria; the Lachish letters show what was going through the minds of the soldiers of Judah in the last days before the Babylonian onslaught. Thirdly, it reveals the life and thought of the neighbours of ancient Israel[140] – which is of interest in itself, and which illuminates the world of ideas within which the thought of ancient Israel developed. And finally archaeology provides essential raw material for those scholars of biblical history, who believe that the first duty of scholarship is to reach a proper understanding of the evidence which the Bible constitutes, and not to prove, or for that matter disprove, the Bible.

Here too, then, the words of Tennyson come to mind, that 'nothing worthy proving can be proven, not yet disproven'. On one level, it is true that the significance of the Bible lies not in the bare facts of history but in its interpretation of history, as a medium of revelation, and that as such it is not open to proof or disproof. But it is still frustrating that archaeology should be so inconclusive even about the bare facts and the cause is disappointingly mundane: the events of the Bible take place for the most part in Palestine, yet the written material – without which historical reconstructions can inspire but limited confidence – which has been recovered thence is meagre, indeed almost non-existent. There one did not write on the almost indestructible clay tablet used in Mesopotamia, nor was the soil as kind to perishable materials as were the sands of Egypt. A deeply religious observer once attributed this combination to divine providence, which so disposed the archaeological evidence as to admit both faith and its opposite, and to leave man's free will unimpaired. It is for this reason that the first news of the Ebla tablets, found in a land which features frequently and prominently in the Bible, electrified both scholar and layman. Does Syria speak where Palestine has been silent? We shall see in a later chapter.

CHAPTER 4

Cuneiform without Tears

The story of the decipherment of cuneiform writing begins in Persia, at a ruined site about thirty-eight miles north-east of Shiraz. There, on an artificial terrace of more than thirty acres, stand a group of ruined palaces, bearing exquisite reliefs and inscriptions. The writing was first reported to Europe in 1602, by Antonio de Gouvea, ambassador of Spain and Portugal to the Persian court, who remarked that 'there is no one who can read it, because the characters are neither Persian, Arabic, Armenian nor Hebrew, the languages now in use in the district; so that everything contributes to erase from memory that which the ambitious king so desired to render eternal'.[1]

It was a time when Europe was re-discovering the Orient. Theologians had come to realize the importance of Hebrew and Aramaic as original languages of the Bible, while concern with its various translations encouraged the study of other oriental tongues; Persian, as well as Syriac, Arabic and Ethiopic, all feature in the London polyglot Bible, published in 1657. That purely secular history too had to be traced back beyond the records of Greece and Rome to the ancient civilizations of the Near East had been shown in 1583 by that outstanding scholar J.J. Scaliger.[2] The maritime powers, as Gouvea's mission shows, had more immediate needs for oriental languages. Thus Thomas Hyde, professor both of Hebrew and Arabic at Oxford, was often called upon by the English government to translate letters and eventually 'to instruct and breed up some young man in the knowledge of the Oriental tongues, as they are in modern use; that there may be a succession of such as may serve the public, in the same manner you have done'.[3]

The first published copy of cuneiform writing consisted of just five characters which were included by a Roman nobleman, Pietro della Valle, in a letter to a friend; it was written in 1621 and published in Rome in 1658. From the horizontal and diagonal wedges in the three middle characters he guessed, tentatively but in fact correctly, that the writing ran from left to right. The term 'cuneiform' (from the Latin *cuneus* 'wedge') seems to have originated in 1700 with Thomas Hyde,[4] who denied, however, that the characters represented any sort of writing. The only material that had yet been published in England (in 1693) consisted of a medley of characters culled at random from several inscriptions by one Samuel Flower, who had since died without explaining what he had done. Hyde, noting that no two characters in Flower's 'inscription' were alike, concluded that they were simply a diversion by someone trying to see how many different patterns he could build up from the wedge form.

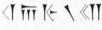

Fig. 1.

Reliable copies of whole inscriptions were first made in 1765 by Carsten Niebuhr, who took part in an expedition sent out by Frederick v of Denmark in 1761 to explore Arabia, and was the only member to escape death by violence or disease. In his account of the journey he reproduced his copies of eleven cuneiform inscriptions in a volume which appeared in German in 1778 and in French in 1780. He noticed two doors that bore identical inscriptions, except that there were two characters which stood at the right-hand of the third line in one copy, but at the left-hand of the fourth line in the other – thus confirming della Valle's guess as to the direction of the writing.[5] He also observed that three different writing systems (or as he put it 'alphabets') were present, and that the inscriptions were usually drawn up in threes, with one representative of each system.[6] That which regularly stood either uppermost or to the left, and could therefore be styled the first, was also the simplest, involving, on Niebuhr's count, just forty-two different signs.[7] It was naturally to have first claim on the attention of future decipherers.

But little progress could have been made without two major achievements in two rather different areas. The first was due to Abraham-Hyacinthe Anquetil Duperron, born in Paris in 1731. In 1754, Duperron was shown a fragment of the Avesta, the sacred literature of the Zoroastrians, which nobody in Europe could read, and he resolved there and then to travel to the East and penetrate its secrets. The Zoroastrian community of Persia, where that faith originated, was by then smaller than that of India, where many had found refuge from persecution after[8] the Arab conquest of Persia in the mid-seventh century AD, and where they are known as the Parsees. How Duperron reached India, where rivalry between the East India Companies of England and France had flared up into unofficial war, by enlisting as a soldier, and how he played on the religious divisions of the Parsees and on the turbulent political background in order to extract information and manuscripts, has been ably described by his biographer, Raymond Schwab.[9] It transpired that the Parsees had a carefully preserved tradition of the pronunciation of the Avesta, and, though they were not sufficiently familiar with its ancient language (parts of the Avesta may go at least as far back as the late second millennium BC)[10] to be able to translate word for word, they extracted its contents with the aid of successive translations and commentaries in Pahlavi[11] (ranging perhaps from the third down at least to the seventh century AD), Sanskrit and their modern vernacular Gujarati. In 1762 Duperron returned to Paris laden with manuscripts and in 1771 there appeared his *Zend-Avesta, ouvrage de Zoroastre*, which included extensive translations into French, a copious index running to nearly two hundred pages of close print, and vocabularies offering French equivalents for about a thousand words each in the language of the Avesta (which he erroneously called Zend) and in Pahlavi. Despite the limitations of his informants' knowledge of both 'Zend' and (to a lesser extent) Pahlavi, Duperron's work contributed enormously to oriental research, and provided a happy hunting-ground for aspiring decipherers of Persian inscriptions.

The decipherment was brought another step nearer by the

French orientalist Baron Antoine Silvestre de Sacy.[12] Besides the inscriptions written in cuneiform, Niebuhr had observed others nearby written partly in Greek and partly in two unknown scripts, but all badly damaged, and he published copies in his *Voyages* (see Fig. 2 for an extract).[13] Comparing these inscriptions and using Duperron's new contributions to Persian philology, de Sacy showed that the unknown scripts represented two different Iranian dialects,[14] and that the content of all three was virtually the same and could be pieced together in full. He was able to translate the inscription reproduced in Fig. 2 as follows:

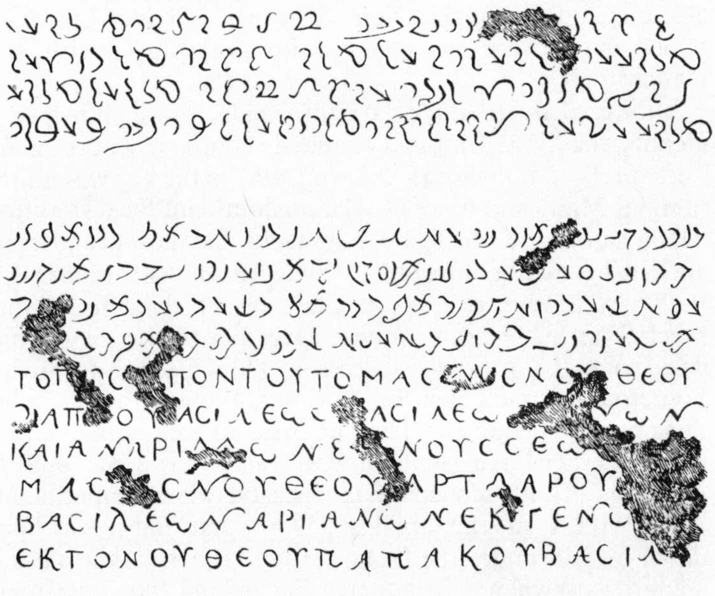

Fig. 2. Inscriptions F, G and H from Niebuhr, vol. 2, tab. XXVIII. They are among those edited in E. Herzfeld, *Paikuli* (Berlin 1924), vol. I, p. 86; F is Middle Persian, G is Parthian and H is of course Greek.

This is the image of the Mazda-worshipping god Shapur, king of kings of the Aryans[15] and non-Aryans, of the race of the gods, the son of the Mazda-worshipping god Ardeshir, king of kings of the Aryans, of the race of the gods, the grandson of the god Papak the king.

Another was an inscription of the said Ardeshir; he too called himself 'king of kings' and mentioned his father by name ('son of the god Papak the king'). These kings were already known to history as the first kings of the Sasanian dynasty (founded *c.* 224 AD) of Iran. It seemed likely that their inscriptions followed earlier models, and that Persian inscriptions of former ages must have run likewise.

Returning to the cuneiform inscriptions themselves, Oluf Tychsen in 1798 supposed that the single diagonal wedge found frequently in the first cuneiform script (see Fig. 3) served to separate words, but that its use was not at all systematic.[16] Soon afterwards the Danish theologian Frederik Münter[17] also concluded that that sign was a word-divider but maintained, in the event correctly, that it was employed with strict regularity.

Münter also settled the date of the palaces, which helped to identify the kings who had founded them and whose names were surely commemorated theron, and so the key was almost in sight. Many had bowed to the predominant local tradition, which named the site Takht-e-Jamshid, i.e. the Throne of the ancient hero-king Jamshid[18] – whence the astronomer J. S. Bailly even ventured to set the date of their foundation precisely at 3209 BC.[19] Others agreed with the view which goes back to Gouvea's successor, Don Garcia de Silva y Figueroa,[20] namely that the ruins were those of the city called Persepolis ('Persian city') by Diodorus of Sicily (first century BC) and other Greek writers, who stated that it was built by the kings of the Achaemenian dynasty, whose imperial rule began with Cyrus the Great in 559 BC, and that it was burnt down by Alexander the Great (at the request, some said, of a courtesan) when he conquered Persia, and thus put an end to that dynasty, in 331 BC.[21] The monuments had been dated later still by Tychsen, to the time of Arsaces, founder of the Parthian dynasty about 247 BC. Münter showed that the ruins agreed so well with what the Greek authors had said of Persepolis and of its Achaemenian founders that they could not reasonably be assigned to any other period. Among the drawings of the reliefs published by Chardin[22] and Niebuhr, he found various groups of men representing the various nations subject to Persia (each group having either a Persian or a Mede at its head), and one of these groups consisted of Ethiopians; but only under the Achaemenians do we know of a Persian empire extending into Africa.[23] Again, Diodorus Siculus (17:71) had reported, at the eastern end of the terrace of Persepolis, a rock hollowed into many chambers into which the sarcophagi of the kings had been hoisted mechanically – which tallied with what Münter had read of Takht-e-Jamshid (or, strictly speaking, of the nearby and obviously contemporary site of Naqsh-e-Rostam, about four miles north-west). These arguments, among others, established beyond doubt that the ruins were those of Persepolis, and dated – together with their inscriptions – to the Achaemenian period.

Münter now turned to the first or simplest script, which he believed to represent a simple alphabet, and tried to decipher some of its characters by two criteria.[24] One was to compare their shapes with those found in known alphabets which he thought were related – not only 'Zend' and Pahlavi but even Armenian and Georgian. On that basis he proposed sign values for several characters, only one of which, however, was correct (*b*), and that largely by accident. His other method, a basic procedure in code-breaking, was to compare and if possible equate the most frequent cuneiform characters with the most frequent letters in what he rightly supposed to be the closely allied language of the Avesta. In theory this might have helped, but in fact it was bound to fail. His Avesta text, drawn from Duperron, was in ordinary Roman letters.[25] What Münter could not have known is that the first type of cuneiform script involved quite a different system. For example, while the vowels *i* and *u* are both explicitly marked with separate signs, the one remaining vowel *a* is not; the sign which serves for *b* alone is also used for the syllable *ba*, and so for *d* and *da*, and so on. Again, some consonants are represented by different signs when succeeded by different vowels, while others are not. For example, three quite different signs exist for *d* before *i*, *d* before *u*, and *d* when not followed by a vowel (the last also serves for the syllable *da*), but only one sign for *b* (or *ba*). No basis existed for comparing the two systems, and Münter failed to add to his one correct sign.[26]

As for the two other scripts which regularly accompanied the first, Münter noticed[27] that for all the repetitions in the first script corresponding repetitions could be traced both in the second and the third, and he concluded that the content of all three was identical – an observation from which the decipherment of the second and third scripts eventually began. Münter could not yet say whether they represented (as he thought more likely) a single language written in three different ways or (as we now know to be the case) three different languages.[28]

The first success in actually reading a cuneiform text was achieved in 1802 by G.F. Grotefend, born in 1775 in Hanover. Grotefend compared two inscriptions which Niebuhr had published and labelled 'B' and 'G':

Fig. 3. Niebuhr's inscriptions B and G.

Of the words into which the sign ⬦ divided the texts, one kept recurring: it consisted of the seven characters

though it sometimes had an eighth one at the end. In both inscriptions it is the second word. It then occurs twice in succession (the second time with an added ending of four characters) as the fourth and fifth words, and is later repeated yet again. On the analogy of the Sasanian inscriptions read by de Sacy,[29] this most frequent word had to mean 'king', and, when repeated,[30] 'king of kings'. Moreover, the name of the reigning king should appear immediately before the first occurrence of 'king' – that is, as the opening word in each inscription – and the name of his father somewhere later on. At this point Grotefend observed that the name of the king at the beginning of 'B'

$$ \bar{\text{IY}}.\bar{\text{IYY}}.\text{EY}.\text{Y}\langle\text{-}\text{-YE}.\langle\bar{\text{IY}}.\langle\langle $$

reappeared, albeit with an extra character near the end, in the third line of 'G'

$$ \bar{\text{IY}}.\bar{\text{IYY}}.\text{EY}.\text{Y}\langle\text{-}\text{-YE}.\langle\text{EY}.\langle\bar{\text{IY}}.\langle\langle. $$

Therefore the reigning king in 'B' was the father of the reigning king in 'G'. But what were the names of these two kings, father and son? Both were of equal length (seven characters each), and the names of king Darius and of his successor Xerxes,[31] well known from Greek historians, seemed to fit.[32] The original forms of the two names, which had no doubt been distorted in the Greek, now had to be recovered. For Darius, Grotefend consulted the Hebrew *Daryāwesh*, and a Greek transliteration *Dareiauēs*.[33] From Duperron's 'Avesta', perhaps together with the Hebrew *Aḥashwerosh*, he arrived at *Khshershe* or the like for Xerxes. Matching these names with the cuneiform characters was not easy (there now seemed too few for Darius and too many for Xerxes), but he eventually proposed[34]:

$\bar{\text{IY}}.\bar{\text{IYY}}.\text{EY}.\text{Y}\langle\text{-}\text{-YE}.\langle\bar{\text{IY}}.\langle\langle$	$\langle\langle\text{YY}.\langle\langle.\text{Y}\langle\text{-}.\bar{\text{IYY}}.\text{EY}.\langle\langle.\bar{\text{IYY}}$
D A R H E U SH	KH SH H Ê R SH Ê

Grotefend must have been especially pleased with his signs for SH and A/Ê, which occurred in just the right places. On the other hand the letters R and H both varied slightly as between Darius' and Xerxes' names, and Grotefend seems to have been confident enough to guess – and later scholarship has agreed – that Xerxes' name, at least in Niebuhr's copy, had been miswritten.[35] He now asked how the word for 'king' was pronounced. He already had five of its seven letters:

$$ \langle\langle\text{YY}\langle\langle.\bar{\text{IYY}}.\text{Y}\langle\text{-}\text{Y}\langle\text{Y}.\bar{\text{IY}}.\text{Y}\langle\text{-}. $$

KH SH Ê H ? ? H

In Duperron, he found *Khscheio* as a royal title in 'Zend'; hence he proposed the values I and O for the two unknown signs, and deduced that the language was identical with that of the Avesta.[36]

The values of more signs could be obtained[37] from the name of Darius' father, which ought to be present in 'B'. Greek sources gave the name as Hystaspes, but which word in 'B' was his name?[38] 'G' had to contain the phrase 'son of Darius the king'; but 'son' was not present in any of its first three lines, in which Grotefend could now account for every word:[39]

Xerxes: king: vali/ant: king: of king/s: of Darius: the k/ing

Therefore, 'son' in 'G' had to be ⎓.⟨⟨⟩⟩.⟩⟩ in the fourth line. But the same word occurred in the fifth line of 'B'; the preceding word, running from the fourth into the fifth line, was then the name of Hystaspes (but expanded with a genitive ending, in the phrase 'Hystapes's son'). Again consulting Duperron for the native form he proposed:

⟩⟩. ⟩⟩. ⟨⟨.⎓⟨⟩⟩.⟩⟩⟩.⟩⟨.⎓⟩⟩
G O SH T A S P

with O, SH and A confirming his earlier results.[40] He was gratified that the name was not accompanied by the title 'king', because Hystaspes is never called 'king' by Greek writers.[41]

Today the names of Hystaspes, Darius and Xerxes are rather differently transcribed as Vishtāsp (roughly, V-I-SH-T-A-S-P), Dārayavaush (D-A-R (A)-Y (A)-V(A)-U-SH) and Khshayārshā (KH-SH(A)-Y-A-R-SH-A). Again, the word for 'king' is now written *khshāyathiya* (KH-SH-A-Y (A)-TH-I-Y(A)). The language has proved to be not identical with Avestan but closely related to it, and is now called Old Persian. But in essence Grotefend's decipherment was correct, and epoch-making for historical research.

Unfortunately Grotefend overreached himself by offering complete translations of both inscriptions. His rendering (left) of Niebuhr's 'B' is here compared with a modern translation (right):[42]

Darius the valiant king,	Darius the Great King,
King of Kings, King of nations,	King of Kings, King of countries,
son of Hystaspes	son of Hystaspes,
the sovereign of the world,	an Achaemenian,
in the constellation of the divine Moro.[43]	who built this palace.

Confidence in the decipherment was badly undermined by this last line, and even more by the rendering which he offered just a few months later of another cuneiform inscription, in which he fancied that he had found the name of Jamshid.[44] Indeed the Göttingen academy, before which all four of his papers had been read, declined to publish any of them. Soon, however, his work on Old Persian gained ever wider acceptance. We shall hear of him again in connection with the two remaining cuneiform scripts.

The years that followed brought steady progress in the decipherment of Old Persian cuneiform.[45] Between 1833 and 1835 the Frenchman Burnouf published a commentary on the Yasna (a component of the Avesta) which advanced knowledge of the language of the Avesta well beyond the frontiers reached by Duperron. Understanding of other Iranian languages, and of the closely related Sanskrit, also improved. Better copies of inscriptions from Persepolis and nearby, including a few not previously known, reached scholars in Europe. One of the inscriptions copied by Niebuhr[46] proved particularly fruitful; it was found to contain a list of nations (or rather lands) under Persian rule, and the recognition of many of these names (e.g. Cappadocia) revealed the pronunciation of yet more characters. However, the Persepolitan inscriptions are brief and repeat the same set phrases, and could provide only limited insight into the language. The best that could be achieved at that point may be illustrated by the translation offered by the Norwegian, Christian Lassen,[47] for the opening lines of the inscription just mentioned; R.G. Kent's translation (1953) is added on the right:

I founded (this, I) Darius, the Great King	I am Darius the Great King,

King of Kings, King of these worthy peoples,	King of Kings, King of many countries,
son of Hystaspes, an Achaemenian	son of Hystaspes, an Achaemenian.
of noble lineage. Darius, King by the favour of Ahuramazda These are those peoples.	Saith Darius the King: By the favour of Ahuramazda these are the countries which...

The translator is within sight of the general sense, but the language and script have not yet been mastered. What was really needed for further progress in the decipherment of Old Persian – let alone the two other varieties of cuneiform – was at least one long inscription of varied content.

Since the early eighteenth century it had been known[48] that a series of cuneiform inscriptions, grouped about a great bas-relief, were engraved on a rock about 1700 feet high[49] at Behistun,[50] about seventy miles west of Hamadan on the road to Kermanshah, and over four hundred miles north-west of Persepolis. The sculptures and inscriptions were carved about five hundred feet above the ground. It is possible that the spot was not quite so inaccessible then as it is now, and that the rock face below was deliberately cut back, when the work was complete, to prevent defacement. At all events, to reach and copy the inscriptions was a 'perilous task, which was left as usual to the private enterprise of an Englishman,'[51] Henry Creswicke Rawlinson. Rawlinson, who was born in 1810 at Chadlington Park, Oxfordshire, and educated at Ealing School – and not at university – not only reached and copied the inscriptions, but also completed the decipherment of Old Persian and went on to pioneer the decipherment of the other two cuneiform scripts, now called Elamite and Akkadian, for which he brought down such abundant new evidence from Behistun.

At the age of sixteen Rawlinson was nominated to a military cadetship in the East India Company's service, and he served in India until selected in 1833 to assist in reorganizing the Persian army. From 1835–9 he held the post of military adviser to the brother of the Shah of Persia, and was stationed at Kermanshah. He then had the opportunity (in the spring of 1835) of copying two inscriptions at Mount Elvend, south-west of Hamadan. All that he knew of research to date was that Grotefend 'had deciphered some of the names of the early sovereigns of the house of Achaemenes', but, out on his own at Kermanshah, he could not find out what inscriptions Grotefend (or any other scholar) had studied, which kings he had identified, or how he read any of the characters.[52] He thus had to start from scratch, and in the event his method resembled Grotefend's.

When I proceeded ... to compare and interline the two inscriptions ... I found that the characters coincided throughout, except in certain particular groups, and it was only reasonable to suppose that the groups which were thus brought out and individualized must represent proper names. I further remarked, that ... the group which occupied the second place in one inscription, and which, from its position, suggested the idea of its representing the name of the father of the king who was there commemorated, corresponded with the group which occupied the first place in the other inscription ... I had [thus] obtained the proper names belonging to three consecutive generations of the Persian monarchy; and it so happened that the first three names of Hystaspes, Darius, and Xerxes, which I applied at hazard to the three groups, according to the succession, proved to answer in all respects satisfactorily.[53]

He travelled to Behistun as often as his duties permitted during the summer and autumn of 1835, and 'used frequently to scale the rock three or four times a day without the aid of a rope or ladder.'[54] A commission deputed to the spot by the French government with express instructions to copy the inscriptions declared in 1840 – apparently unaware of Rawlinson's achievement – that the task was impossible. Rawlinson himself, however, considered the difficulties to be 'such as any person with ordinary nerves may successfully encounter'.[55] He thus relates how he copied the Persian text, which is situated for the most part directly underneath the central relief:

On reaching the recess which contains the Persian text of the record, ladders are indispensable in order to examine the upper portion of the tablet; and even with ladders there is considerable risk, for the foot-ledge is so narrow, about eighteen inches or at most two feet in breadth, that with a ladder long enough to reach the sculptures sufficient slope cannot be given to enable a person to ascend, and, if the ladder be shortened in order to increase the slope, the upper inscriptions can only be copied by standing on the topmost step of the ladder, with no other support than steadying the body against the rock with the left arm, while the left hand holds the note-book, and the right hand is employed with the pencil. In this position I copied all the upper inscriptions, and the interest of the occupation entirely did away with any sense of danger.[56]

By 1836 at the latest he had copied the first two paragraphs with remarkable accuracy, and had also deciphered eighteen signs.[57]

Fig. 4.

For some reason Rawlinson never cared to explain in detail how he achieved either this or any of his later feats of decipher-ment. In 1847 he remarked: 'I am neither able, nor is it of any consequence after the lapse of so many years, to describe the means by which I ascertained the power of each particular let-ter, or to discriminate the respective dates of the discoveries.'[58] Perhaps the seemingly endless toil was an experience which he preferred to forget. He later recalled how 'for twelve weary years – broken by only one brief visit to England – I resided, in an exhausting climate, cut off from all society, sparingly supplied with the comforts of civilization, and, in fact, doing penance in order to attain a great literary object'.[59]

However, his own statement[60] about the names which he first discovered, together with the remarks of Sir E.A. Wallis Budge,[61] who knew him personally, allows us to recover the spirit, if not the letter, of his method. At Mount Elvend he had read the names of Hystaspes, Darius and Xerxes, and his readings must have been approximately as follows:

VI SH T A S P   D A R(A) YA VA U SH

KH SH YA A R SH A

In the Behistun inscription, he recognized the second word as the name of Darius. In so long a text Rawlinson hoped that Darius' ancestry would be traced further back than at Mount Elvend, and that he might encounter some of the names in Herodotus 7:11, where Xerxes I, determined to invade Greece, is made to say: 'No worthy scion am I of Darius, Hystaspes, Arsames, Ariaramnes, Teispes, Cyrus, Cambyses, Teispes and Achaemenes, if I do not avenge me on the Athenians!'[62]

Rawlinson was not disappointed. At the end of line 4 and the beginning of line 5, he found

𒈠𒊑𒠿𒈠𒍑
A R SH A ?

who must be Arsames; therefore ►𝅀𝅁 = M. In the middle of line 5, he found

𒈠𒊑𒄿𒅀𒀀𒊑𒀀𒈠
A R I YA̦A R A M ?

who must be Ariaramnes; therefore ⤵ = N. In line 6, he found

𒄩𒈠𒈨𒉌𒍑
? KH A M N I SH

who must be Achaemenes; but as A was already known, Rawlinson put ⟨► = H (A). At the end of line 5 and the beginning of line 6, he found

𒋾𒅖𒉺𒀀𒅖
? I SH P A I SH

the Greek Teispes. Thus 𒋾 had to be a sort of *t*, but different from the T he already had. He eventually decided on the sound of *t* in nature or *c* in cello, and the sign C is conventionally used.

He could also recognize P-A-R-S-I-YA 'Persia' in line 2, as the reader is encouraged to check.

During 1837 Rawlinson finished copying the first two hundred lines or so, and also completed a manuscript in which he transliterated and translated the first two paragraphs, and which he sent to the Royal Asiatic Society, London. It immediately won him international renown, and from that point on Rawlinson was in active correspondence with Lassen and Burnouf, and generally kept abreast of European research, which supplied him with information he badly needed on the related language of the Avesta (Burnouf's Yasna commentary being invaluable) and on Sanskrit. During 1839, he completed transliterating and translating the rest of the two hundred lines he had copied, and one can only speculate how he achieved these further results. The additional lines yielded about thirty more names – mainly of provinces of the Persian empire, but also of former kings, and of Darius' generals and foes – which were known from Herodotus and other Greek writers, and which no doubt enabled Rawlinson to read many more letters. He gladly acknowledged[63] that he also learnt much from his contacts with European scholarship – though any discussion about who first discovered how to read which sign when would be odious and futile. In his notebooks, which now lie in the British Museum, one finds draft after draft[64] of transliteration and translation of hundreds of lines, testifying to the unflagging effort necessary to reduce the script and language to order.

These results too he communicated to the Royal Asiatic Society,[65] but he was prevented from seeing through any publication by the outbreak in 1839 of the Afghan War, in which he served with distinction until 1842, being mentioned several times in despatches, and eventually (in 1844) awarded the CB. He was then sent back to India, and to renewed adversity. During the war he had been responsible for nearly £1,000,000 of British government money, and the boat laden with all the bills and vouchers relating to that expenditure caught fire on the journey back. Rawlinson was nevertheless strictly required to present full accounts and receipts. It took him six months – during which he also found time for 'a severe attack of brain fever' – to reconstruct the accounts from memory and obtain duplicate vouchers from all payees.[66] Only at the close of 1843, when he came to Baghdad as 'British

Political Agent in Turkish Arabia', was he able to resume his cuneiform studies. In 1844 he finished copying the 414 lines of Old Persian text at Behistun, and then completed the decipherment and translation of the whole. He forwarded to the Royal Asiatic Society in February 1846 a complete copy of the Old Persian text, a transliteration, copious linguistic notes, and a translation so fine that only the occasional phrase has since needed correction.[67] In August he sent off an additional note setting forth the mysterious workings of the 'alphabet' – certain consonants being represented by different signs according to the vowel following – but in this result he was pipped at the post, for the same discovery had been announced on 9 June by Dr Edward Hincks,[68] a graduate of Trinity College Dublin, and rector of Killyleagh (Co. Down), who contributed decisively to the decipherment of all three cuneiform scripts. It was at all events Rawlinson who first presented to the world an accurate translation of several hundred lines of cuneiform. Henceforth Old Persian would be well understood, and supply the key to decipherment of the two remaining scripts.

The earliest researchers saw that the second cuneiform script possessed about 100 characters (we now know[69] of about 123), and Münter inferred that there must have been a separate sign for each syllable.[70] Here no word-divider existed, but one very useful signpost in this unfamiliar terrain was discovered by Grotefend; on comparing texts in this script with their Old Persian counterparts, he found that a vertical wedge ❚ was placed before proper names (both of people and of places)[71] – which could thus be located and, once again, utilized to open the decipherment.

A start was made in 1844 by a Danish scholar of Sanskrit, Niels Westergaard.[72] The text which helped him most was one that he had copied himself; the previous year he had visited Persia in search of antiquities and found, engraved on Darius' tomb at Naqsh-e-Rostam, close by Persepolis, an inscription executed in all three cuneiform scripts. His first step, once he had assembled all the examples he could find of the second cuneiform script, was to locate the names which occurred in the accompanying Old Persian texts. His next was to search for these names, with the aid of the vertical wedge,

in the texts of the second kind, and thus to work out how to
read the various signs which the second script employed to
render them. Thus in the inscription which he had copied at
Naqsh-e-Rostam, he found Darius' name at five points in the
Old Persian, and at each corresponding point in the second
text he found

This too had to be the name of Darius, but how was each sign
read? He noticed that the second sign recurred further down
in other names (identified by Ⲓ), the pronunciation of which
he knew from the corresponding Old Persian text:

H Ä R I W Ä   (now read Haraïva)

B A K H T R I S   (now read Bākhtrish)

Thus Ⲏ had to be *ri*, in which case the first sign in Darius
was *da* and the last sign in 'Bakhtris' was *s*. By such reasoning
Westergaard proposed values for eighty-two signs (though not
more than twenty have stood the test of time).[73]

Applying to the remainder of the text the sound values
yielded by the names, Westergaard soon found that it could
not possibly be (as Münter and others had been inclined to
suppose) Old Persian in a more complicated script. It was
evidently a wholly different language, for which he used
the name Median, though scholars took a long time to
agree what to call it, and many other names (such
as Scythian or Susian) have been used.[74] The standard term
today is Elamite, as many royal and other public inscriptions
in this language, from this and from earlier periods, have since
been discovered at various sites in ancient Elam, especially at
its capital Susa.

Westergaard carefully compared the patterns of repetition
in the Old Persian and Elamite texts; thence he often suc-

eeded in identifying a group of signs in Elamite as the equi-
alent of a particular word in Persian, and so built up a voca-
ulary and gained some insight into the grammar. He was
andicapped by the fact that both he and Lassen, with whom
e collaborated, had attained (as shown on p. 80) only a
imited understanding of Old Persian. Thus he translates Ela-
nite *naari* (today read *nanri*) by 'noble' though it actually
neans 'says'; he had found – quite rightly – that this Elamite
vord corresponded to Old Persian *thātiy*, which indeed means
says', but which Lassen had mistranslated 'noble'. But on the
vhole he made an admirable start, even grasping the general
ense of one Elamite inscription which had no Old Persian
quivalent;[75] he worked out that Darius was boasting of his
uilding achievements at Persepolis, though Westergaard
hought that he was referring to the principal terrace and not,
s we now know, to a new fortress.

In 1846 Hincks was able to advance somewhat further. He
worked through the comparison between the renderings of
ames in Elamite and Old Persian for himself, with surer in-
uition than Westergaard, and also with a better understand-
ng of Old Persian.[76] But the most valuable material for
lecipherment was at Behistun. In 1844 Rawlinson had copied
ot only the remainder of the Old Persian but also the entire
Elamite text, with even greater difficulty.[77]

Rawlinson's notebooks include much work on Elamite. In
the Old Persian text at Behistun one paragraph was so
lamaged as to be almost illegible, and he substituted a transla-
ion which was based on the Elamite text, and has proved
lmost faultless;[78] it relates how a rebellion in Parthia and
Iyrcania was crushed by Hystaspes. But he never published
is researches, for he realized that the third script held the key
o far richer treasures, and so in 1851 he handed over his
apers to Edwin Norris, Secretary of the Royal Asiatic
Society, who published his own results in 1855. Like Westergaard, he used names as his principal basis for inferring
he readings of signs,[79] and the Behistun inscription now put
nore than a hundred at his disposal. In about thirty cases the
pronunciation he proposed for a cuneiform sign has since been
liscarded, but the rest (about seventy) are accepted, and his
ranslation has required no more than occasional amendment.

In general, however, Elamite is the least understood of the three types of cuneiform writing. Though Genesis 10:22 traces Elam's ancestry back to Shem, Elamite is certainly not a member of the Semitic family of languages, to which Hebrew and Arabic belong, nor has it any other known relatives. Those few texts that are accompanied by a version in a language that is well understood – either Old Persian or Akkadian (the language of the third cuneiform script) – are our only reliable guide to its recovery; the rest is guesswork. Many basic issues remain unresolved, e.g. whether or not Elamite was a dead language in the time of the Achaemenian kings and whether voiced and voiceless[80] consonants (such as *b* and *p*, *d* and *t*) were perceived as distinct (as in English, in which *bad*, *bat*, *pad*, *pat* are quite different words) or not.[81]

Thousands more Elamite texts from the Achaemenian period, and many others in earlier forms of Elamite, have since been discovered, but our ignorance of the language leaves them largely obscure. They include a treaty (?) with Naram-Sin, dedications of cult objects from about 1200 BC. delivery notes and letters from the seventh century, and a hoard of 'Achaemenid warehouse records'.[82] All these texts explain why Elamite was included in the inscriptions of the Persian emperors; the tradition of Elamite writing had continued unbroken down the centuries, and when the Achaemenians gained control of Elam they entrusted their records to Elamite scribes and recognized Elamite as an official language.

Finally, hundreds of inscriptions (mostly on clay tablets) dating right back to the third millennium BC, probably between 3000 and 2200, have been discovered at Elam, and the script has been termed Proto-Elamite. An attempt at decipherment by W. Hinz,[83] who believes them to be written in the Elamite language, has had a cool reception, and there is still little agreement as to their language or interpretation.

Rawlinson's decision to concentrate on the third cuneiform script is easily understood. As early as the seventeenth century, della Valle not only sent back to Europe his copy of five cuneiform signs from Persepolis but also brought back (in 1626) some inscribed bricks from the vicinity of Hilla on the

Euphrates (about sixty miles south of Baghdad), where he correctly located the ruins of Babylon, and also from Muqayyar,
ancient Ur. All bore cuneiform writing; and during the succeeding centuries many more inscribed bricks and cylinders
reached Europe, mostly from the Hilla district. The first man
to conduct a formal excavation in Mesopotamia was Joseph
de Beauchamp, who in 1784 hired native workmen to dig
among the ruins of Babylon; such efforts were renewed by
Claudius James Rich, the East India Company's Resident at
Baghdad, who conducted more thorough excavations in Babylon (in 1811), and augmented his collection of antiquities
when he visited ancient Assyrian sites in the neighbourhood
of Mosul, such as Nimrud (ancient Calah) and Kuyunjik
(ancient Nineveh). Now more than one eighteenth-century
writer[84] noted that the writing on at least some Babylonian
bricks much resembled the third cuneiform script at Persepolis, which therefore came to be known as the Babylonian
script;[85] and though the Babylonian inscriptions appeared to
differ among themselves, and the Assyrian inscriptions seemed
different again, Grotefend argued that the script and also the
language of all of them was essentially the same, though it
varied somewhat with time and locality, and therefore the
same as the Persepolis inscriptions of the third kind. It was
thus becoming clear that the third cuneiform script attested
in Persia held the key to the inscriptions that were steadily
trickling in from present-day Iraq. But in 1843 in the Mosul
area there began the excavation of Khorsabad (ancient Dur-
Sharrukin) under the French consul at Mosul, Paul-Emile
Botta, and in 1845 that of Nimrud under Sir Austen Henry
Layard. Cuneiform texts began to flood in, and the prospect
of what might be revealed if only they were deciphered aroused
feverish excitement.

Thus the decipherment of the third cuneiform script posed
a far more urgent problem than the other two, and attacks
were launched on several fronts. The first steps were obvious
enough from the straightforward comparison of the Old Persian and Babylonian texts of the simplest inscriptions from
Persepolis. Fig. 5, for example, reproduces Westergaard's
copy of the Babylonian text which accompanied the Old Persian inscription 'G' in Fig. 3:

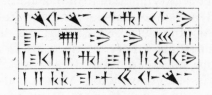

Fig. 5.

The meaning is known from the Old Persian: 'Xerxes, grea
king, king of kings, son of Darius the king, an Achaemenian.
To discover how 'king' is represented, we have to ask wha
occurs four times, with the second and third occurrence:
(which together mean 'king of kings') in immediate succes
sion; and the answer, somewhat disconcertingly, is the singl€
sign ⪢ . Hence the daunting possibility that the script pos
sessed some signs (technically termed *logograms*)[85] whic]
stood for whole words (like our & 'and', 4 'four'). At all event:
we can now break up the text into units, of which we knov
the meaning of each, without as yet knowing how t<
pronounce anything. The first line must begin with 'Xerxes
and the last must consist of 'Achaemenian'; in both, however
we first meet a vertical wedge, which must therefore, as in Ela
mite, indicate a personal name. Thus the sign ⟨, and there ma}
well be others, is not pronounced but serves to indicate a par
ticular class of word; such signs are called *determinatives*. W<
then have three names:

         ◣⟨⊦◣ . ⟨⊦⫤⟨ . ⟨⊦   Xerxes (1.1

         ⊒⟨⟨ . ⟨⟨ . ⫤⟨⟨ . ⊨⟨⟨ . ⟨⟨ . ⫫⊩⟨   Darius (1.3

         ⟨⟨ . ⫶⫶ . ⊒⟨⟨-⫠ . ⟪ . ⟨⟨⊦◣   Achaemenian (1.4)

and in these the signs seem not to have been logograms o₁
determinatives but to have actually been pronounced, togethe₁
making up the full names. All that remains is ⊒⟨⊦ ⫫⫫ i₁
the second line, which must mean 'great', and ⟨⟨⟨ ⟨⟨ at th€
end of the line; of these, ⟨⟨⟨ should indicate that the pre
ceding ⪢ is plural, and ⟨⟨ should mean 'son'. And s<

the whole inscription has been 'read', but we are very far from having mastered Babylonian cuneiform; indeed, inscriptions for which no Old Persian crutch exists remain almost as impenetrable as before.

One starting point was to ascertain whether Babylonian might be akin to any known language family. A clue was sought in the names which the Bible preserves of Babylonian and Assyrian monarchs, such as Merodach-Baladan, Nebuchadnezzar, Tiglath-Pileser, but these had so suffered in transcription (the first, for example, is in fact *Marduk-apla-iddina* 'Marduk has given a son') as to be useless for the purpose, and suggested to different scholars affinities with Persian, Sanskrit and even the Slavonic languages.[87] In 1843 the Swede Isidore Löwenstern suggested the Semitic family, since the Bible calls Ashur (Assyria) a son of Shem (Genesis 10:22).[88] This proved correct, although the reasoning was precarious; for Genesis 10 also calls Elam a son of Shem, though Elamite is not Semitic, and Canaan a son of Ham, though the language of Canaan is Semitic; moreover it regards Nimrod, who reigned over Babel and 'built Nineveh', as a grandson of Ham.[89] All of which, incidentally, is not the fault of the Bible, whose classification of nations seems to be geographical and partly political rather than linguistic; scholars have long acknowledged that the tag 'Semitic' for the language family it denotes is more convenient than scientific.

The decipherment was completed, at least in its essentials, by 1851; and it seems preferable to survey the work of each major contributor in turn, rather than attempt a strictly chronological account, which would involve whisking the reader to and fro between Dublin, London and Paris as each new paper was read.[90] The various contributions of each scholar would in any case take some time (it was often a matter of years) to reach his rivals, and even longer to be adopted by them.

Hincks started out, as in the first researches in Elamite, with the names in trilingual inscriptions. We have just seen how these could be located in the Babylonian text once the accompanying Old Persian was read; and Hincks was aided by Grotefend's remark that ⎸ was the determinative for personal and ⟩⟨ for geographical names.[91] He realized that names might not always be pronounced identically in Old Persian and

Babylonian; today, for example, we know that Cyrus and
Darius were called Kurush and Dārayavaush in Old Persian
but Kurash and Dariyamush in Babylonian. But the names
did have to be similar; and so he strove to assign to the various
characters such values as would result in the best possible
degree of overall similarity between the Babylonian names and
their Old Persian equivalents. He added to his list of values
by employing what may be called the substitution principle,
to which decipherers in general often resort. One looks for a
text, or at least for a considerable stretch of text,[92] which
occurs in two inscriptions (or even in different parts of the
same inscription) in identical form except for one variation
at a particular point; one can then follow up the possibility
that the two different signs, or sequences of signs, which
the two inscriptions offer at this point are equivalent or
in some other way interchangeable. He also had a third
criterion, namely that characters common to the Elamite
and Babylonian scripts had 'the same value, or nearly so',
in both.[93]

His results, presented to the Royal Irish Academy between
1846 and 1850, showed amazing insight. He discovered that
every character that was not a logogram or determinative
stood for a full syllable, never for one consonant alone;[94] and
he drew up syllabic values[95] – of such patterns as *u*, *sa*, *si*,
su, *as*, *sib* – for about eighty cuneiform signs 'of which about
forty are absolutely correct, while the rest are more or less
approximately right'.[96] He also set forth the principle of *homophony* – that in some cases two or more outwardly distinct
signs expressed the same syllable.[97] And as early as 1846 he
read the first Babylonian word that was not a name: 𒀀 𒈾 𒆪 ,
shown by Old Persian parallel texts to mean 'I'. He knew from
many names (such as *A-hu-ru-ma-az-da-a*') that the first sign
was *a*; the second he may have inferred from his reading[98]
of the closely similar Elamite sign 𒈾 as *na*. He had seen
the third in an inscription from Murghab, just north-east of
Persepolis; it was the first character in the name of Cyrus (or
Kurush according to the Old Persian parallel), so he
pronounced it *ku*. The resemblance between the whole word
– *anaku* – and the Hebrew pronoun *anoki* 'I'[99] was unmistake-
able, confirming that the language was Semitic.

Hincks also discovered more logograms, and explained their usage in detail. Some were accompanied by a syllabic sign (to which the term 'phonetic complement' is applied) to indicate the true pronunciation; in the same way the English logogram 3 can be pronounced either 'three' or 'third' (as in '3 May'), but in the latter case we often add the phonetic complement *rd*. Hincks' example was the logogram ◁𝕀𝕀𝕀 'heart' (though he thought it meant 'territory'), which was followed now by the sign for the syllable *bu* and now by that for *bi*; he could not pronounce the whole word, but he realized that it could end with either *-bu* or *-bi* as grammar dictated.[100] Again, two logograms could on occasion be combined to yield a third, whose meaning could possibly (not certainly) be guessed from those of its components, but not its pronunciation – just as in English the pronunciation of the composite logogram 12 cannot be deduced from that of 1 and 2. So Hincks observed that 𝔼 stood for 'son' and ⟨ for 'woman', and concluded that 𝔼 ⟨ meant 'daughter', but he was aware (even though he could not pronounce any of these words) that one could not arrive at the pronunciation of the word for 'daughter' simply by reading out in succession the words for 'son' and 'woman'. He also identified more determinatives, clarifying their use, and showed, for example, that one of them (indicating 'land') was placed not before but after the word to which it related.[101] He saw that some signs were used in more than one way. For example ∬ often stood for the syllable *a* but could also mean 'son' (see p. 90) – rather like the sign 'I' in English;[102] and ⊢ might be pronounced *an*, or it might be a logogram meaning 'god' (being then pronounced *ilu*),[103] or it might be a determinative placed before a particular god's name (in which case it was not pronounced at all).[104] All these principles set forth by Hincks are now fully accepted, though many details have naturally required correction.

Another aspect to be investigated was the outward form of the characters, both in the inscriptions from Persepolis and in the many others which contained Babylonian cuneiform; for only by careful analysis and comparison could one hope to read the latter even when the former were once fully deciphered. Here Hincks made an auspicious start. He examined two inscriptions that had been recovered from Babylon, one in characters similar to those of Persepolis, the other in a far more complex and archaic script (now called Old Babylonian) which also featured in many of the other inscriptions then known; and he discovered that both contained the same text (see Fig. 6) – though the resemblance is far from obvious – and was thus able to draw up a table in which seventy-six of the hitherto mysterious archaic characters were assigned equivalents in the script of Persepolis.[105]

Meanwhile, and to the same end, Botta was examining meticulously the many hundreds of characters he had encountered at Khorsabad. He aimed to discover the variant forms of which each sign was capable, and then to draw up a list of the signs that were truly different – just as a future decipherer of modern English handwriting would need to know that t, $\mathcal{T}$ and t were mere variants of the same sign, and f, f and f of another, quite different sign. In this he made remarkable progress, by means of the substitution principle and the cautious study of outward resemblance. He also identified, partly by the latter method, scores of characters at Khorsabad with their equivalents in Achaemenian inscriptions from Persepolis and elsewhere.[106] This work was to prove invaluable in the study of the different varieties of Babylonian cuneiform writing – but not until the Achaemenian inscriptions had themselves been mastered.

For the moment, Botta could not pronounce a single character; but he did recognize a few logograms in their Khorsabad forms. He noticed, for example, a character ⟶ which often occurred[107] at the beginning of an inscription and was followed by ❙ (which introduced a name) but which only rarely featured in the body of the text. He wondered whether it meant 'king' and was thus the counterpart of ⟶ at Persepolis; and the general similarity in form confirmed it. This result was ingeniously exploited by Adrien de Longpérier, Keeper of Antiquities at the Royal Museum in Paris,[108] who found that the 'king' sign once occurred along with: ⟶ ⟶ ⟶ Thus the first part of the king's name, which begins straight after the vertical wedge, was written – and presumably pronounced – just like the word for 'king'. Whose could this name be? Longpérier recalled that one Hebrew word for 'king,

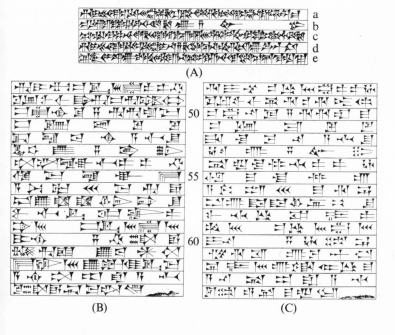

(A): Last five complete lines (left-hand side) of the cylinder published by
   Sir Robert Ker Porter, *Travels in Georgia …*, (London 1821–22), pl. 78.
(B): Corresponding portion of the East India House Inscription, accessible
   in H.C. Rawlinson and E. Norris, *The Cuneiform Inscriptions of Western
   Asia I*, (London 1861), pl. 53–58, col. III, lines 48–64.
(C): Transcription of (B) into the 'ordinary Babylonian character' by
   Rawlinson and Norris, pl. 59–64.

The texts agree closely but not exactly. Each line of (A) happens to begin
at the same point as a line in (B), thus: (a) 48, (b) 51, (c) 54, (d) 59 (but
here considerable variation occurs), (e) 62. The reader may however find it
helpful first to compare (A) with (C). The inscription commemorates the
building works of Nebuchadnezzar II (605–562 BC) in Babylon and
Borsippa. The extract above refers to Ezida, the temple of Nebo at
Borsippa, and concludes: 'The temple I fittingly beautified, and, that it be
admired, I filled it with splendour.' Both originals now lie in the British
Museum (nos. 90908, 129397).

Fig. 6.

'prince' is *šar*, and that an Assyrian king called Sargon was mentioned[109] in the Bible (Isaiah 20:1); and so he discovered how to pronounce (albeit approximately) the word for 'king', and also whose monuments the French were excavating at Khorsabad. True, this was an isolated result, but it was achieved without the aid of any parallel text, and stands as a worthy example of the sort of ingenious reasoning which the decipherment of Babylonian cuneiform would have called for had there been no bilingual inscriptions.

Rawlinson's first remarks on Babylonian cuneiform appeared in 1847, when he reported that by comparing the Old Persian and Babylonian forms of names in the inscriptions then available, he had worked out a 'tolerably extensive alphabet'. He was, however, far from satisfied with this, seeing 'our only key to the decypherment of the Babylonian alphabet'[110] in the Behistun inscription; and this was no exaggeration. The trilingual inscriptions were by far the most satisfactory, if not the only, basis on which to begin the reconstruction of the unknown language and its writing system; the scanty and repetitive material as yet known might (and in fact did) yield many important results, but not the sort of proficiency in language and script which would make unilingual Babylonian texts readily intelligible. And so in 1847 he returned from Baghdad to the Behistun rock:[111]

The Babylonian transcript at Behistun is still more difficult to reach than either the Scythic or the Persian tablets. The writing can be copied by the aid of a good telescope from below, but I long despaired of obtaining a cast of the inscription; for I found it quite beyond my powers of climbing to reach the spot where it was engraved, and the craigsmen of the place, who were accustomed to track the mountain goats over the entire face of the mountain, declared the particular block inscribed with the Babylonian legend to be unapproachable. At length, however, a wild Kurdish boy, who had come from a distance, volunteered to make the attempt, and I promised him a considerable reward if he succeeded ... [The boy eventually managed] to cross over to the cleft by hanging on with his toes and fingers to the slight inequalities on the bare face of the precipice, ... passing over a distance of twenty feet of almost smooth perpendicular rock in a manner which to a looker-on appeared quite miraculous ... He had brought a rope with him attached to the first peg, and now, driving in a second, he was enabled to swing himself right over the projecting mass of rock. Here with a short ladder he formed a swinging seat, like a painter's cradle, and, fixed upon this seat, he took under my direction the paper cast of the Babylonian translation of the records of Darius ... I must add, too, that it is of the more importance that this invaluable Babylonian key should have been thus recovered, as the mass of rock on which the inscription is engraved bore every appearance, when I last visited the spot, of being doomed to a speedy destruction, water trickling from above having almost separated the overhanging mass from the rest of the rock, and its own enormous weight thus threatening very shortly to bring it thundering down into the plain, dashed into a thousand fragments.

Rawlinson did not, however, restrict himself to the Behistun text. He found that it shared many phrases – which turned out to be stock annalistic expressions – with other recently discovered inscriptions, notably a black obelisk which Layard had discovered at Nineveh in 1846, and he soon decided to work on these at the same time. Naturally, however, his first step was to compare the names which he had found (no doubt with the aid of determinatives) in the Babylonian text at Behistun with their Old Persian counterparts. 'More than eighty' names were available, and the comparison – which, as noted in connection with the work of Hincks, was no straightforward task – 'supplied the means of determining with more or less of certainty, the value of about one hundred Babylonian characters'.[112]

It would be wrong however to infer that Rawlinson had succeeded so early in identifying the syllables which all these characters denoted. His use of the term 'alphabet' will have been observed; and at this stage he in fact treated most cuneiform signs as single alphabetical letters, with syllables in a small minority. One of his notebooks shows an early attempt to compile what he calls an 'alphabet'; most of the characters receive such values as *a*, *b*, *d*, *h*, *i*, *k*, *kh*, and only a few are regarded as syllables (such as *hi*, *ras*, *var*). Again, the name of Darius' foe Gaumata, which consists of four signs now transcribed *Gu-ma-a-tu*, became in his analysis *G-m-a-t*.[113] As a result, most of the signs which in fact denote a syllable consisting of a consonant and vowel (in either order) appeared to him to indicate the consonant alone; and as each consonant enters into several such syllables, he was often compelled to assign the same English letter to many different cuneiform signs, which must have all seemed wholly interchangeable at the writer's whim. But this apparent superfluity did not deter him, and his error may have furthered his progress. Many languages (including English, as any stenographer will know) can still be read even if most of the vowels are missing, and this applies especially to the Semitic languages, many of which are regularly written in alphabets of twenty to thirty consonants, with vowels but rarely marked. Rawlinson soon convinced himself that Babylonian was a Semitic language; moreover, he was proficient in reading the Arabic, Syriac and perhaps also the Hebrew scripts without vowels; and so the consonantal skeletons in which his earliest transcriptions of Babylonian appeared would have been rendered only marginally easier for him to penetrate if he had instead recovered all the vowels correctly – and a great deal more difficult if (as was then likely) he had got many of them wrong.

Unexpectedly, he now proceeded 'to collate inscriptions and to ascertain ... from the variant orthographies of the same name ... the homophones of each known alphabetical power'. This is of course the substitution principle once again; he often found the same name differently spelt in different passages, and if he was able to read it (or part of it) on any one occasion, he could deduce the value of any sign(s) which appeared to alternate with the sign(s) he already knew. He thus 'added nearly fifty characters to those previously known through the Persian key'.[114] He would probably not have achieved this remarkable total of additional values were it not for his mistaken idea that so many signs were alphabetic. Babylonian has a system of cases (rather simpler than that of Latin) with the three endings -u, -a, -i. In many names, therefore, three possibilities exist for the final syllable – for example, Su-bar-tu, Su-bar-ta, Su-bar-ti 'Assyria' – for which three different signs are therefore liable to be used. Now as far as Rawlinson was concerned, if he could recognize any one of the three (taking the example above) as one of his signs for t, he could add the others also to his collection of t signs. Eventually of course he realized that the signs were in fact syllables, carefully differentiated; but at this early stage, when he was making do with hardly any vowels, he lost very little in intelligibility by lumping them all together as *t* – and similarly for the many other syllabic signs.

It was probably at this stage, when he was analysing names, that he discovered the principle of *polyphony*, that many cuneiform signs are capable of two or even more distinct values. Thus he found that one sign could be read either *khi* or *da*, another as either *tar* or *khas*,[115] and so on. This discovery was greeted with disbelief, as we shall see, but it has since been accepted as an essential feature of the script.

At the same time he had also been investigating the vocabulary of Babylonian, by such comparisons as were described on p. 90. He thus obtained from the Behistun inscription 'a list of about two hundred Babylonian words, of which we know the sound approximately, and the meaning certainly'. But beyond that he managed, by 'an extensive comparison of similar or cognate phrases', to add 'about two hundred meanings certainly, and a hundred more probably, to the vocabulary already obtained through the Babylonian translations'. He thus applied the substitution principle to vocabulary as well as sound; and he thought that these five hundred words included 'all the most important terms in the language'.[116]

By now he was in sight of his final goal, to penetrate the script and language well enough to elucidate the Behistun inscription as well as all the others he had studied, but a great deal of work remained. He had various guidelines, each of which however could be bent, though he did not know how far. Every sign had to be given a fixed and consistent value; but a minority – or so he (correctly) hoped – had two or more. The Babylonian text at Behistun bore the same meaning as the Old Persian; but there were bound to be differences of idiom, of terminology,[117] and even – as it turned out – of content.[118] The language was Semitic, and should therefore resemble such known languages as Hebrew and Arabic; on the other hand, it had like any other language many words and other features peculiar to itself, and Rawlinson's notebooks record his painful first steps in recognizing them – for example the verbs *kev* 'to say' and *ves* 'to do' (the forms in use today are *qabû* and *epēšu*).[119] And so we continually find

him preparing a draft transliteration and translation of whatever passage he could, and then drawing up all manner of lists
on the basis of it – lists of cuneiform signs with their latest
values, of names in their latest forms, of common nouns, of
forms belonging to the same verb, of first person singular past
tense forms of different verbs – everywhere striving to discern
greater regularity than before, and then returning with whatever knowledge he had thus gained to a new attempt to trans-
literate and translate. And so he re-worked his material time
and again, going round not, as any lesser man would have
done, in circles, but rather in an ever-widening spiral, until
he had reconnoitred the whole terrain. The decipherment of
Babylonian was, in its essentials, completed when he published
the Behistun inscription in 1851 – text, transliteration, translation, and a full list of signs.[120]

Many questions as to the details of Rawlinson's work and
his indebtedness to other scholars will probably remain un-
answered. One would like to trace his progress step by step
from his early supposition that most of the signs represented
alphabetical letters to his sign-list[121] of 1851 in which every
sign is taken as a whole syllable. This move well illustrates
how the successful decipherer must know when to stand his
ground and when to abandon a position in order to make a
further advance; some of Rawlinson's rivals had also begun
with the idea that the signs were alphabetic, but clung to it
as a dogma – largely because the other Semitic languages they
knew were written alphabetically – which led them fatally
astray.[122] Another point is that Rawlinson's adoption of 'syl-
labism' brought him over to the position taken up in 1849–50
by Hincks, with whose work Rawlinson was certainly
acquainted, and who once insinuated that Rawlinson owed
him more than he cared to admit.[123] Again, Norris once remarked that the researches of Rawlinson and himself into
Elamite sometimes provided (on account of the resemblance
between characters in the two systems) the value of a Babylonian character.[124] But it would be as idle as it would be
churlish to question Rawlinson's originality in deciphering the
Behistun inscription and thereby laying the very foundation
stone of Assyriology.

The application of this new knowledge to unilingual Babylonian texts was pioneered by Rawlinson himself, who, as stated, had begun work on them even while deciphering the Behistun inscription. Even before his publication of the latter, he produced[125] what was partly a translation and partly a summary of the Black Obelisk, which commemorates Shalmaneser III (859–824 BC) – though Rawlinson, for reasons soon to be explained, misread the name as Temenbar. With no bilingual key, the unfamiliar words which confronted him in each new inscription had to be explained through their context and through whatever analogies he could find in the related languages – especially Hebrew, less often Aramaic and Arabic. These first labours on unilingual inscriptions were probably the most strenuous of all; in 1850 he declared:

I will frankly confess, indeed, that after having mastered every Babylonian letter, and every Babylonian word, to which any clue existed in the trilingual tablets, either by direct evidence or by induction, I have been tempted, on more occasions than one, in striving to apply the key thus obtained to the interpretation of the Assyrian Inscriptions, to abandon the study altogether in utter despair of arriving at any satisfactory result.[126]

But the sustained efforts of Rawlinson and his contemporaries – notably Hincks, and Jules Oppert in Paris – and of the generations of scholars since, have yielded an exceedingly satisfactory result. With the sheer mass of documentation,[127] which often yields multiple copies, written at different periods, of the same text, scholars can now follow in detail the form of each character as it varied with time and place, and usually an expert need only look at the script on a tablet to be fairly sure when and where it was written. As to the syllabic values of the signs, research[128] has been complicated through the realization that the range of syllables represented by a given sign varied with time and place, and even with literary genre.[129] For example, one particular sign[130] is read exclusively *ul* under the Akkad dynasty, but *tur* in Assyrian (northern Mesopotamian) texts from about 1800 BC, while from the fifteenth century onward its usual value is *kib* or the like. Hence, for each different period and locality, scholars have tried to ascertain which syllable(s) each sign may indicate. This effort has involved further application of the basic principles (e.g. that of substitution), together with great

patience and ingenuity. Much has also been learned from texts
used in the actual training of scribes; many were found in the
library of the Assyrian king Ashurbanipal (668–c. 627 BC), excavated at Kuyunjik (Nineveh) in 1850–4, and many more have
been recovered elsewhere from earlier periods right back to
the age of Hammurapi. Some of these group together signs
which were pronounced similarly (such as *bu ba bi*); others
are exhaustive lists of signs with the value(s) of each spelt out
in elementary syllables; and many more types occur.[131] Agreement on sign values has now been reached, for the most part;
but debate has been lively over the years, with at least one
third of all the values ever proposed being later discredited,[132]
and has been repeatedly extended through the discovery of
new archives, as at Nuzi and Ugarit.

The language too has yielded its secrets. Its development
over the centuries and the variations between the dialect of
southern Mesopotamia (to which the term 'Babylonian' is now
restricted) and that of the north ('Assyrian') are now tolerably
well known. It is now called Akkadian, as inscriptions first
appear in quantity under Sargon and his dynasty.[133] So
abundant is the documentation that the meaning of most
words can be adequately fixed through the many contexts in
which they occur. There are of course limits to the precision
one can expect; for example, we know that *azupīru* was a
garden plant used as a spice and for medicinal purposes but
we cannot yet identify the species and similarly we cannot
quite pin down the screeching nocturnal *eššebu*-bird.[134]
Doubts also arise where the cultural gap is particularly wide.
For example, the word *melammu* often means 'splendour'.
Apparently every god possessed a (?) *melammu*, emanating
from his head (in the Creation Epic, when Marduk went forth
to smite Tiamat, whom he eventually split in two and thus
fashioned heaven and earth, 'his fearsome *melammu* covered
his head'), and we also hear of the *melammu* of temples and
kings. What then when we read of demons who 'cannot be
recognized either in heaven or on earth' and 'make clear as
the day (i.e. see clearly) the secrets of the bed' because 'they
are covered with a *melammu*'? One scholar concludes that
melammu means 'mask'. This he connects with the well-docu-
mented practice of conjurer-priests to don masks when com-

bating demons, who must be fought with their own weapons;
in relation to the gods, however, the word came to denote a
crown of glory or the like, and was ultimately 'spiritualized
into ... supernatural glamour'.[135] Another scholar however
maintains that 'splendour' will suit all these passages; even
the demons possess an uncanny radiance which dazzles the
onlooker, so that they see but cannot be seen.[136]

By and large, however, Akkadian is now well understood.
Several volumes have appeared of two great dictionaries;[137]
and on a more mundane level, students can be expected to
translate passages from English (one university recently set 'O
God our help in ages past' in its BA examination) into Akkadian. It is even repaying its initial debt to Hebrew, the known
vocabulary of which has been augmented, and many biblical
passages newly explained, through Akkadian. For example,
in the tragic story of the Levite and his estranged concubine
in Judges 19, most translations state in v. 2 that she had 'played
the whore [Hebrew *wattizne*] against him', though there is no
other hint that she had been anything but chaste right up to
the time of the outrage in v. 25. Ingeniously, Professor Sir
Godfrey Driver proposed to re-interpret the Hebrew word
through the Akkadian *zenû* 'be angry',[138] and the New
English Bible accordingly translates: 'In a fit of anger she had
left him.' Perhaps not every Akkadian-based reinterpretation
in that admirable new version is quite so felicitous – as at
Isaiah 41:14, where 'Israel poor louse' has replaced 'ye men
of Israel' (Authorized Version) by an appeal to Akkadian *mutu*
'worm, louse', the Hebrew original being *mətē*. It may be
noted in passing that of the many philological treatments
(Akkadian is of course only one of the languages used) which
have resulted in novel translations in the New English Bible,
not all have won general approval, and some seem never even to
have been explained to the scholarly community; at Zechariah
13:5, for example, an eminent Semitist recently admitted that
he 'had just no idea' how the translators had arrived at:
'I am a tiller of the soil *who has been schooled in lust* from boy-
hood.'[139]

The problem of polyphony deserves special mention,
because it contributed richly to early scepticism on whether
such a system as Rawlinson had reconstructed could ever have

been put to practical use, and, even if it had, whether scholars could ever agree on its decipherment.[140] To anyone first leafing through the standard reference books, in which the values in use in all periods and areas are consolidated,[141] the difficulties do seem overwhelming; and it is true that the scribes were occasionally tempted to display their erudition and to employ very rare values, which we cannot always recover, for the characters. This sometimes happened when a scribe wrote his name, genealogy and title at the end of a tablet,[142] and another, well-known example is furnished by a tablet which describes the manufacture of red-stone coloured glass. Here the scribe's motive is often said to have been to preserve a trade secret, but other possibilities – to demonstrate the antiquity of glass-making technology in his native Babylonia or simply to show off – are just as likely.[143]

Usually, however, the scribes play fair and if we restrict ourselves – as any ancient scribe was restricted – to a given time and place, the problems become manageable, though still very far from simple; the majority of the signs will have just one value, and only a very small proportion will have more than two. The context will usually leave no doubt as to the value intended – just as no practical problem is posed in English by 'lead', 'refuse' or 'agape'. Failing that, doubt may be dispelled by a second copy of the text. A notable instance occurs in a poem about a righteous sufferer which is often styled 'The Babylonian Job' – though, as W.G. Lambert notes, it differs from Job in that far more space is devoted to the eventual restoration of the sufferer's fortunes than to the problem of his sufferings, and 'The Babylonian *Pilgrim's Progress*' might be a better title.[144] The hero concludes his catalogue of woes, according to Lambert, with the hope that *Samas-su-un i-rim* 'their [i.e. the sufferer's whole family's] Sun[-god] will have mercy' – bringing to mind Job's 'I know that my redeemer liveth.'[145] However, the sign which Lambert read *rim* also has the value *kil*, which, if adopted,[146] would replace *irīn*, 'has mercy', by *īkil* 'darkens', so that the whole passage ends in unrelieved despair: 'their sun will grow dark'. The reading was eventually settled by a newly discovered copy in which the offending word was spelt out with *three* signs which must be read *i-ri-im*; *īkil* is thus excluded.[147]

To take a specific example, the Code of Hammurapi uses some two hundred characters. Of these some fifty may take more than one value; in the majority of these cases the alternative values are all closely akin (such as *ga/qa, aḫ/iḫ, is/i s/iz*), while only about twenty are capable of denoting wholly unrelated syllables (such as *ḫar* and *mur*, or *uṭ/uṭ/ud* and *tan*).[148] All this is certainly complicated, but not hopeless, and there seems in fact to be only one word of which the reading is in serious doubt. It occurs in §127 of the Code, in the penalty for a man who 'has caused a finger to be pointed at a priestess or a married lady and cannot justify it'; in the presence of the judges either *i-na-ad-du-ú-šu* 'they shall cast (or drag) him' or *i-na-aṭ-ṭù-ú-šu* 'they shall flog him', before shaving half his head. And so those who scoffed that polyphony would make of the cuneiform script *'un inextricable gâchis'*[149] have been brilliantly confuted.

It is a paradox that whereas Persian names supplied the decipherer's first clue, native Mesopotamian names long continued to baffle him, partly because the context was rarely of any help, and partly because many such names were written in a mixture of logograms and syllabic signs. The name which Rawlinson read as Temenbar on the Black Obelisk was spelt with four characters having the syllabic values DI MA NU BAR; but its correct pronunciation had to be ascertained from a list of names, spelt out first in the customary fashion and then syllable by syllable, from the library of Ashurbanipal. It transpired that the DI sign could be read as a logogram, meaning 'welfare, peace', and was then pronounced *shulmu*, which with the following MA. NU read *Shulmānu*, a divine name. The BAR sign was then also used as a logogram, meaning 'first' and read *asharēd(u)*. The full name was therefore *Shulmān(u)-asharēd*, 'Shulmanu is chief', which became Shalmaneser in the Bible. Again, the name of Gilgamesh was first read Izdubar, and Rawlinson thereupon identified him with Zoroaster.[150] The queen of Ur (about 2600 BC) whom Woolley found buried close by her husband, together with some sixty attendants and a multitude of treasures so that they should lack nothing in the afterlife, has long been known as Shub-ad, but the name should probably be read Pu-abi.[151] Similarly Shulgi of Ur was formerly called Dungi; the name

Behistun Inscription §5

MAN† da– ri– ia– mush sharru* ki–a–am i– qab–bi ina § silli** sh
Darius (the) king thus saith in (the) protection o

GOD† ú– ri– mi– iz–da– a' ana §–ku sharru* GOD† ú– ri– mi– iz–da– a
Auramazda I king Auramazda

sharru–tu*‡ ana §–ku id–dan–nu
kingdom I he granted

'Thus saith Darius the king: Under the protection of Auramazda I am king
Auramazda hath granted the kingdom unto me.'

Code of Hammurapi §16

shum–ma a–wi–lum lu wardam* lu amtam* ḫal– qá– am
if (a) man either (a) slave or (a) bondmaid lost (i.e. fugitive)

sha ekallim** ù lu mushkēnim*** i–na bi– ti– shu
of (the) palace or (a) private citizen in house–his

ir– ta– qí– ma a–na shi– si– it na–gi– ri– im
has harboured –and at the summons of (the) crier

la ush–te– ṣí– a–am be–el bītim* shu–ú id– da– ak
not he has brought (him) out the master of house that shall be slain

'If a man has harboured in his house a fugitive slave or bondmaid belonging
to the state or to a private citizen, and not brought him out at the summons
of the public crier, the master of that house shall be slain.'

Explanation of Symbols

† determinative, preceding names of the class indicated.
* logogram; the number of asterisks indicates the number of component
signs.
‡ logogram combined with syllabic sign.
§ sign with disyllabic value.

' indicates the glottal stop. ḫ is sounded like *ch* in Scots *loch* or German *nach*. On *q* see below. *ṣ* is distinct from *s*, the nature of the difference is uncertain, but the analogy of Arabic suggests that in the articulation of *ṣ* the back of the tongue was raised and its tip held behind the lower teeth.

What appear to be accents (as in *qà*) do not in fact indicate shades of pronunciation. In view of the problem of homophony (p. 92), the various cuneiform signs which may express a given syllable have been arranged in a conventional order (which reflects their frequency and also the order of their discovery), so that, for example, the many signs that can be read *u* are distinguished as u_1, u_2 ... It is accepted practice, however, to omit the subscript 1, to replace 2 by an acute and 3 by a grave accent, and to write actual numbers only from 4 onward.

Fig. 7.

of the reformer-king of Lagash may well have been not Uruka-gina but Uruinimgina;[152] and such examples could easily be multiplied.

By way of illustration, Fig. 7 presents §5 of the Behistun inscription and §16 of the Code of Hammurapi, which may be compared with Deuteronomy 23:15f.

Old Persian, Elamite and Akkadian might have seemed enough; but as early as 1850 Hincks sensed that the cuneiform tradition went back a stage further. He first observed that cuneiform was not well suited to the Akkadian language. For example, the Semitic languages possess a series of so-called emphatic consonants;[153] thus, whereas English has just two consonants formed by closure between the back of the tongue and the soft palate, namely *k* and (hard) *g*, they also possess a third, denoted *q*, for which the closure is made farther back than for the other two.[154] Hincks detected the presence of *q* as well as *k* and *g* in Akkadian, but found no special signs for the syllables in which it occurred; instead, the signs for syllables containing *k* or *g* were pressed into service. Similarly he found that *ṭ*, another emphatic consonant, distinct from *t*,[155] occurred in Akkadian but had no signs of its own. He concluded that the language of the inventors of cuneiform writing was not Akkadian, and suggested (wrongly) that it might belong to the Indo-European family.[156]

At the same time he was intrigued by various characters each of which could express either a word or a syllable which

bore no apparent relation to that word. His discovery that ⊷⊬
could express both the word 'god' and the seemingly un-
connected syllable *an* has already been mentioned. Similar
anomalies familiar from the history of writing in his native
Ireland suggested an explanation.

The Irish letters were at first chiefly used in the copying of Latin
texts. In Latin manuscripts, the letter *s* with a peculiar mark, which
may be represented by *s'*, was used to express the word *sed* ['but'].
In course of time the same mark was used in Irish manuscripts to
express *akt*, the Irish equivalent of *sed*. And by a further progress,
it was used to express this sound, when it no longer signified 'but',
but was a portion of a word of totally different meaning. Thus, *ts'*
was used for *takt* 'to come'.[157]

In a later paper he compared the use of Latin words or
abbreviations in English: £ stood for *librae* but was read
'pounds', and *e.g.* for *exempli gratia* but was read 'for
example'.[158] Here, then, Hincks found further evidence of the
borrowing of cuneiform signs from another language. If a
single sign could express both a word and a syllable between
which no connection could be traced in Akkadian, then,
Hincks suspected, both functions of the sign – its meaning as
a word and its pronunciation as a syllable – must have been
taken over from the earlier language, in which lay the reason
why the two should go together. In this particular case, ⊷⊬
must have denoted 'god' and must have been pronounced *an*
in the earlier language also.[159] These deductions by Hincks
were soon brilliantly confirmed; and his comparison of the
role of this language with that of Latin in western Europe –
a classical language which nations treated with lasting respect
and from which they derived their own writing system and
much of their culture – could not have been more apt.

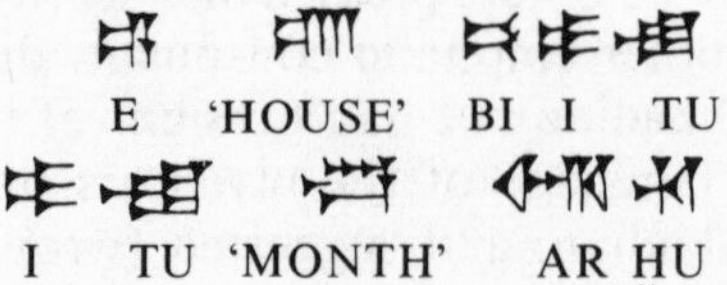

E   'HOUSE'   BI I   TU

I   TU 'MONTH'   AR ḪU

Fig. 8.

In the same year Rawlinson too remarked that the cuneiform script had not been invented by the Akkadians but 'evidently betrays an Egyptian origin'.[160] He was wrong to think
of Egypt; but the library of Ashurbanipal, which was just then
being excavated, soon provided him with plentiful information about the language from which cuneiform had been borrowed. Although it had long ceased to be spoken – perhaps
as early as the period of the kings of Akkad[161] – the study
of it remained an essential part of the training of all Akkadian
scribes for as long as the cuneiform tradition endured, and
Rawlinson discovered all manner of 'text books' which they
had devised. Many contained three columns, of which two
typical entries are shown in Fig. 8. In the centre column Rawlinson recognized a series of logograms used in Akkadian writing, and to the right he found the corresponding Akkadian
words, fully spelt out in syllables. But what was the first
column? The signs were easy to pronounce, but the words that
resulted seemed quite unfamiliar. Rawlinson soon had the
explanation. For various entities, such as 'house' and 'month',
the older language possessed words which were normally
expressed in writing by a single character. These ways of writing the words were borrowed into Akkadian, whence the mysterious logograms; and they are registered in the middle
column. Now the first column spells out, in elementary syllables, how these words were pronounced in the older language. These 'textbooks', then, not only elucidated a whole
series of logograms used in Akkadian, but also gave the
pronunciation and the meaning of the cuneiform signs in
which the older language was written. He must soon have discovered that the sound values of the signs in the two languages
were often but not always identical, and that, as in Akkadian
but to a lesser extent, some signs in the older language had
more than one value. He also found paradigms showing how
verbs were conjugated in both languages, and bilingual literary
texts in which each line appeared first in the older language
and then in Akkadian translation, and even unilingual texts
in the former.Its grammar and vocabulary however placed it
in neither the Indo-European nor the Semitic language family.
As early as 1855 Rawlinson appreciated the historical importance of the people who had spoken that language and had

taught the Akkadians the art of writing, and he declared that it was they who had 'built all the primitive temples and capitals of Babylonia, worshipping the same gods, and inhabiting the same seats as their Semitic successors'.[162]

This older language – 'older' meaning merely that it was earlier reduced to writing – now had to be found a name. Because many Mesopotamian kings used the title 'King of Sumer and Akkad', and because the name Akkad appears in the Bible (Genesis 10:10), the term 'Akkadian' was widely adopted for some decades,[163] though it is of course very differently used today. Oppert protested, as early as 1869, that Sumer should have been chosen rather than Akkad, but his view did not prevail until 1889, with the discovery of a tablet which referred to the language as *li-ša-an šu-mi-ri* 'the language of Sumer'[164], and, three years later, of Ashurbanipal's boast[165] that ' I read the curious text of the obscure Sumerian (which is) difficult to translate into Akkadian.' And so a people whose name had been lost for thousands of years was re-discovered and could speak again. Even the Bible had preserved no clear trace of their name. An identification with Shinar (Genesis 10:10 etc.) is tempting, but the change from *m* to *n* is odd, and the names are even more different in the original Hebrew.[166] Another suggestion is that in the name Sumer – more properly *Shumer* – the final consonant was left unpronounced, and the resulting *Shume* entered the Bible as Shem, just as the full name of the city called Ur in the Bible was Urim.[167] But the change of vowel is puzzling, nor is it easy to understand in historical terms how Sumer could have been regarded as the ancestor of the 'Semitic' peoples.

Meanwhile a far stormier controversy had broken out in 1874, when the French scholar Joseph Halévy published his theory that the Sumerian language and people never existed at all. What passed for Sumerian writing, Halévy argued, was in fact written in the Akkadian language but in an ingenious cryptic system invented by the Akkadian scribes. Once archaeology had reached down to the purely Sumerian levels, the existence of that people and their language was (or soon became) indisputable; but in 1874 the only evidence was provided by philology, and the issue cannot have seemed clear-cut if only because Halévy's views were espoused by three leading

Assyriologists, among them the eminent Friedrich Delitzsch (who recanted however in 1897). Sir E.A. Wallis Budge suggested that Halévy's refusal to believe in the Sumerians sprang from his being 'proud to proclaim that his remote ancestors were kinsmen of the Hebrew patriarchs whose home was Babylonia, and that they were the founders of all civilization in Mesopotamia',[168] and some have agreed with him.[169] It is odd, however, that none of these writers goes on to explain the (albeit temporary) anti-Sumerian stance of Friedrich Delitzsch, who expounded his thoughts on the Jews and their scriptures lucidly enough in his book *The Great Deception*.[170]

Overwhelming evidence against Halévy's theory came from the French excavations made from 1877 onward under G. de Sarzec at Lagash. Here thousands of unilingual Sumerian texts came to light, which could hardly all have been written in code, and thousands more flooded in from the American excavations between 1889 and 1900 at Nippur. Moreover, the physical features of the people depicted on the statues and reliefs at Lagash differed clearly from those on Assyrian monuments.[171] And so the reality of the Sumerians has not been doubted since the present century began.

The investigation of Sumerian progressed steadily from the first; no decipherer could have asked for a better key than the wealth of Sumerian-Akkadian 'textbooks'. The first unilingual text, of twelve lines, was published in 1871 by A.H. Sayce.[172] A fundamental work – consisting of an extensive grammar and sign-list, together with transliterations and translations of nearly eighty Sumerian texts, a quarter of them unilingual – was published in 1873–9 by François de Lenormant, and has been followed by a century of distinguished research.

In structure, Sumerian is agglutinative; that is, it possesses many particles which are liable to be formed into lengthy chains, within which they must stand in a fixed order. One might encounter such a form as *ḫu-mu-na-ni-ib-dù* 'surely he built it for him therein'. Here *ḫu* corresponds to 'surely', *mu* is a particle whose function is still uncertain, *na* signifies 'for him', *ni* 'therein', (*i*)*b* 'it', and *dù* 'build' or (as there seems to be no special particle to indicate the subject 'he' and the past tense) 'he built'; and the order has to be just so. Contrast English, where the constituent elements of such a phrase enjoy some mobility (for example, we could have begun the English version with 'he' or 'therein') and are therefore perceived as separate words. Two main dialects of Sumerian are well attested, and at least one more is known to have existed;[173] how the language evolved with time has also been ascertained, at least in part; but all attempts to relate Sumerian to other known languages have failed.[174] Many other agglutinative languages exist – examples are Finnish, Turkish and Mongolian – but none seems related to Sumerian. The languages of the Indo-European and Semitic families are not, of course, agglutinative, and it need hardly be remarked that the supposition that Sumerian is a common ancestor of both, on which Dr John Allegro bases his curious theories about Judaism and Christianity, is untenable and has long caused philologists to wonder why so many libraries classify these writings under non-fiction.

Scholarship has not, however, yet achieved a command of Sumerian comparable to that of Akkadian. The basic difficulty is that with no known related language virtually no information can be gleaned, and no guess verified, outside the closed field of cuneiform literature, where the evidence is not always easy to interpret. (A rare opportunity of investigating Sumerian through means other than cuneiform is provided by a handful of fragmentary Sumerian and Akkadian texts accompanied by Greek transliteration, of which five were published in 1902; although they seem as late as the second or first century BC, they have much to tell us about the sounds of both languages, and demonstrate to the sceptical that the decipherment of Sumerian is not just an elaborate delusion).[175] Among the cuneiform sources, the bilingual Sumerian–Akkadian texts on which one must primarily depend are not altogether reliable; the oldest do not go back beyond the early second millenium, by which time Sumerian had been a dead language for centuries, and was only imperfectly remembered. One feature suggesting that the memory of it was distorted is the enormous number of homonyms – for example, sixteen different words all read *gar*, eighteen read *gur*,[176] and the words for 'one' and 'six' both read *ash* – which occur in the language as the 'textbooks' present it, but which a living language, even if it had (as many suppose) a system of musical tones like Chinese, could hardly have tolerated. Hence the importance of the newly discovered Sumerian–Eblaite texts, which should record Sumerian as a spoken language.

With our present knowledge, receipts and other administrative texts are more or less intelligible, but literary texts are still too problematic for anything more than a tentative translation. A fair example can be drawn from the so-called 'Myth of the Pickaxe'; the translations offered for lines 18–24 by two eminent Sumerologists, S. N. Kramer and Th. Jacobsen, are here set side by side:[177]

The head of man he placed in the mould,	In the hole (which he thus made) was the vanguard of mankind
Before Enlil *he* (man?) *covers* his land,	(And) while (the people of) his land were breaking through the ground toward Enlil
Upon his black-headed people he looked steadfastly.	He eyed his black-headed ones in steadfast fashion.
The Anunnaki [attendant deities] who stood about him,	The Anunnaki stepped up to him,
He placed *it* (the pickaxe?) as a gift in their hands,	laid their hands upon their noses (in greeting),
They soothe Enlil with prayer,	Soothing Enlil's heart with prayers,
They give the pickaxe to the black-headed people to hold.	Black-headed (people) they were requesting (?) of him.

The first line in Sumerian runs *sag nam-lú-ulú ù-šub-ba mi-ni-gál*, and the treatment of it typifies the differences between the two scholars, who agree essentially on only one word out of the four, namely the second, translated 'man(kind)'. To *sag* Kramer assigns its primary meaning 'head', while Jacobsen takes it figuratively ('vanguard'); *ù-šub(-ba)*, usually 'brick-mould' (Kramer), has been generalized to 'hole' by Jacobsen; finally, for the *gál* element in *mi-ni-gál* both 'to place' (transitive) and 'to be' (intransitive) are well attested meanings. The many divergences of this sort have led to two wholly different interpretations of the passage.[178] Kramer sees the pickaxe as Enlil's gift for man's use. He admits – perhaps with the first two lines especially in mind – that his translation might seem 'sodden, stilted and obscure', but he is anxious, given the limits of present knowledge, 'to hew close to the literal word'. Jacobsen, who has allowed himself greater freedom, finds instead an account of the creation of the first men; they had developed like plants in the earth, the crust of which Enlil now breaks with the pickaxe, and man shoots forth. Scholarship has yet to reach a confident verdict between these two treatments – and the various others that have been proposed.

That text is thought to have been composed about 2000 BC; but as we move farther back into the third millennium, with no bilingual texts – until the Ebla discoveries are fully known – to guide us, Sumerian presents ever greater difficulties, which are felt the more keenly as inscriptions in Akkadian peter out. About a thousand texts dating from about 2600 BC were discovered at Fara (ancient Shuruppak, see map on page 23) in 1902–3, and some five hundred more, roughly contemporary, came to light in 1963–5 at Abu Salabikh (of which the ancient name is not yet known, recent suggestions being Eresh[179] and Gishgi[180]). Many are economic, and at least partly intelligible, but there are also literary texts, notably hymns, of which very little is understood. In studying the latter, some scholars have experimented with assigning to many of the characters values which they never take elsewhere, in the hope of ultimately obtaining something which will make sense as Sumerian; no consensus, however, has yet emerged.[181] Here, then, decipherment is still in progress, and much work remains to be done on this, the oldest literature known – or ever likely to be known.

Many still earlier texts have been recovered from Mesopotamia, notably at Uruk and Jamdat Nasr,[182] and are even more baffling. They have been investigated by the Russian scholar A.A. Vaiman. The first difficulty which leaps to the eye is that many more characters occur here than in later texts; at first sight, at least, they exceed 1,000.[183] One must begin, then, by working out, just as Botta did when he first encountered cuneiform, which signs are interchangeable variants, and how many truly different signs exist; Vaiman reports that his researches have reduced the number to some 800. Even this, however, is rather more than the number of characters that appear in later texts, which is about 600; apparently many of the characters then current fell out of use before the period at which texts become properly intelligible to us, so that we can hardly hope to discover how they were read. Many more, however, must have continued in use, and so we may seek to identify as many of these archaic characters as we can with characters familiar from later texts. This is no straightforward task, since time changed considerably the outward form of the characters, as we shall see; Vaiman claims to have identified 250 of these most ancient characters with later cuneiform signs. A complete translation, therefore, may never be feasible; but that, at least in terms of literature, is probably no great loss. The little that has been deciphered[184] (see Fig. 9) consists of humdrum receipts and the like: 'fifty-four bulls [and] cows', or '[To] the diviner: 290 GAR long, 62 GAR broad, 10 BUR and 2/10 IKU [in area]' – evidently the dimensions of a field.[185] The outward appearance of the texts confirms that most were 'mere lists of objects pictorially jotted down on clay-tablets with the numbers of each beside them, indicated by a simple system of strokes, circles and semicircles'.[186] It was evidently the need to keep track of the busy economic life of the Sumerian city-state – the export of manufactured goods, the transport and storage of surplus grain, transactions between individual citizens – that led to the first writing in Mesopotamia, and indeed in the world.[187] It is tempting to suggest a date for the beginnings of this writing, but very hazardous; many think tentatively about 3100 BC.[188]

Who were its inventors? The earliest texts whose language can be established are in Sumerian; they belong, as we shall see, to the Jamdat Nasr collection, which is not quite so ancient as some of the tablets from Uruk. Many scholars see no reason to doubt that even the earliest texts were read in Sumerian, and that it was the Sumerians who invented writing. However, of those who hold that the Sumerians first came to Iraq in the closing centuries of the fourth millennium (a problem discussed on p. 19), some ascribe the invention, and even the most ancient tablets, to the supposed earlier inhabitants of Iraq; here it has been contended (but not by any means proved) that cuneiform could not have been designed for

Sumerian because it does not fit the language well enough[189] – just as Hincks showed for Akkadian.

Though their meaning is so little understood, these texts do provide a starting-point from which the history of cuneiform can be traced. As Fig. 10 shows, many words were first expressed by simple pictures,[190] which might be subject to various devices (as when an animal was represented by its head alone, or a part of the human face was indicated by shading) or combinations (as when 'mouth' and 'water' together meant 'drink'); wholly abstract signs also occur (like the signs for 'friendship' and 'enmity' in Fig. 10). But the all-important step, without which one cannot speak of writing but merely of pictures and mnemonics, is what Gelb has called phonetization;[191] the symbol which represents a word is used to express the sound of that word even when the word itself is not present. For example, if a writing system had to be newly invented for English, the words 'bee' and 'leaf' could be represented by drawings of those objects; but with phonetization one could also use the 'bee' sign for the verb 'be', and combine it with the 'leaf' sign to express 'belief' – two words for which pictorial symbols could hardly be devised.[192] This step may

Texts from Uruk (Level IV), ed. Falkenstein

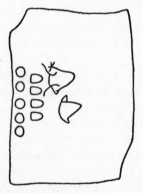

No. 339 (Reverse)
'54 bulls (and) cows'

No. 15*
'2 gazelles [of] the DI-lady (lit. the feminine wearer-of-clothes DI†) [to] the butcher [of the city of] Uruk'

Texts from Jamdat Nasr, ed. Langdon

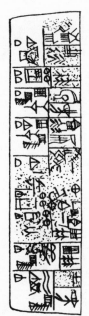

No. 22 (Flat side, III)
Largely unintelligible apart from the occurrences
of the name En-líl-ti. 'Enlil (grants) life'
composed of three signs:

EN 'lord'; the sign may depict a tower
surmounting a barn.‡

LÍL 'air', perhaps expressed by a drawing of a
reed wall, through which air wafted. ‡ Enlil of
course means 'lord of the air'.

TI 'arrow', used for its homonym *ti(l)* 'life';
see below.

No. 100 (Convex side, IV)*
'[To] the diviner: 290 GAR long, 62 GAR
broad, 10 BÙR 2/10 IKU [of field]'

* Translated by Vaiman.

† Vaiman believes the DI sign to be present but has not embodied it in a
   translation.

‡ As suggested by A. Deimel, *Šumerisches Lexicon*, (Rome 1928–37).

Fig. 9.

first have been taken to meet the administrative need to
represent the name of each citizen accurately enough to avoid
confusion.[193] The earliest example yet known comes from
Jamdat Nasr (about 2900 BC?), in a name which consists of
symbols denoting the god Enlil followed by a picture of an
arrow. From Enlil and 'arrow' little sense can be extracted;
but in Sumerian the words for 'arrow' and 'life' are
pronounced identically, as *ti*[194] and so the name surely means

The Evolution of Characters from the Earliest Texts (c. 3000 BC to c. 600 BC)

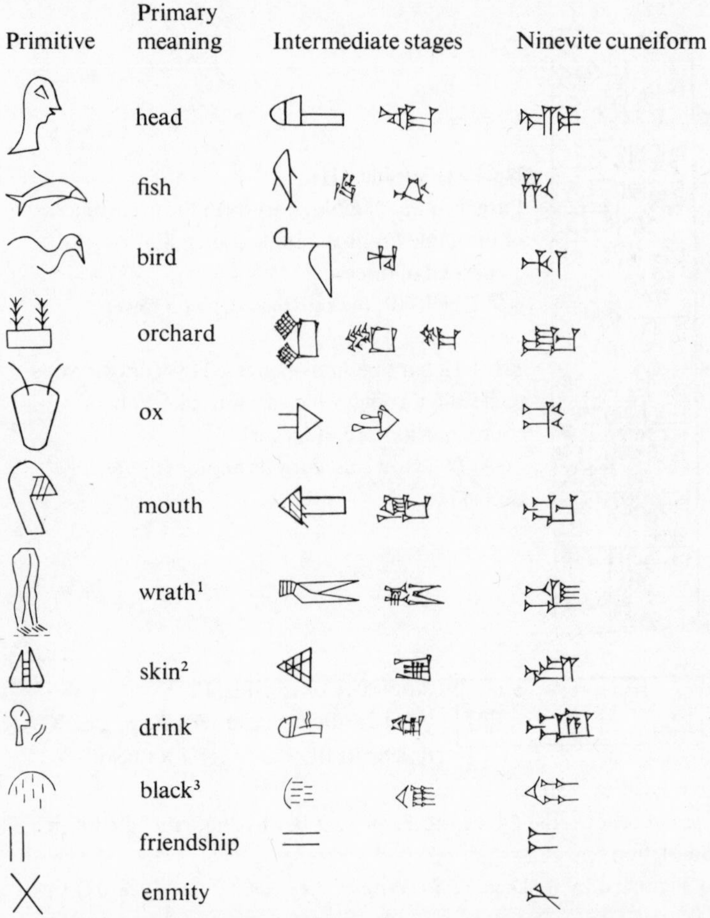

Primitive	Primary meaning	Intermediate stages		Ninevite cuneiform
	head			
	fish			
	bird			
	orchard			
	ox			
	mouth			
	wrath[1]			
	skin[2]			
	drink			
	black[3]			
	friendship			
	enmity			

[1] Perhaps thought to reside in the viscera or bowels (compare our 'spleen'); legs were added to indicate the lower half of the body (Deimel).

[2] The symbol may have been a wooden frame on which hide was worked (Deimel). In the fifth century this sign was complicated to

[3] The semi-circle represents the vault of heaven, whence darkness descends (Labat).

NB This figure concentrates on developments in Assyria; many signs evolved differently in Babylonia. See further R. Labat, *Manuel d'Epigraphie Akkadienne*, (5th ed., Paris 1976).

Fig. 10.

Enlil (grants) life', with the 'arrow' sign representing not an arrow but simply the sound *ti*. At least from that point onward, the writing is demonstrably Sumerian.

Among other devices, we note that many of the signs were used for more than one word.[195] Thus a drawing of a leg could express not only the word *du* 'leg' but also *túm* 'bring', *gin* 'go' and *gub* 'stand'; again, the figure of a plough stood not only for *apin* 'plough' but also for *engar* 'ploughman'. That signs could be read in more ways than one was therefore accepted from the first. To avoid confusion, two further devices arose. Sometimes a sign (technically termed a determinative) was added, but not pronounced, to indicate the general class to which the word belonged. Thus, when the word denoted by the 'plough' sign was *engar*, the sign for 'man' could be placed before it, but when *apin* was intended, the sign for 'wood' could be prefaced instead. Many determinative signs came to be used even in cases where there was no confusion; thus the 'wood' sign later occurs regularly before all sorts of trees and wooden objects, and a vertical wedge functions as a determinative before all personal names – as the decipherers were glad to discover. Another device was to follow an ambiguous sign with a second sign that pointed to the true pronunciation; for example, when the word intended by the 'leg' sign was *gub*, then one could place straight after it the sign that expressed the word *ba*, which in fact means 'give' but which here served simply to eliminate all the alternatives (such as *gin*), which did not end in *b*. This is the phonetic complement, discovered, as we saw, by Hincks.

Such was the writing system of the Sumerians, and soon, probably early in the third millennium, the Akkadians adapted it to their own quite unrelated language. Unfortunately, they used the Sumerian signs in more than one way. Sometimes they took over the sign for a Sumerian word and employed it without further ado for the corresponding Akkadian word. Thus, for example, the sign which indicated the Sumerian word *ìr* 'slave' was simply adopted for the Akkadian word *ardu* 'slave'. Such, then, as Rawlinson noted, is the foreign origin of the logograms in Akkadian, and it was thence too that they borrowed determinatives and the principle of the phonetic complement. But beyond that they took one great creative step: they analysed their own words into syllables, and expressed each syllable by a Sumerian character. This meant that nearly every Sumerian character was designated to express one or more of the syllables that occur in Akkadian. The syllables assigned to the characters were, by and large, identical or similar to the sounds of the words they expressed in Sumerian, or, less often, of their equivalents in Akkadian.[196] Thus the sign which denoted 'mouth', for which the Sumerian is *ka* and the Akkadian is *pu*, acquired such values as *ka*, *ga*, *qa*, *pi*, *pe*[197] – though at no one time and place were all five available. More prolific was the sign for the Sumerian word *kur*, meaning either 'mountain' or 'land'; the Akkadian for 'mountain' is *shadû* and for 'land' *mātu*. Hence the sign took on such values as *kur*, *qur; shad*, *shat*, *sad; mat*, *mad*, *nat*, *lat* – but, once again, never all together.

There were remarkably many differences between the values which the characters could assume in different areas, and even in the same area at different times.[198] A possible explanation is that when the idea of using the Sumerian characters for Akkadian syllables first developed, different Akkadian-speaking areas worked out their own detailed solutions to the problem of which syllabic values should be assigned to which characters; different localities then tended to preserve different traditions as to the value(s) of each character; and in the major centres of power (such as Babylon), political developments would, every so often, bring to the fore a hitherto obscure local tradition of writing. As luck would have it, the system was at its most complicated, with polyphony at its height, in the middle third of the first millennium – from which period dates the Babylonian text at Behistun.

These changes in the function of the characters had been accompanied by changes in their outward form, largely due to the adoption of clay (which was inscribed with a reed stylus) as the writing material.[199] The scribes must have begun by holding the clay tablet in the left hand and the stylus in the right. The most natural point at which to start writing was then the top right-hand corner, and so the text was first written from right to left,[200] usually (if it was of any considerable length) in vertical columns; this arrangement is shown in Fig. 11(a), where the sequence of characters is represented sche-

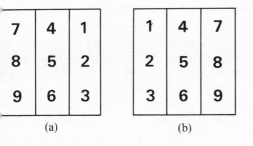 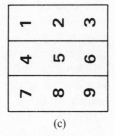

| | (a) | | | (b) | | | (c) | |

Fig. 11.

matically by 1 2 3 ... The scribes soon found, however, that the right hand, when inscribing the later columns was liable to smudge the earlier ones; and so the practice grew up of starting at the top left-hand corner – except on stone inscriptions, to which this problem did not apply, and which continued to be written in the old fashion well into the second millennium. A clean break with earlier practice, as suggested in Fig. 11(b), would however have been unacceptable. Instead, the scribes rotated each character anti-clockwise, and arranged them horizontally in rows, as in Fig. 11(c); they thus avoided smudging, and yet if the finished tablet was simply turned around, it looked just like the tablets written in the time-honoured way.

But the characters in their new positions lost most of the realism they may have had as pictures, and were soon liable to be modified further. Drawing any continuous outline tended to heap up the clay in front of the tip of the stylus, and so the scribes came to prefer to press the stylus into the clay in a single movement. They could thus produce a fair range of different marks, as the edge or corner of the stylus entered the clay at different angles. Not all these were equally convenient; in writing from left to right some (such as ◄) would have involved turning the stylus around. They chose, therefore, to confine themselves to a small number of strokes, namely ► ➘ ⊤ ⟨ and rarely ✓ and to build up each character by as many of these as were necessary.[201]

It is of course at this stage that the writing can truly be called cuneiform ('wedge-shaped'). By confining themselves to this small range of strokes, the scribes could not hope to preserve anything of the pictorial nature of the characters, but they still took care to distinguish the characters from one another. A complex process of evolution now ensued. The number of strokes in each sign tended to be reduced; horizontal and vertical strokes came to predominate, at the expense of diagonal strokes; one sign might be re-modelled on the analogy of another; other, seemingly arbitrary, tendencies sometimes came to the fore, as when many signs were embellished with additional strokes in the time of the later Achaemenian kings; and local differences grew up. The development of a small sample of characters is shown in Fig. 10.

After this complex evolution, it is no wonder that the Assyrians themselves referred to cuneiform writing as a 'secret treasure' or 'mystery'.[202] Quite apart from the use of the signs as logograms and determinatives, the syllables they express seem infuriatingly arbitrary; the script which was standard in seventh-century Nineveh (and which students today usually learn first) is typical in its profusion of signs of similar form which are utterly different in sound – as is evident if one strips down a fairly complicated sign – and vice versa (Fig. 12). And yet the system served the scribes well enough (and many of today's students have found it far easier to memorize, say, the

shik	qi(n)	la	ku	shu	ma	is	tab	ash

ash	esh	ish	ush	sha	she	shi	shu	mash	dish

Fig. 12.

seventh-century Nineveh signs than they had feared), and although it steadily lost ground from the seventh century onward,[203] cuneiform survived, albeit in ever more limited use, at least as far down as 75 AD.[204]

Cuneiform was also adopted by the speakers of other languages – the Hurrians, the Hittites (who used the script to write not only their own language but also those of neighbouring peoples, and of the Hattians, whom they displaced), the Urartians and the Elamites. With the exception of the Hittites, they largely dispensed with logograms and with polyphony of signs, and produced far more convenient systems; for example, Elamite in the Achaemenian inscriptions has just over a hundred syllabic signs, of which at least ninety have a single value only, plus a mere handful (less than twenty altogether) of logograms and determinatives. As has happened so often, the foreigners who borrowed the system improved on it and developed it in a way that the natives, hidebound by tradition, never could.[205] The idea of making signs with wedges, but not the characters and values themselves, was also adopted to create the various 'letters' in two systems which approximated to an alphabet – that of the Canaanites at Ugarit, in the fifteenth and fourteenth centuries BC, and that of Old Persian, which script is often said to have been invented at Darius' command,[206] though it may instead have developed from the scribal traditions of Urartu.[207] But the Persians set up their inscriptions not only in their own language but also in Elamite and Akkadian, and thereby left the key with which men one day would learn to re-enter a world long forgotten, and to reach back to the beginnings of recorded history.

CHAPTER 5

Tell Mardikh

In 1963, Paulo Matthiae, an archaeology graduate with a special interest in ancient art, was sent out by the Institute of Near Eastern Studies at the University of Rome, to select an excavation site in Syria. He was received with every courtesy by officials from the Department of Antiquities, some of whom, however, were a trifle taken aback by his appearance. They had expected some venerable sage and were confronted instead by a fresh-faced young man whose unruly shock of blond hair made him look even younger than his twenty-three years, but they were impressed by the professionalism of his approach, the range of his knowledge and his almost oppressive earnestness. What he lacked in years he made up in gravitas.

He was taken on what was virtually a grand tour of Syria and must have found its geography as dramatic and varied as its history, for one can within half an hour move from an almost Alpine landscape of snow-capped hills to torrid, wind-blown desert and from lush plains to gravelly steppe. There are also extremes of temperature, not only between the different regions of the country, but within the same regions, creating different landscapes at different seasons, and anyone who travels through Syria in April might fail to recognize it in July.

The country may be roughly divided into four main geographical areas. There is first a narrow well-watered coastal plain, nowhere more than twenty miles wide and which vanishes altogether where the mountains come down to the sea. The climate is typically Mediterranean, with miles of sandy beaches and abundant crops of olives, vegetables and citrus. A little inland one has the mountain ranges stretching from north to south and rising to about four thousand feet. The western slopes receive abundant rainfall and have a considerable farming population engaged in the cultivation of vines, olives, tobacco and cotton. The eastern slopes are rather less favoured and peter out into plateaux and plains. Then there is the northern area, watered by the Balikh, the Euphrates and Orontes, which contains Syria's richest agricultural land and the main centres of population and has, since earliest times, been famous as a source of wheat and barley, and wine, and of textiles. And finally to the south-east, one has the rock-strewn steppes of the Syrian desert, now rising to about three thousand feet, now falling away into shallow depressions, to merge finally with the great deserts of Arabia.

The country is about the size of England and Wales and has a population of about six million. About a third of Syria is uninhabited and uninhabitable, the result possibly of overcultivation and de-forestation, for there is abundant evidence to suggest that ancient Syria was more fertile than it is now. The situation of the country as the gateway to the Mediterranean and at the cross-roads between the warring powers of Mesopotamia and Egypt has made it the battleground of almost every great empire in history. It has felt the tread of Sargon and Caesar, Alexander the Great and Napoleon and many an army which came to battle remained to enjoy the comforts of its cities and the abundant produce of its hillsides and river valleys, and not a few have left evidence of their stay in the form of tells.

A tell is an artificial mound accruing from a long period or successive periods of settlement and is to be found commonly in those parts of the world where the building material – in this case mud brick – is so cheap, abundant and expendable as not to be worth reclaiming. The mud-walled dwelling – and millions of them are in use throughout the East to this day – is in fact a disposable house, so that when a set of buildings crumbles or is destroyed, people simply level out the ruins (sometimes they don't even do that) as a foundation and build on top, so that in the course of time a hill rises above the surrounding plain and, where the site is abandoned, the sand blows in from the desert and the tell assumes the familiar rounded aspect of a sugar loaf.

The Syrian landscape is dotted with such tells, as if blistered by the fierce summer heat, and Matthiae examined a number before arriving finally at Tell Mardikh some thirty miles south of Aleppo, and just off the main road to Damascus. He was first of all attracted by its very size, for it is a large tell, some hundred and forty acres in extent and rising to a height of fifty feet. The Syrian authorities, moreover, were anxious to attract an expedition to the area, firstly because they had reason to believe that it was of more than casual interest and secondly because they had been troubled by the depredations of grave robbers, who had been probing the site under cover of darkness. Grave robbers, though a nuisance and a menace, are, in a sense, folk archaeologists, receivers of local lore, and the very fact that they were active in the area suggested that it had secrets to yield. The mere scratching of the loose, wind-blown top soils revealed potsherds going back to the Middle Bronze Age as well as earthen ramparts of equal antiquity. And in 1955 a farmer's plough had turned up a double basalt trough, not unlike a large, stone kitchen sink, which could be dated about 1900 BC. The originality of the reliefs it bore – on the front, a king pours a libation, while both sides show scenes of marching warriors, and lions' heads with mouths open in a silent roar – belied the usual view of Syrian art as a mere reflection of Mesopotamian, Egyptian and Anatolian influences.

Syria's Byzantine, Roman and Hellenistic past had been fairly well documented and Matthiae hoped to find something going back to an earlier date, perhaps as far back as the end of the second millennium BC, when the Phoenicians established themselves by the coast and the Aramaeans in the heartland of Syria. Tell Mardikh held out a promise of even greater antiquity, and he expressed a desire to begin digging as soon as an expedition could be assembled and equipped.

Rome was at first hesitant.[1] A basalt trough, no matter how ancient or impressive, does not constitute a civilization. Moreover, Matthiae, though able and zealous (and, what can count for as much as both in Italian scholastic circles, of good pedigree – his father was a distinguished art historian), was, they felt, a trifle immature to direct excavations at a site the size of Tell Mardikh, especially as his training was almost entirely academic and his experience of field work had been confined to prehistoric sites in Italy. They were also troubled by his very prognostications, for if Tell Mardikh should indeed have the prospects he claimed, then it called for the attention of a senior man, especially as a major find at an overseas site could have diplomatic implications which perhaps only a senior man could handle. Matthiae himself, however, felt confident that he could cope with any problem which might arise and he enjoyed the ready support of his teachers, but nevertheless he agreed to be guided in his first seasons by some senior colleagues and Professor Sabatino Moscati, who was then head of the Institute of Near Eastern Studies at Rome University and Professor Floriani Squarciapino, an authority in classical topography, helped him to build up a team and to oversee his initial efforts.

There is more to a dig than digging and the excavation of an historic site calls for more skills than the erection of a major edifice; apart from the specialists necessary to evaluate the importance of a find, who were drawn from several different disciplines, Matthiae had to recruit architects, surveyors, engineers, draughtsmen, technicians and administrators. By the time his team – which included his wife, Gabriella Matthiae Scandone, a trained Egyptologist – was complete, he had some two dozen people round him, all drawn from Italian universities.

Labour was recruited on the spot. Aleppo itself is a major trade centre at the heart of a prosperous cotton growing district with a large population, but as one moves south, water becomes sparse and the soil infertile. The area turns a light greyish green after the winter rains and wild flowers erupt in colourful profusion, but the vegetation fades as the clouds recede and by the summer the dual-carriage highway is like a pair of black streaks across the white sands. Beyond the highway, minor roads of beaten earth, hardly more than goat-tracks, weave their way to the occasional village with mud habitations like elongated bee-hives, which, from a distance, look more like an outcrop of rock than human dwellings. As one gets nearer one notices more substantial dwellings of concrete or stone, with a balcony and grill-work, the upper storey painted a faded green, the home of some local notable, or a family with relatives abroad, though the bee-hives tend to be cooler in the summer and less cold in the winter than the grander dwellings.

The village that lies between the site and the highway, also called Tell Mardikh, is fairly typical of the region. Its population of three or four hundred lives, as it has always lived, mainly on its hardy flocks of sheep and goats which roam the area, with bells tinkling from their necks, snatching at the scattered shrubs and somehow thriving on them. Men and women, the latter often with small children to their backs, work in the fields and coax a sparse harvest of cereals and melons out of the gravelly soil. Well-fed chickens scratch around the village street and emaciated dogs slumber in the shade. One sees few old men about – in contrast to an English village – possibly because people do not survive to old age in this part of the world, or if they do, they are still at work in the fields.

The arrival of Matthiae and his colleagues has done surprisingly little to affect the calm pattern of Tell Mardikh life. Their encampment is about half way between the village and the tell but is not quite of it. They have not turned native (beyond sporting kefiahs and drinking arak) and the natives have not turned Italian (though some Arab labourers have been sighted with spaghetti in their pitta). The excavations have, however, provided a useful source of employment and the excavators a ready market for produce and the village has become one of the most prosperous in the district. An uncommonly large proportion of its children have got shoes and they are no longer startled or agog at the constant stream of Fiats and Volvos bouncing through their narrow pot-holed streets heading for the dig, which is rapidly becoming a place of pilgrimage. Scholars have been coming and going since the first stone was turned. Now there is a constant stream of press men and camera crews. The tourists must follow and Dr Afif Bahnasi, Director General of Antiquities, has promised a library and lounge for visitors.[2]

An archaeological expedition is never a year round affair and in Tell Mardikh the season lasts a mere ten weeks, from the beginning of August until the rains descend about the middle of October. Most of the principals involved have teaching duties during the year; it would in any case be difficult to keep a team together for much more than ten weeks at a time, for the work is demanding and occasionally tedious, the conditions are spartan, the amenities few, the isolation vexing and after an extended period, what may have begun as an adventure can end as an ordeal.

At first Matthiae used the Baron Hotel, Aleppo as his headquarters. The Baron, an imposing edifice of white limestone, with lofty rooms completed in the early years of the century, was amongst the first hotels in Syria with western standards of comfort and eastern standards of hospitality and was praised as such by T.E. Lawrence, but Matthiae found the thirty-mile journey to Tell Mardikh time-consuming and tiresome. There was no possibility of finding adequate accommodation within Tell Mardikh itself and he therefore arranged for the construction of a two-storey building, somewhat on the lines of a French Foreign-Legion Fort, with dwellings in a linked quadrangle round a central courtyard and gates which could be locked at night. Between the main quadrangle and the outer gate was a second courtyard which contained a work area and storage space. Two sides of the quadrangle contained the offices, workrooms and studios of Professor Matthiae and his colleagues, a third contained the bedrooms, showers and toilets and a fourth the kitchen and dining rooms. Outside the dining room stands a sort of tabernacle, its walls of reed-matting, a tarpaulin for its roof, its floor covered with Turkish carpets, its corners strewn with cushions, at the centre a wood fire, with bronze jugs of coffee steaming amid the embers, where members of the expedition relax after a day's work. It is their mess-room, their club and possibly because of their very isolation a sense of family develops between them which is impenetrable to the visitor and which, indeed, is almost on guard against him. The family evolves over the course of successive seasons and those who cannot feel fully a part of it drop out to make room for those who can. When the members leave in the autumn they require some time to adjust themselves to the realities of the outside world. Some never do and Professor Matthiae in particular occasionally gives the impression that he takes Tell Mardikh with him wherever he goes.

Archaeology can have a similar effect even on the casual

visitor. As one's efforts gather pace one has the sensation of
descending through the centuries. A top layer three feet thick
may represent a mere century of accumulation. But as one goes
deeper and deeper the effect of the descent is almost intoxicat-
ing, for one is surrounded by clay, mud, basalt, all of them
porous and they seem to exhale the past as one moves among
them. To tread even among the top soils can be an overwhelming experience. Mr Ramsay Homa, a London businessman
and art historian who visited the site in 1976, compared its
impact to his first glimpse of the Parthenon. But it was not
the sight of the excavations which gripped his imagination so
much as the thought of them, the feeling that there amidst the
dust might lie the very beginnings of recorded history.[3] One
hurries to the cold showers at the base camp to be restored
to reality. Some never are.

The day begins early and the Arab kitchen hands are busy
before the first pink glow of morning has brightened the sky.
By 5.30 am Matthiae is in the dining room, warming his hands
on a cup of coffee, giving an occasional sip, too impatient to
sit down. His colleagues, somewhat more relaxed, help themselves to bread, cheese, olives, cucumber, peppers, onions. The
coffee is abundant but thick as mud and not unlike it in flavour
('it's made out of ground-down Tell Mardikh tablets,' said one
visitor). By 6 am Matthiae is out by the tell with his assistant
taking the roll-call of Arab labourers. The wages paid by the
expedition are well above the local average and in the first seasons there was a scramble for jobs, but gradually something
like a permanent work force has evolved whose members
return season after season and who have come to regard their
employment almost as a proprietary right, so that when they
can no longer continue at their jobs they pass them down to
relatives.

Until recently it was quite common for one supervisor in
an archaeological dig to direct the efforts of a hundred or more
labourers, as if they were coolies building a highway, so that
important finds were sometimes overlooked and others
damaged by the heedless application of pick and shovel.
Nowadays the ratio of supervisors to labourers is commonly
about one to ten and not infrequently one to five or six (de-
pending on the nature of the job), so that everything is sifted

and scrutinized and layers of soil are as carefully pulled back as layers of fat in a surgical operation.

Several of Matthiae's assistants are young women and some of the Arabs did not take kindly to receiving orders from dainty little nymphs in frayed shorts and dolly glasses. The fact that to some of the young Italians all Arabs looked alike, or at least were called alike – Mohammed, mostly, or Ahmed or Mahmoud – could also occasion embarrassment, for it was not always certain who was who and a Mahmoud trained to do one job sometimes found himself doing another intended for Ahmed, but all such difficulties were straightened out within a season or two and, once the dig was in full swing, Matthiae found himself in command of an effective work force, though one might not always think so from a casual visit to the site.

An archaeological expedition on site reminds one, at first glance, of a film crew on set. Several people may be shouting mutually contradictory orders (sometimes at each other), one or two may be actively at work, three or four are moving hither and thither and a great many others are standing around (or even lying around). All that is missing is the mobile canteen dishing out cups of tea, though as a matter of fact someone arrives in the course of the morning with cold drinks. One does not get the impression that it is a hive of industry, but that arises largely out of the delicate nature of the work. One cannot apply a bulldozer to an archaeological dig (even though one is frequently tempted to do so). If one cuts away the side of a tell, as has sometimes been done, one finds civilization after civilization – say Crusader at one level, Byzantine at another, Hellenistic, Persian, Assyrian and so on, back to the earliest dawn of history – flattened and stacked, one below the other, like the different layers of a vast multi-decker sandwich, and embedded within each one sometimes finds small objects, bones, flints, the handle of a jug, the base of a figurine, the head of an arrow, which declare their age. Every spadeful of soil is therefore examined and sifted and hardly a stone is left unturned; one looks down into the digs to find men on all fours beavering away with little straw brushes like overzealous housewives cleaning their kitchen floor. If anything important, or which looks as if it might be important, is discovered, all work stops as the experts rush in to give their opinion and the inexpert crowd in to look. It is these cries of discovery – what one might call the Eureka syndrome – which give archaeology its peculiar drama, and which elevate what is for the most part drudgery, into a vocation, but which all adds to the impression of somewhat erratic effort.

Matthiae adopted the method perfected by Dame Kathleen Kenyon in her Jericho expedition,[4] which is to say, he divided his site into sectors and sub-sectors, each about four metres square, with a small team burrowing away in each. The sub-sectors (or squares as they are usually called) are intersected by balks a metre thick – strips that are left unexcavated, and at which the arrangement of the strata can be inspected intact. The work is painstaking and laborious and as the soil is removed, a description of it is recorded by the supervisor, as, for example, 'Level 1, white, dusty limestone'. All finds, pottery, flints, metal, carvings, bones are placed in containers marked according to their locations (say 'Layer 1, sector 2, sub-sector C'). As soon as one layer is cleared and another comes into view a new entry is made in the record and any finds are put in different containers. The fewer the finds the quicker the progress and the success of an expedition is often in inverse ratio to the area uncovered.

Sometimes orderly progress is thwarted by the discovery of soil or objects which bear no relation to the surrounding layer, suggesting that a hole must have been dug at some time, either as a rubbish pit or for a burial. It is here that the balks are of particular importance, for they are a visual record of the levels already excavated, and comparison of these will alert one to anything which has been deposited at a level which does not correspond to its true age. Apart from the written record of each layer and square, draughtsmen make scale drawings and then come photographers so that as ground is cut away from under one's feet, one has detailed records of every stage of the dig.

Work at Tell Mardikh begins at an hour of the day when one can still be numbed by the cold. The labourers are kept warm by their exertions. The supervisors stand hunched with their collars raised about their ears against the chilly mist. Then, as the day brightens, they straighten up. The odd, muffled exchanges of the early hours become animated and snatches of Italian and Arabic ring through the dry air. The top soil, kept firm by the dew of early morning, becomes as dry as talcum. Every movement stirs a small cloud and as the morning proceeds, everyone is covered in a fine white dust. By noon the temperature can reach a hundred in the shade, but of shade there is almost none – save for those labouring in the depths of the dig – and blobs of sweat cut channels through the dust on every face. Voices become quieter, exchanges less frequent, movement less assured.

At 1 pm work stops for the day. Shovels are stacked and the labourers set off on foot down the road to the village. Matthiae and his colleagues return to their encampment in a small fleet of cars and vans. Everything which looks as if it might be significant is brought back in rubber panniers and straw-baskets for closer scrutiny and the tell is left silent to its solitary guard, who lives with his wife and child in a small stone cabin nearby and who patrols the perimeter with a shot-gun.

The outer sands of the tell are thick with potsherds which outside the Near East might be pounced on as treasure but which Matthiae discards as insignificant. They are mostly Byzantine or Roman or Greek, but in any case under two thousand years old and moreover, there is sufficient of them to pave the road to Damascus. Among the first principles which an archaeologist has to establish is his system of priorities. He has limited time, limited funds and limited personnel. He cannot scrutinize everything and there is, therefore, a brisk and sometimes arbitrary process of selection on site.

The secondary and tertiary processes take place in camp. Everything brought back from the tell is washed and scrubbed by a small army of Arab women working in the outer courtyard and is then laid out in the sun to dry. Sherds with unusual markings or signs of great antiquity are retained for further examination, as are comparatively recent pieces sufficiently related to each other to be pieced together. In the afternoons, after they have showered and changed and lunched and rested, Matthiae and his assistants concentrate on what might be described and which, indeed, often looks like an intricate jigsaw puzzle. In one cell a technician is pasting related sherds into a whole. In another a draughtsman is drawing some completed vessels. In a third a photographer is photographing them. In a fourth an anthropologist is bent over some bones. In a fifth an epigrapher is scrutinizing some inscriptions, each trying to place the object before him in some slot in time and thereby attempting to read the story of Tell Mardikh. And, as in a jigsaw, each piece placed makes it easier to place subsequent pieces, so that if the process of identification is at first slow, it accelerates as the work proceeds and as the workers become expert. Here too the Eureka syndrome comes into play, more so perhaps than on site, for on site people are working among the ores, while at camp they are handling the refined products and they do so with veneration, like pilgrims among religious relics.

The most exciting discoveries find their way to Matthiae's desk where he sits poring over them fondly, as a man might pore over a portrait of his children. He will try and interpret their significance or return them for a while to a colleague for a possible second opinion. Finally all the finds, the exciting ones as well as the unexciting, are crated in long, coffin-like wooden boxes and sent to Aleppo, where they are buried in the vaults of the local museum.

The most precious discoveries – numerous though they may be – are of course the cuneiform tablets and they are treated with special care. Epigraphers can, if they wish, obtain a sight of them at camp, but otherwise they work from photographs (which are often easier to follow than the originals). Nevertheless, there are reports that some Ebla tablets have already come onto the market and Professor Pettinato was startled to discover what looked very much like one of his tablets in an American museum. Tell Mardikh is not particularly well-guarded and anyone familiar with the layout of the site can do his own digging and come away with the occasional fragment. Museum curators are not always the most scrupulous of men and neither are antique dealers. Nor are they always the most discerning of individuals and it is not too difficult for a man with one tablet to obtain a mould and make others and we may in future years come upon far more Ebla tablets than were ever raised in Ebla.

In the past, archaeological finds tended to be divided between the host country and the museums and learned societies which sponsored the expedition, though the host country always got the first pick. It was the prospect of spoils which enabled expeditions to finance their work in the first place. There is no such division of spoils in Tell Mardikh and no one suggested there should be and a special pavilion is being added to the Aleppo museum which will eventually enable them to go on display. The Syrian Department of Antiquities is nominally in control of the excavations and there is usually an official from the Department at the camp. Relations between Professor Matthiae and the Syrian authorities are excellent.

The whole company foregathers for dinner about six. The food is abundant and well-cooked and is served briskly and efficiently by young Arab boys. Abu, the Druze cook and major-domo, a large and robust man with black curly hair and gold teeth, moves round the dining room like a Yiddishe momma.

'Food is no good?' he asks a visitor who has refused a second helping.

'Is good.'

'Then eat more.'

The cuisine is oriental and spicy and bottles of chianti and arak pass to and fro among the company. Conversation is animated and almost everyone talks at once, except Matthiae, at the head of the table, who hardly talks at all and sits amidst his fellows like a spectre at a feast. He shows animation only on site, as if anything above ground is of only passing relevance.

After the meal the company retires to the reed hut for coffee and cigarettes and Abu joins them, puffing at an ornate narghillah and smiling with affable bemusement. He is obviously fond of the young, rapidly-talking Italians, but is not quite sure what to make of them, and why they, or anyone else for that matter, should want to come a thousand miles to dig up pieces of broken pottery which are as common to his part of the world as discarded beer-cans in Europe.

There is no electricity in Tell Mardikh and all illumination is provided by paraffin, hurricane lamps and pressure lamps which buzz quietly in the soft night. By eleven the reed hut is empty and there is a tinkle of running water in the concrete guttering as people prepare for bed. In the dining room the table is laid for breakfast. On the ramparts, a sentry is half asleep, propped up on his rifle. A couple who have discovered something more precious than Bronze Age pottery embrace in a quiet corner. One light after another flickers out and three sides of the quadrangle are in darkness. In a corner of the fourth a light shines brightly. Matthiae is in his study, bent over the day's discoveries, matching them one against another, putting this piece under a magnifying glass, dabbing at that piece with chemicals, or detaching a sliver and placing it under a microscope, in a restless attempt to extort their secrets. He has ways of making them talk.

CHAPTER 6

Eureka!

Tell Mardikh looked smooth and rounded from a distance. As one drew near one became aware of irregular forms under the sand, of humps and bumps, cavities and declivities, like a gigantic film-set kept under wraps. The outlines of what was presumably a city wall were clearly visible and on the crown of the hill was the sharp projection of what could have been a citadel. One of the mysteries of Tell Mardikh is how so large and accessible a site with so many intriguing features could have remained unexamined for so long.

An American expedition from Princeton University visited the area in 1904–5,[1] but it was more like a lightning tour than an excavation campaign and they had no inkling of the treasures they had missed. A French expedition headed by G. Tchalenko approached the area in the early fifties but paused only on its periphery,[2] and in archaeological terms therefore the Italians were touching upon what was almost virgin territory. One says almost, for as Professor Matthiae points out the tell had been ravaged by what he delicately called *explorateurs clandestins*,[3] but who may be simply described as grave robbers. They must have found their efforts singularly unrewarding, for one of the mysteries of Tell Mardikh which has yet to be explained is what its ancient inhabitants did with their dead, because, although the expedition has now been on site for fourteen years, very few graves have so far been unearthed.

Before the expedition settled down, the Italians examined a dozen other tells in the area which seemed pregnant with prospects, all within a twelve miles radius of Tell Mardikh.[4] They had no time to do more than to scratch around the surface, but they found ceramics which showed evidence of extensive settlements in Roman and Byzantine times and they were particularly intrigued by Tell Touqan and Tell Afis. The former is a large tell with the outlines of a high wall encircling the perimeter and an inner wall round the raised area of the tell, which may have formed a citadel. Gaps in the outline of the outer wall suggested the main gates. They found a flat clay statuette of a woman, in a style characteristic of the beginning of the second millennium, and the remnants of miniature chariots in clay. Tell Afis is believed to be the site of Hadrach mentioned in Zechariah 9:1ff., along with Damascus and Hamath (modern Hama). From the distance it looked like a gigantic woman's breast, but as one comes nearer one can see that, like Tell Touqan, it has a lower tier and an upper one. The Italians found numerous fragments, indicating that the area had been settled in the early part of the second millennium, but the great days of Tell Afis were a thousand years later; a stele found there in 1903 celebrates the victory of Zakir, 'King of Hamath and Lu'ath', over a coalition led by 'Barhadad son of Hazael, King of Aram', the Ben-hadad of 2 Kings 13:3, about 800 BC. At one site after another, gaps in the pottery record or even layers of ashes suggested that a raging fury had stormed into the area and had laid waste a large part of Syria. The identity of the fury and the time of its coming was to become a major preoccupation of the Italian expedition.

The reconnaisance of the surrounding tells took up much of their first season and left them with little time to get far with Tell Mardikh. They were, however, able to complete a survey, and found that like the other tells it too was composed of two main tiers – the lower city, just thirteen feet higher than the surrounding countryside, and the acropolis, rising to about fifty feet. A raised band almost equally high encircled the tell, covering the ancient city-wall. The tell was over half a mile long but rather less in breadth, tapering sharply at its extremities. In the surrounding enclosure they noted four depressions which, they believed, probably hid the city gates. One of their early discoveries was a well dug to a great depth which still contained water. They also found potsherds in abundance, often of a refined quality of a light yellow colour, which could be dated to the second half of the third millennium with the decorations typical of the period, painted horizontally in red, brown or black and cut in spirals on a lathe. Others were entirely hand-made and covered in a greenish glaze.[6] Pottery typical of the early second millennium was also found both in the lower town and the acropolis.

The first soundings were made at a point on the southern perimeter. A trench initially four yards wide was cut into the ridge that enclosed the tell, and thence further trenches were opened both towards the east and the west. They found large stones and unbaked bricks belonging to an ancient wall, as well as a bronze arrow-head and the remnants of large clay jars decorated with incised horizontal bands cut through by a wavy line.[7]

A second trench was cut near the western slopes of the acropolis where they discovered a heap of large stones covering the circular mouth of a well, which adjoined an underground area about ten feet in diameter, surmounted by a dome-shaped roof cut out of solid rock. Inside they found fragments of a basalt statuette of a man seated – or enthroned – and the remains of a sculptured basalt basin, similar to that found in 1955. Different fragments depicted the heads of a roaring lion and a bull-man, and a bearded figure offering sacrifice. Matthiae attached particular importance to those fragments as 'a precious documentation' of indigenous Syrian art at about 2000 BC.[8] The statuette (the head of which was missing), with typically Syrian clothing carved in relief, seemed about a century later, and it too testified to a distinctive local tradition. But time and sand had worn away any indication of who or what the figure represented.

Also unearthed, at various spots, were some seventy terracotta figurines, almost all fragmentary, ranging in date from about the third century BC right back to the twenty-third. There were male and female figures, and animals – including a bull, a dog and an ape – and also chariot wheels. Their crude workmanship gave the impression that they could have been made by children playing with clay, but their purpose was probably religious – perhaps as offerings to the gods, or to avert evil forces.[9]

Life in Tell Mardikh, Matthiae deduced, must have reached an abrupt halt about 1600 BC, as no pottery attributable to any later date was found – until one reached the Persian (*c.*

535–325 BC) and Hellenistic periods (c. 325–60 BC), during which the acropolis alone showed signs of having been reoccupied.

At the end of the first season Professor Matthiae felt able to conclude:

> On first examination Tell Mardikh appears extremely interesting in testifying eloquently to the flourishing culture of inland Syria between the end of the third and the beginning of the second millennium BC. The culture represented here ... is characterized as far as it is possible to judge in the present state of research, by the density of its urban centres, the quality of its art, the impact of Mesopotamian influences and by the great size of its urban defence system.[10]

He felt fairly hopeful that the sand of Tell Mardikh hid no mean city, but some years were to elapse before his hopes were fully confirmed and in the early years the discoveries tended to be fairly commonplace. Most of the broken pieces of earthenware with which the tell was littered, though regarded with excitement at first, proved to be of Greek or Roman origin which, in the context of the distant millennia towards which Matthiae was reaching, was of little interest.

The excavations on the southern perimeter eventually revealed the main gateway of the city. Its outer entrance, flanked by two pairs of buttresses with orthostats, was about forty feet deep and led to an open courtyard some fifty feet long which in turn was succeeded, on a zig-zag pattern, by two other entrances protected by three pairs of buttresses.[11] The raised band that surrounded the tell proved to be about two miles long and to consist of red earth and limestone fragments pressed together in alternating layers of varying thickness. The wall that it covered reached a height of fifty feet and spread to a thickness of about one hundred and thirty feet at its base.[12] Fortifications so elaborate suggested a large population and great wealth and an unhappy history of harassment.

Their second season yielded many more such finds. One day a workman digging in a trench cut into the south-western slope of the tell, clanked his spade against an unusually firm object. He got down on all fours to scrape the soil away and came upon what at first sight looked like the remains of an ornate pavement. Others quickly rushed to his side, and gradually uncovered first the throne, and then the back of a seated figure. They dug all around it to reveal arms, legs, shoulders, but all that remained of the head was an ornate beard whose ringlets came down to the chest. It was probably a divinity, though if mortal, obviously a person of high rank. There was a cup – or possibly some symbol of office – in one hand and he wore an ornate robe with irregular geometric patterns of a type not infrequently found on Mesopotamian statues.[14]

They photographed the figure as it was found on site, and raised it carefully with a feeling of awe and reverence. The comparatively good state of the ornamentation at the back had roused the hope that there might be some inscriptions on the front. They scrutinized it microscopically, but were disappointed. The statue was silent. They made a careful search for the head but found no sign of it, which suggested that its headless state was the result of wilful disfigurement. Was it a discarded deity? Professor Matthiae considered every possibility and speculated whether it was a live king at a banquet, a deity receiving libation or perhaps a dead king presiding over a funerary rite, and on balance he inclined to the first view.[15] The statue had been found little more than two feet below the surface of the trench, but careful examination of the style of the beard and robe and of the throne suggested a date between 2050 and 1850 BC. It had, a trifle irreverently, been brought into use as a building material.[16]

They also found yet another double limestone trough, not unlike the original one which had brought Matthiae to Tell Mardikh, with three of its four sides carved in relief depicting various mythical scenes – a royal banquet, a procession of sheep, goats and antelopes, a bearded nude warrior (with unusually prominent genitals), grasping by the tail a dragon gushing forth water. It was found in a temple on the acropolis and was believed by Matthiae to date from the twentieth or nineteenth centuries BC, though the images were in many ways similar to those found on Mesopotamian monuments going back to the late third millennium.

One small discovery which had at first caused great excitement was the fragment of a jug imprinted, evidently by means

of a seal, with a cuneiform inscription. Experts pored over it
for days but were able to identify only two cuneiform signs
which, in the absence of any context, were not enough to indicate even in what language (Akkadian or Sumerian) they were
written.[17] Beyond that they found a bone needle, necklace
beads and a cosmetic container in stone, and *bullae* used to
cover cylinders and jars and, presumably, to indicate their contents or ownership.

In their third season they uncovered a substantial part of
the acropolis temple which Matthiae believed was the principal place of worship of the town in the first half of the second
millennium. It had a tripartite plan on a longitudinal axis and
numerous courtyards whose proportions and design bore a
striking resemblance to the temple of Solomon, though it
was of course built much earlier. Matthiae dated it to the
early second millennium BC and saw in its architecture an indigenous style independent of Mesopotamian influences,[18]
though Professor Sabatino Moscati of the University of
Rome, who had helped Professor Matthiae set up the expedition, felt that the discoveries in general continued to reflect
Mesopotamian themes and showed 'the spread of Sumero-
Akkadian civilization into the heart of Syria'.[19]

While working on the temple they began uncovering a
neighbouring edifice which, from its situation on the crown
of the hill, seemed to be a citadel but which, on closer examination, proved to be the remains of a magnificent royal palace.
Here, too, Matthiae noticed an indigenous Syrian style. It was
an imposing structure employing large limestone monoliths
of the type used in the south-west gate, with ascending terraces
and spacious courtyards and ante-rooms. One courtyard was
of beaten earth, the antechambers were paved with a fine
strong, stone conglomerate, while their walls were covered
with light-grey plaster. In later seasons they were to uncover
a second courtyard, the various sectors being linked by well-
preserved narrow winding passages. They also uncovered a
few private houses consisting of a small entrance area leading
to a hallway giving access to two or more rooms.

Primitive mud dwellings abutted on the palace which looked
as if they could have served as servants' quarters, but they
belonged to a much later period and Matthiae concluded that

they were a squatters' encampment built after the palace was destroyed, and that at some time during the second millennium a semi-nomadic type of life had replaced the urban social structure of Tell Mardikh.[20] They also found a small temple, almost a family chapel, away from the acropolis in the lower part of the town, consisting of a single room built on bed rock. The walls were of rubble and faced with orthostats. This must have been the original site of the basin found in 1955, since a missing piece was found on the stairway leading in.[21]

The number and variety of the finds was considerable but by 1968 they still had nothing outstanding to report. They were approaching their fifth season and felt as if they had only scratched the surface of the tell. Moreover, they were encountering physical difficulties. One can guard a site against robbers, but one cannot put it under tarpaulins between seasons, and when the winter rains descend – as they do in great torrents in this part of Syria – and the winds blow in from the desert, silting up trenches and filling up shafts, much of the work of the preceding seasons can be obliterated. Archaeology on such an exposed site is frequently a matter of taking two steps forward and one step back – and sometimes even two steps back. Their discoveries to date were considerable but they had found little to distinguish Tell Mardikh from many other Near Eastern sites, and they may have felt that they were doing little more than shifting sands from one part of the wilderness to another. More ceramics were uncovered, more sculptured fragments, more figurines – and then, another headless statue. They had found quite a number by now so that at first it caused no particular excitement. Then, as they scraped away the packed soil and lime incrustations round the top, they found an inscription, not like those on the earlier documents too fragmentary to be read, but twenty-six lines of cuneiform writing, the last nine of them incomplete.

The figure was of basalt and a comparative study of its artistic features (such as the beard and the cloak) suggested to Matthiae a date in about the twentieth century BC.[22] Pettinato, who was then in Heidelberg, was brought over to read the inscription, which was in Akkadian and which read:

For the goddess Eshtar, a basin did Ibbiṭ-Lim, son of Igrish-Hepa, king of the people of Ebla, bring [into the temple]. He whose name Eshtar caused to shine in Ebla, even Ibbiṭ-Lim, [had sculpted] a statue for his life and for the life of his children ...[23]

Eshtar, whose name eventually appeared in Greek guise as Astarte, was the Venus of the Orient and was revered through-out the Near East over many centuries as the goddess of love and procreation and, a little improbably, war. The name Ibbit-Lim was a blank to everyone. He appears in no known records and had never been heard of before, but the most exciting part of the inscription was the two references to Ebla. Did they mean that Tell Mardikh and Ebla were one and the same?

Professor Mario Liverani, a member of the expedition, had suggested after the very first season that the archaeological remains found at Tell Mardikh showed that it had flourished towards the end of the third millennium and the beginning of the second, and had then been more or less abandoned, which tallied with what one knew of Ebla. But it also tallied with what one knew of several other lost cities, and such evidence, as Liverani himself pointed out, was therefore inconclusive.[24] The Ibbit-Lim statue, however, was another matter and Pettinato, having combed through all available evidence on Ebla, thought its identification with Tell Mardikh 'very probable'. Matthiae was more tentative: 'It seems possible that Tell Mardikh should be identified with Ebla.'[25] Professor Michael Astour, an American authority on ancient place names, however, felt otherwise.

A dedicatory inscription on a votive statue identifies the votary and the place of his (or her) origin; it does not necessarily identify the place where the statue was erected. In absence of supporting in-scriptional evidence the find at Tell Mardikh of a statue dedicated to a deity by a prince of Ebla demonstrates just two things; that the city which stood on the site of Tell Mardikh was important and had a renowned temple; and that the relations between this city and Ebla were friendly at the time when the statue was dedicated.[26]

He went on to argue that the true Ebla was probably buried some ninety miles to the north-east of Tell Mardikh, over the Turkish border. Here was an academic debate which could have continued for generations, but it was settled in dramatic form some six years later.

It is, in a sense, the job of the archaeologist to push back the frontiers of history and, as a result of his efforts, what is prehistoric to one generation becomes part of recorded knowledge to another, but he has tended to be rather individualistic in his dating methods. One knows in general terms what the Stone Age, the Chalcolithic Age and the Bronze Age represented, except that different places had their different ages at different times – some, for example, are not quite out of their Stone Age even now. Moreover, each period has sub-periods such as early, middle and late which are further sub-divided into early early and middle early and early middle and so on without any clear demarcation of where one ended and another began, so that one man's Intermediate Early Bronze–Middle Bronze could be another man's Middle Bronze I. As a result it has become the common practice of every major expedition to introduce its own dating system applicable to the conditions of that particular site, and Matthiae did the same at Tell Mardikh.

He had carried out soundings a short distance south-west of the acropolis which he pushed almost as far as bed-rock and had come up with pottery dating back to the second half of the fourth millennium BC. This period he called Mardikh I. He had also discovered evidence of a great conflagration with thick layers of ash both in what he called the acropolis and the lower city, which he was able to date back to about the year 2000 BC and he therefore called the preceding millennium, Mardikh II. There was evidence of further conflagration at about 1600 BC and he called the intervening centuries Mardikh III. The destruction which ended this phase may have been due to the depredations of the nearby kingdom of Yamhad, with its capital in Aleppo, though it was most probably the work of the Hittites. Later fragments indicate that the city was rebuilt, but settlement became sporadic. Its walls, essential to the sustenance of the population, were neglected and became unusable, which limited growth and the city fell through declining stages of significance, with evidence of Persian, Greek, Roman and Byzantine occupation, until it was finally swallowed by the surrounding wilderness. Matthiae traced the various periods and defined the years 1600–1200 as Mardikh iv; 1200–535 as Mardikh v and 535–60 BC as Mardikh vi. Thereafter, to all intents and purposes, Ebla was no more and remained hidden from human reckoning till he raised it from its sleep.

Matthiae's dating method owed a lot to the system of controls devised by the Chicago Oriental Institute during its expedition to the Amuq plain, near the Mediterranean city of Antioch from 1932 to 1938 (in which year it passed from Syrian to Turkish rule). The expedition had unearthed artefacts ranging from 2000 right back to 5500 BC and had identified ten different phases corresponding to the different character of the finds, and labelled them from A (the earliest) right down to J. The Americans in turn were able to relate their discoveries to the artefacts uncovered at other sites – notably in Egypt and Mesopotamia – to pin down the approximate chronology of each phase. Matthiae now compared his own discoveries to those of the Amuq and by the incidence of some type of pottery rather than others was able to work out their various dates. For the first ten years of his expedition the most significant phase, as far as Matthiae and his colleagues were concerned, was Mardikh iii. Most of their major finds, especially those within the palace and temple precincts, fell within that period.

In archaeological terms Syria had for long been the Cinderella of the Near East. Egypt had been opened up to the scholar by the arrival of Napoleon and his savants in 1798. Bricks stamped with cuneiform, some of which reached Europe as early as the seventeenth century, attracted attention to Iraq which in 1842 witnessed the arrival of the first of many archaeological expeditions, and of course the interest in the Bible brought an endless succession of archaeologists to Palestine. Syria, on the other hand, had received comparatively little attention, and most of the sites chosen, such as those at Mari, Brak and Chagar Bazar, though within the present borders of Syria, were all part of ancient Mesopotamia. Others, such as Byblos and Ugarit, lay on the coast and could not be taken as representative of inland Syria. In 1963 the Orientalist, W.J. Van Liere, observed that there still remained within Syria 'many cultural centres, capitals and citadels and kingdoms ...

untouched by the spade'. He, however, thought that any such discoveries would necessarily be 'of lesser importance'.[27] After five years' work, Matthiae was in a position to contradict him. The royal palace with its courtyards and corridors, its inner chambers and outer chambers, its basalt orthostats; the principal temple, an elaborate structure a hundred feet long with an ornate vestibule, a nave and an inner shrine, and numerous religious requisites, including a circular basalt table (its legs carved in relief with figures of naked goddesses), which might have served as an altar; the small temple in the lower city; the mighty ramparts, the massive gates, all indicated that in Ebla they had come upon a major centre of civilization. They were also bringing up a gratifying number of sculptured fragments many of which confirmed Matthiae in his belief that it represented not merely another essentially Mesopotamian settlement, like Mari, but a distinct Syrian entity.

Inscriptions, however, continued to be disappointingly rare. Apart from the Ibbit-Lim statue they discovered the inscribed heads of two lances belonging to the seventeenth century BC, giving their owner's name and occupation (mercenary and scribe, respectively),[28] and a handful of clay cuneiform fragments, apparently contemporary with the Ibbit-Lim statue.[29] Their condition made them virtually undecipherable, but their very presence raised hopes of more to come which might be less fragmentary and more readable, unless, of course, the fragments had been brought in from another town, and they redoubled their efforts.

They were tunnelling away through the ages, each group in their own small sector and in 1973 soundings on the south-west slopes of the acropolis revealed impressive structures in mud-brick, which looked rather like fortifications. Further digging in 1974, however, showed that here was another royal palace – belonging to the earlier period Mardikh II, i.e. the third millennium. It soon yielded rich finds – a sceptre of wood and gold, and masterly wood-carvings of a girl, and of a king wielding an axe. Matthiae himself became almost obsessed with the place, moving from this corner to that, turning over stones, probing into trenches, almost like a cat in search of its quarry, knowing it is there somewhere, but not certain exactly where or how to get at it. Then, one hot summer's day,

when the mound was white with the noon-day heat and everyone shrank away to the darkest corners of the dig, a workman
began tugging at what seemed to be another terra-cotta
fragment, and came away with an entire clay tablet, four inches across. It did not take a minute to rub away the soil to
reveal a face covered with cuneiform characters set out in their
characteristic rows. Others were found in the same room –
forty-two in all. Some were completely blackened, indicating
that the palace had at some time been destroyed by a fire which
had in fact served to harden the tablets and had left them in
excellent condition. Matthiae promptly cabled Pettinato –
who had moved from Heidelberg to Rome in the previous year
– with news of his discovery.

Pettinato arrived excitedly amidst the sands and stood scrutinizing the tablets with a look of bafflement on his face. What
was this he saw before him? The two languages expected in
cuneiform were Sumerian and Akkadian. He found Sumerian
in plenty, but flanked often by expressions in a language which
was neither Sumerian, nor Akkadian, nor, indeed, any tongue
he had ever encountered, and although the Sumerian told him
something, the presence of the other language made it impossible for him to understand any tablet in full.

He found the key he was looking for in the formulae with
which the tablets closed. Many ended with two signs which
could be read in Sumerian as DUB ('tablet') and GAR ('lay
down, set') and made reasonable sense: 'tablet drawn up' or
the like. Two other tablets, however, ended with two quite different signs. If they too were Sumerian, one could be read either
as G Á L (which is capable of a wide range of meaning: 'throw;
open; place; dwell; be') or IG ('door'), while the other could
be read as either DÚB ('dash in pieces') or BALAG ('a type
of musical instrument'). As there seemed no good reason for
these tablets to end with a reference to dashing a door in pieces
or throwing a musical instrument or any of the other combinations, Pettinato concluded that they could not be Sumerian.
But what of Akkadian? In Akkadian the former could be
pronounced *ik*, *eg* or *ek* as well as *ig*, and the latter *tub* as
well as *dub*. Here again none of the possible combinations
made sense. One of them, however, namely *ik-tub*, raised some
hope. In pattern it resembled many Akkadian verbs in the past

ense, like *igmur* '(he) completed', *irpud* '(he) ran'. Most verbs
in Akkadian, as in other Semitic languages, consist of a root
of three consonants which have to be filled out with vowels
(and often with additional consonants) to yield the various
forms actually used; for example the Arabic root KSR 'break'
gives *kasara* 'he broke', *yaksiru*, 'he will break', *maksūr*
'broken' and so on. Now *iktub* would be a perfectly good
past tense verb in Akkadian if only that language had a root
KTB. Unfortunately it does not, but other languages, originally spoken in areas west of Mesopotamia (e.g. Hebrew and
Arabic) do have a root KTB, meaning 'write'. Perhaps, then,
Pettinato reasoned, he had come upon a language with grammatical forms not unlike Akkadian but with a vocabulary
which differed somewhat from that of Akkadian and included
some items known from more westerly languages; *iktub* would
then mean '(he) wrote', coming close enough to the Sumerian
formula. This was a daring suggestion because there was no
evidence that speakers of any West Semitic language (i.e. a
Semitic language other than Akkadian) were present in northern Syria before about 2000 BC, and it was widely believed that
the inhabitants of Syria at this remote period were not Semites
at all but 'of unknown ethnic affiliation'.[30] It was also
disturbing that neither of these 1974 tablets seemed to indicate
who it was who supposedly 'wrote', but Pettinato thought this
might be economy of words, as when we write 'paid' on a bill
without mentioning the subject.[31] This was however confirmed in the following year with the discovery of texts in
which *iktub* did have a subject (e.g. *en-ma ti-ra-il* dub-sar *i k-
tub* 'Thus Tira-Il the scribe wrote').[32]

With this Pettinato was almost able to say 'Eureka!' He at
first named the newly identified language 'Palaeo-Canaanite'
because he was struck by the vocabulary which it shared with
later attested languages of Canaan (i.e. Syria–Palestine), such
as Hebrew and Ugaritic, but later called it 'Eblaite', a term
which indicated simply that this was the language of ancient
Ebla – the identification of which with Tell Mardikh won universal acceptance after the discoveries of 1975, as we shall soon
see – and which begged no questions. The Eblaite language
was not, however, used as a rule to write the entire text of
any document. A substantial proportion – which naturally

varies from one document to another and, according to
Pettinato, is on average eighty per cent – was written in
Sumerian logograms, on the same principles as in Akkadian
If read orally, however, the text would have been pronounced
wholly in Eblaite, with each written Sumerian element re
placed by an Eblaite equivalent.[33]

When the forty-two tablets in the royal palace were raised
dusted and read, Matthiae was convinced that they could no
be the end of the story, but he was by then near the end o
his season. When he and his colleagues returned in 1975 the
could hardly contain their excitement at the prospects which
they were confident lay before them and within a matter o
days they uncovered in a room seventeen feet long by twelve
feet wide, an entire library of tablets, heaped one on top of the
other, mostly lined up as before without keeling over. The
had been stacked on wooden shelves, propped up against
wooden supports. The holes in the floor which had held the
supports were still clearly visible, though all the timber had
vanished in the fire which destroyed the palace. The tablet
had come crashing down. Many were shattered by the impac
and had crumbled to dust. Others were cracked but still
legible. Many were blackened like overdone toast. The
majority were intact. Matthiae gazed upon his find with some
thing like disbelief. He had been hoping for something like
this, but had not expected his hopes to be fulfilled with such
dramatic suddenness. The discovery he said, was 'like a kind
of earthquake which has put very many things in doubt'.[3]
His wife, Dr Gabriella Matthiae Scandone, was similarly over
whelmed. 'We had never conceived of finding so large and
beautifully preserved a library,' she declared. 'I couldn't *believe*
we had discovered such an immense, beautiful, important
treasure. Even my husband, who rarely loses his *sang-froid*,
found it an emotional experience. He suddenly felt like an
archaeologist of the last century must have, like Botta dis
covering the archives of Ashurbanipal or Hilprecht the tablet:
of Nippur.'[35]

After being photographed on site the tablets were brought
back to the base camp. They filled the registry, the photographer's room, the two rooms reserved for the draughtsmen
the three reserved for the archaeologists. They filled the studies

and store-rooms. They overflowed into the bedrooms. Dr Scandone, who assisted as the expedition registrar, brought in three students to help her. They divided into two teams and work went on round the clock. About 14,500 tablets had been found in the main palace archive by the summer of 1977.[36] By then small caches were appearing all over the place. Six hundred tablets were found in one ante-chamber, eight hundred in another, about a thousand in a third. In an open court adjoining the palace, which was possibly an audience chamber (it contains a podium of rough bricks covered in white plaster which may have supported the throne), some thirty tablets were strewn on the floor, as if someone had dropped them in a hurry. There were times when workmen in the palace couldn't sink a spade into the ground without hearing it clink against a tablet.

Pettinato, who had been contemplating the small cache found in 1974 at leisure, now found himself facing an avalanche. Most of the tablets are at least two inches across. Not a few, however, are more than a foot square with thirty columns on each face with some three thousand lines, while even the smaller tablets – which likewise are inscribed on both sides – can hold over a thousand. Pettinato was helped by the fact that many of the tablets have a brief indication of contents on their edge, like the title on the spine of a book, but even so the task was a daunting one. Nevertheless by 30 October 1975 he had some ten thousand tablets catalogued and classified under their various economic, administrative, historical, literary and lexical headings.[37] And it was necessarily a one-man operation, for although there are a number of scholars with a knowledge of Sumerian (a language which still has large unexplored areas), Pettinato alone had the key to 'Eblaite'.

Some of the meanings which Professor Pettinato was to read into the tablets were later to become the subject of heated debate, but one controversy which had been simmering ever since the discovery of the statue of Ibbit-Lim was finally put to rest. Ebla was undoubtedly Tell Mardikh: the inscriptions on some three hundred tablets emanating from the 'King of Ebla' confirm it. As for Ibbit-Lim, he had reigned some centuries after the great fire which had destroyed the palace and with it, it would seem, the Eblaite language, for the inscription on his statue was entirely in Akkadian. Matthiae and Pettinato had come upon the true zenith in the history of Ebla. Period III, which is to say the first half of the second millennium in which they had vested most of their hopes and which had generated most of the excitement hitherto, was but a denouement. The real story of Ebla, or of what one might now call Greater Ebla, lay in Period II, and more particularly in the second half of the third millennium. Matthiae had searched for a city and had found what he was to describe as an 'empire'.[38]

CHAPTER 7

The Merchant State

The business of Ebla was business and of the tablets examined to date, the large majority – about thirteen thousand – are hardly more than ledgers, day-books and inventories. They, in the main, make very dull reading, but they do yield a few surprises one of which is the very size of Ebla. It appears that it was a most prosperous trading area of 260,000 people which, in the third millennium BC must have made it one of the largest conurbations in the Near East, or anywhere else.[1]

The late Sir Leonard Woolley calculated that, when the present century began, the old cities of Aleppo and Damascus had a population of about 160 to the acre,[2] and argued that the population densities in the cities of ancient Mesopotamia – and, we may suppose, Syria – must have been about the same, and thus Ebla proper, with an area of 140 acres, would have had a population of around 22,400, and the total suggested by the tablets must have included outlying settlements and suburbs, and perhaps even distant colonies.

More surprising than the size of Ebla was the size of the bureaucracy administering the community which, according to one tablet, was 11,700,[3] or four and a half per cent of the total population (which may also explain the size of the archive: where others communicated by word of mouth, bureaucrats even then, preferred to have it in writing). Another tablet refers to the eight different parts of the city in which people worked, and lists some of the principal officers and their dependants. Four of the sectors are referred to simply as the first to fourth districts, while the rest are described as the 'Palace of the king', 'Palace of the city' (which could have served as some type of public forum), the 'Stables' (?) and a sector which, on one interpretation, was some sort of servants' quarter and, according to another, was rather ominously called the 'House of the bull'.[4] It is likely that the four latter sectors, which were crowded round the acropolis, were concerned with central government, and the rest with local government.

The fourfold division of the lower city seems reflected in the appearance of the site today. Matthiae had observed in his first season, that the great earthen rampart encircling the tell, was interrupted by four depressions, to the north-west, north-east, south-east and south-west, where four city gates must have lain.[5] Now the earthen rampart, and the two gates excavated so far (in the south-west[6] and south-east[7] corners) date from a later time (about 2000 BC) than the tablets (which belong to the middle of the third millennium) and if, as soundings at points quite distant from one another suggest,[8] the area occupied in these two periods was virtually the same, the rampart and gates of the later period may well have followed the line of the earlier one. Thus, we can perhaps locate today four gates which gave access to these four districts of the lower city.

In a number of tablets we encounter such phrases as 'Gate of Rasap', 'District of Rasap', 'Gate of Sipish', and 'District of Dagan'. It is deduced that three of the districts and corresponding gates were associated with three of Ebla's principal deities,[9] all of them already well-known – Ra-sa-ap, surely pronounced Rashap,[10] god of pestilence and war, later identified by the Greeks with Apollo; Sipish, deity of the sun, whether masculine (cf. Akkadian Shamash) or feminine (cf. Shapsh at Ugarit); and Dagan, perhaps originally a god of weather[11] and fertility,[12] known from the Bible to have been worshipped as Dagon by the Philistines. The fourth gate may have been called 'Gate of the City', an expression noticed by Pettinato in two tablets,[13] perhaps indicating an outstanding monumental structure;[14] the corresponding deity was apparently Baal.[15] While no quarter of the city appears to have had a god particular to itself or, what might be called, a patron god, it is possible that some gods had a more popular following in some areas than others, which would explain why each quarter (and each gate) was named after a different deity. What god went with which gate is not clear and Professor Matthiae, after much subtle speculation suggests, 'with all possible reserve', that the south-east gate was named after Rasap, the north-east after Sipish, and the south-west after Dagan.[16] What is certain is that the symmetrical layout of the city, planned well back in the first half of the third millennium as a great circle cut into four quadrants was, even by the standards of much later times, a remarkable feat of urban design.

The head of state was *Malik* or king, of whom five or six are named in the tablets, but his authority seems to have been circumscribed by the *Abbū* (Eblaite, meaning fathers) a council of elders enjoying numerous powers and responsibilities which extended even – as Pettinato put it – to 'the management of the royal family'.[17]

Professor Pettinato believes that the monarchy was not hereditary and sees proof of this in the fact that the king was anointed, though why he should regard this as proof is uncertain, for in ancient Israel (cf. 2 Kings 23:30), where the monarchy was hereditary, kings were likewise anointed.[18] It is said that one of the kings had thirty-eight sons,[19] which suggests that he may have had more than one wife. The first-born, as a rule, ran internal affairs[20] and appears to have functioned as co-regent when occasion required. The second son looked after foreign affairs, while one of the kings – as yet unnamed – appointed his sons as viceroys of the outlying towns.[21]

The Queen of Ebla appears to have enjoyed an exalted position in the state hierarchy,[22] which does not, in itself, however, tell one much about the position of women in general. It is known that in Mesopotamia women were more emancipated and were subject to fewer handicaps during the period covered by the Ebla archive than they were in later times (the change seems to have set in about 1600 BC). They could own land or other property in their own right, to sell or bequeath as they wished, could take legal action independently of, and even against, their husbands, could train as a doctor or scribe,[23] and it is possible – indeed probable – that Eblaite women were equally 'liberated', but to date nothing has been published from the archive to confirm this view.[24] The position of female slaves was no doubt different again, but nothing is yet known of slavery at Ebla, which presumably played a major role in the economy.

What is perhaps more unusual is the extent of what one might call Ebla's literary services.[25] It had a school for scribes which attracted foreign students and there are clay tablets showing the early struggles of pupils with the intricacies of cuneiform script. We have first of all tablets with the careful marks of the master, and others with the unsteady hand of the pupil. Not a few close with the sign X in the hand of the master, which meant much the same then as it does now.

The career of a scribe called Azi may be followed from a sequence of tablets bearing his name, the first of which he wrote under the supervision of a *dub-zu-zu*, or 'knower of tablets'. Later he appears as a *dub-zu-zu* in his own right and finally emerges as one of the highest officers of state.

Several hundred of the Ebla 'textbooks' survive,[26] including lists of cuneiform signs grouped now by similarity of appearance and now by sound. There are also syllabaries which list Sumerian words and give, in each case, first, the single (possibly compound) sign which indicates the word and, secondly, a phonetic breakdown into syllables. Thus, for example, the sign for *ashgab*, meaning 'currier', is followed by three signs reading *ásh*, *ga*, *bù*, while the sign for *nagar* meaning 'carpenter' is followed by signs reading *na*, *ga*, *lum*. These syllabaries which once told Ebla scribes how Sumerian was pronounced render precisely the same service to scholars today. It is true that many such syllabaries were already known, but there are many Sumerian words, the pronunciation of which was lost and which, thanks to the Ebla tablets, has now been recovered. What is far more important is that the syllabaries previously known all dated from the nineteenth century BC or later, long after Sumerian had ceased to be a spoken language,[27] while the Ebla texts are the first to reveal how Sumerian was pronounced as an actual, living language.

One achievement of Sumerian learning was to draw up lists which were then copied time and again – lists of gods, of professions, of objects of various classes. This tradition is well represented among the Fara and Abu Salabikh texts,[28] and long continued in the academies of Mesopotamia; it can perhaps be traced even as far back as *c.* 3000 BC, among the Uruk texts.[29] The lists played an important part in the education of scribes, and are therefore of obvious interest to the modern scholar, but their wider significance is debated. Some consider them just one more expression of the Mesopotamian tendency – said to show itself in other aspects of the culture, such as the design of temples – to accumulate and to elaborate;[30] others see them as systematic attempts to classify and to categorize, and thus as marking the beginnings of science – lists of plants or stones being first steps in the development of botany and mineralogy, and so on. Be that as it may, many such lists, in Sumerian, have been discovered at Ebla – lists of metals and precious stones, of wooden and metal objects, of plants and trees, lists of animals, two lists of birds, several lists of fish, lists of professions, personal names and geographical names.

It is not surprising that Pettinato had found, at the last available count,[31] that more than a hundred of these texts corresponded to lists already known from Fara and Abu Salabikh, two of which call for further comment. The first is a list of more than sixty professions, already attested in five copies all of which however were defective; two well-preserved copies have now been identified at Ebla, and have enabled Pettinato to reconstruct the first sixty-three entries in full.[32] The first few are devoted to the highest officers of the state, and the order in which they are listed (which surely reflects the order of precedence) will help us to understand the position and function of each. The other text, first discovered at Abu Salabikh, had been identified as a geographical list, but there was no knowing where the places were, apart from some feeble indications pointing to the south of Iraq;[33] another copy has been found at Ebla, and Pettinato believes that nearly all the places named fall within Syria–Palestine, and deduces that the list 'was drawn up in Syria – more precisely at Ebla'.[34]

Many of these lists, however, are unique to Ebla – though one may speculate how many were composed and handed down within the confines of Ebla alone, and how many circulated widely over Syria and Mesopotamia, but happen to have first turned up in a copy preserved at Ebla. In one list, the items are grouped into fifty sections according to their initial element – first those beginning with *nì*, then those beginning with *ka* – and so on;[35] and similar schemes of ordering are found among many other Sumerian word-lists at Ebla. These are by many centuries our earliest examples of that mode of arrangement, called 'acrophonic', and is for the cuneiform scribe the equivalent, or rather forerunner, of our alphabetical order.

Most exciting of all are the bilingual word-lists, in Sumerian and Eblaite. They are the earliest dictionaries known to history; the oldest bilingual lists discovered hitherto (Sumerian/ Akkadian) dated from the Old Babylonian period, i.e. later than the twentieth century BC. Pettinato has identified more than one hundred such texts at Ebla. The Sumerian words they contain are arranged acrophonically, and each is accompanied by an equivalent in Eblaite. Many of these lists have turned out to be duplicates of one another, and Pettinato now considers them all to be copies or extracts from three basic Sumerian-Eblaite 'dictionaries', which he hopes to reconstruct. He estimates that they contained altogether three thousand words, each given in both languages.[36] These three basic bilingual dictionaries were themselves no doubt based on lists in pure Sumerian, to which the Eblaite equivalents were added, rather than supplied from the first.[37] Many scribal exercises are based on these 'dictionaries'; Pettinato singles out one tiny tablet which bears just one word in Sumerian (*nam-mi*) and in Eblaite (*ù-nu-šum*), meaning, of all things, 'femininity'.

Other works produced by Ebla's academy were unilingual lists in Eblaite alone,[38] and paradigms showing how Eblaite verbs were conjugated.[39] All in all, the scholastic texts discovered at Ebla promise to advance enormously our knowledge both of Eblaite (and thence of other Semitic languages) and of Sumerian.

A new and unexpected light has also been thrown on cultural relations between the cities of the third millennium BC. Two of the lexical texts were written down, according to the colophons they bear, 'when the young [i.e. junior?] scribes came forth from Mari'.[40] Apparently an academic conference was held at Ebla, and attended by scholars from Mari and, presumably, other cities too. Elsewhere we hear that Ebla entertained scribes from Emar, while the author of what has been identified as a mathematical text came from Kish. Some of these lexical lists, so important to Sumerian studies, may have been hammered out at these very international conferences, though they also suggest that scholars tended to have a nomadic streak even then and many may have been drawn to Ebla by its prosperity.

There was much work for the scribe in the pernickety attention to detail or rather in the meticulous stock-control. Thus, for example, one tablet[41] lists the 174 officials and their 403 dependants entitled to half a *gubar* of corn (the *gubar*, a measure first encountered in Ebla, was equivalent to about half a bushel). Another lists the rations apportioned to some of the members of the palace staff:[42]

... 390 *gubar* of flour, rations for the staff, for the month of Kamish; 540 *gubar* of flour, rations, for the staff, 250 *gubar* of flour, food of the palace, for the journey to Zabu in the month of Beli ... 103 *gubar* of flour, an offering of the Queen unto Gura, in the month of Adamma ... 80 *gubar* of flour, rations for the weavers ... 50 *gubar* of flour for the house of Ihsup-Damu ...'

Agents sent abroad were usually allotted bread, beer, wine and oil, and the diet certainly to modern eyes was unexciting – except perhaps for the beer, which may have been known and enjoyed beyond the gates of Ebla. Among the cuneiform lists later current is a list of beers,[43] including one called *ebla*, pronounced just like the name of the city; could it have been the beer which made Ebla famous?

Ebla's craftsmen were skilled in the working of timbers, metals and precious stones and the city was the centre for an extensive trade in wheat, barley, grapes, cattle and other agricultural goods. But it was above all a textile centre and there are many tablets recording the delivery of clothing material and finished garments to members of the royal household and various court dignitaries and priests as well as their export to many parts of the Near East.[44] Professor Freedman lists the itinerary of one commercial traveller who set out from Ebla and journeyed as far as Sinai, stopping on the way to display his wares at Byblos, Sidon, Acre, Carmel, Dor, Ashdod and Gaza. One finds reference to many hundreds of places with which Ebla had trade connections including Cyprus, Hazor, Megiddo and Jaffa and numerous places long since forgotten in the valleys of the Euphrates and Tigris and beyond them to the plateau of what is now Iran.[45]

A number of tablets have been discovered with a bearing on Eblaite law. Professor Freedman (whose findings, however, have not been confirmed either by Matthiae or Pettinato),[46] speaks of a law which awarded damages of five lambs for a blow inflicted by hand; the seduction of an unmarried virgin could result in an unspecified fine payable to her parent or guardian, while the penalty for raping a virgin was death. (In the Old Testament the attacker had to marry his victim, which was a life sentence for them both.)[47]

It is clear that Ebla reinforced her trade links with conquests and used conquests to establish trade links, as may be seen from a despatch[48] sent by Enna-Dagan, a victorious Eblaite commander who had been rewarded, probably by Ar-Ennum,[49] with the throne of Mari:

The town of Aburu and the town of Ilgi, which are in the land of Belan, I besieged, and I vanquished the king of Mari; I heaped up piles of corpses in the land of Labanan. The town of Tibalat and the town of Ilwi I besieged, and I vanquished the king of Mari; I heaped up piles of corpses in the land of Angai ...

The letter continued in much the same vein, and by the end Enna-Dagan has conquered more than a dozen towns (one of them, he says, 'for the second time', which does not say much for his success the first time), reported eight times that he vanquished the king of Mari, and left no less than thirty piles of corpses in his trail. The king of Mari is named as Iblul-Il who had been heard of before the Ebla discoveries,[50] but scholars were unaware that, according to the tablet, he was also king of Ashur – the city on the Tigris, about sixty miles south of Mosul, which, ironically, was later (c. 1800 BC) to annex Mari, and ultimately became the centre of an Assyrian Empire.

One phrase in the despatch – 'I liberated the commercial colony' – suggests that Mari had sparked off the war by taking a 'commercial colony' belonging to Ebla (apparently in the vicinity of Emar);[51] but the basic point at issue was probably the control not only of Syrian trade, but all trade passing through Syria. The tribute imposed by Ebla was massive and one tablet speaks of 2,193 minas (rather more than a ton) of silver, and 134 minas and 26 shekels (say 150 pounds) of gold[52] – of which fifteen per cent went to Enna-Dagan by way of commission. Other Eblaites followed him on the throne of Mari, including one Shura-Damu, a son of Ebrum, which suggests that Ebla's dominion over Mari persisted through several decades – though Professor Matthiae believes instead that Mari soon regained her independence but was later again subdued by Ebla.[53] Yet the scholars of Mari and Ebla conferred amicably, and it is conceivable that the large archive found at Mari, though written in pure Akkadian, may have owed something to the influence, centuries earlier, of the Ebla school for scribes.

Ashur, though part of Iblul-Il's dominion, did not succumb to Enna-Dagan and, perhaps a generation later, we find Ebrum[54] entering into a treaty with a king of Ashur called Du-ud-ià. Curiously, the king-list in which the Assyrians set down their own tradition on the rulers of Ashur[55] begins with the names of seventeen kings who 'lived in tents', and who are widely regarded as mythical, or at least as having nothing to do with Ashur,[56] and the first of whom is said to have been named Tu-di-ia. Pettinato plausibly identifies him with the Du-ud-ià of the treaty and snatches him out of the mists.

Of the treaty's contents, two somewhat different notices have been published, both by Pettinato and both in 1976. According to one,[57] the tablet begins with a list of Ebla's leading citizens and its main subject is the foundation of a new *kāru* – i.e. harbour and commercial centre. The regulations involved are set forth in detail, and the new centre, though unnamed, might well be Kanesh, whose commercial importance is attested as far back as the twentieth century BC.[58] The other article[59] states that the introduction contains a list of the cities and fortresses 'in the hand of the king of Ebla', to which Ashur's merchants are now to have access, and that the tablet goes on to describe the joint foundation by Ebla and Ashur of various commercial centres in Anatolia and northern Syria and indicate the importance of their trade links.

As was usual in the ancient Near East, the treaty closes with a curse, warning of the consequences which would befall the signatories should one or the other fail to abide by its provisions:

The moment that he does not respect the treaty, may the god Sun, the god Adad and his own personal god disperse his decision in the steppe; for his messengers who set out on a journey may there be no water, may you have no stable abode, may you undertake a trip of perdition!

In other words, may you get lost. The fact that the warning on this particular tablet is addressed to Ashur leaves the impression that it may have been a vassal of Ebla, but it is possible that a parallel version of the curse – directed against the latter – lies buried in the ruins of Ashur and that it was a treaty between equals.

There are records of other treaties including those made with the kings of Hama, Tuttul (present day Hit, in Iraq) and of Emar.[60] The latter married a daughter of the king of Ebla and received several towns as a dowry.[61]

Professor Pettinato has found numerous references to Carchemish in the tablets, one of which assigns 'a "divine"[62] garment for the wife of Iddi-Kamish ... who is going to Carchemish'. Another, which comes from the preamble to the treaty with Ashur discussed above, declares that 'the *kāru* of Carchemish is in the hand of the king of Ebla'. The very occurrence of the name in these third millennium texts is significant, for, although Woolley's excavations had demonstrated the existence of Carchemish in the third millennium, the name had not been found earlier than the Mari archive (*c*. 1800 BC), and scholars had wondered whether Carchemish might have been known by a different name in the third millennium. Pettinato also has an intriguing suggestion about the origin of Carchemish. That city, already at the period of the Ebla archive, contained a *kāru* which has in fact been excavated to reveal 'a quay with a brick-lined watergate flanked by mud-brick walls on stone foundations'.[63] Kamish was the name of a principal god at Ebla (see p. 165). Pettinato therefore analyses the name Carchemish (*Kàr-kà-mi-iš*) as the *kāru* (quay) of Kamish (*Kàr* + *Kà-mi-iš*). Because Ebla is (as yet) the only known centre of Kamish worship at this time, Pettinato suggests that Carchemish was founded by Ebla, which would render more plausible the statement just cited, that the commercial centre of Carchemish was 'in the hand of the king of Ebla'.

Ebla showed a ready tolerance for deities of every variety, foreign and domestic, male and female and Pettinato has, at the latest count, identified no less than five hundred gods and goddesses who enjoyed a following,[64] some of whom were thought to be more godly than others, but all of whom were accepted as divine. To the western mind brought up on monotheism, a disposition to accommodate so many gods suggests almost an adherence to none and one does have the impression that Ebla, for all its gods (possibly because of them), was not overawed by them.

Some evidence of Eblaite thought and belief is provided by its art and architecture as well as the tablets. The layout of the royal palace, for example, is different from that found in Mesopotamia. At Ebla, the various sectors – administrative, residential and so on – were found side by side or back to back[65] crowded together about the northern and eastern sides of the great open space known as the 'Audience Court' (so called because it contains a podium, where the royal throne was apparently set). In the Mesopotamia of this period, on the other hand (which is to say the middle of the third millennium), the trend was to build one huge self-sufficient enclave in which living quarters, shrines and administrative and other buildings were all brought together in one tight enclosure.

This tendency to integrate is reflected in the very language of Mesopotamia in which one can get sentences like:

If a woman who is dwelling in a man's house causes her husband to enter a contract that no creditor of her husband shall seize her, (and) causes a tablet to be executed (to that effect), if that man had incurred a debt before he married that woman, his creditor shall not seize his wife.[66]

While in those ancient languages of Syria and Palestine known to us (e.g. Hebrew), sentences are loosely strung together.

The Court, Matthiae believes, extended westwards to connect the palace with the lower town to the west, providing a meeting-place between the rulers and the people, and a focus for social life. It would be wrong to infer from the failure to include a temple among the palace buildings that there was a separation between church and state, but it does suggest that the former was discouraged from becoming too closely involved in the affairs of the latter, and we may expect to find that the Ebla archive was in the hands of the laity, and the scribes were laymen.[67] As most of the tablets were, as we have seen, concerned with trade the western reader might infer that here was one area where god and mammon did not mix, but there is no evidence that Ebla harboured such lofty ideals. There were so many gods in its pantheon that they mixed in everything – divine ubiquity being sustained by numbers.

Pettinato identified some twenty mythical texts, featuring gods already familiar from Mesopotamia – Enlil, Enki, Inanna, and Utu and Suen (an earlier form of Sin), gods of the sun and the moon respectively.[68] They are spoken of in Eblaite,[69] but the myths which surround them are free translations of Sumerian myths.[70] In one fragment, said Pettinato, there is 'an account of the creation of the universe which closely resembles Genesis 1'.[71] According to one report, he added that the heavens, earth, sun and moon were created in that order in both accounts, and also announced the discovery of a Flood story, in which 'Enlil sent six days of water'.[72] The fact that the gods here are Sumerian (or Akkadian), and therefore not the principal gods of the city – as distinct, for example, from the gods who gave their names to the gates – renders the question which all mythology should elicit particularly relevant here: how far do these myths reflect the religious feelings of Ebla, rather than its literary creativity? One sometimes gets the impression that they arise from the latter rather than the former.

The monthly flour rations mentioned above tell one something of the Eblaite calendar and Eblaite gods. It was a lunar calendar of twelve months, with a thirteenth intercalated where necessary (rather like the Jewish calendar) to adjust the time to the solar year.[73] Four of the months were related to seasonal events such as 'the month of the Corn Harvest', the month of 'Deliveries' and the month of 'Provisions',[74] while the rest bore the names of gods. The year, Pettinato believes, began in September with the month of *Beli*. The name means 'my lord' but Pettinato believes that it stands for the ubiquitous Dagan,[75] who features in Scripture many centuries later as the Philistine god, and who was chief god of the Eblaite pantheon. December, appropriately, was called after Adad or Hadad, the lord of tempests and benign rainfall; July after

Eshtar[76] (philologically equivalent to the Phoenician goddess Ashtoreth), and August after Kamish, who appears two thousand years later as Chemosh, the warlike god of the Moabites. Two of the months, rather surprisingly, bear the names of Hurrian deities, Ashtabi and Adamma.[77] The Hurrians, at this time, were thought to have been confined to an area of Mesopotamia between the Tigris and the Zagros mountains,[78] and although they soon began a long westward trek they did not, as far as was known, penetrate Syria until about the eighteenth century BC.[79] The fact that Hurrian gods are not only found in Ebla but that they were so established in popular lore as to have found their way into the calendar, suggests that the westward march of the Hurrians may have begun many centuries earlier than anyone had imagined. It also shows the remarkable readiness with which the Eblaites were disposed to assimilate strangers in their midst, gods and all.[80] Two months are known by the somewhat improbable expressions the 'month of the cities' (January) and the 'month of the ban, taboo' (Eblaite *hurmu*, cf. Hebrew *ḥèrem*). The former suggests some sort of festive gathering[81] (like the Hebrew pilgrimage festival), the latter something dark and sombre and as yet wholly mysterious.[82]

A student of archaeology, five thousand years hence, might be tempted to conclude from a study of the Gregorian calendar that twentieth-century Europeans still worshipped Janus, Mars and Juno and an inscription reading say, Thursday, 5 August 1976, AD might be taken as proof that the Scandinavian thunder-god, a Roman Emperor and Christ himself shared a place in their pantheon. It could be as dangerous and misleading to read too much into the names used in the Eblaite calendar, except that it was of recent creation and was, according to Pettinato, instituted by King Ibbi-Sipish.

Most of the personal names deciphered by Pettinato consist of a phrase incorporating a divine name such as Damu (the Sumerian god of healing), Lim (an Amorite god), Il (the aged, almost superannuated head of the Ugarit pantheon), or Malik, meaning king, who may have had some relationship to the dark and mysterious Molech whose cult involved child child sacrifice, and against whose worship the Hebrews were repeatedly warned (Leviticus 18:21). A noun, MLK, mean-

ing 'sacrifice' has been identified in Phoenician, whence the
suggestion that the Hebrew *molek* is not a name after all but
means simply 'sacrifice', and that such phrases as 'give unto
Molech', 'commit whoredom with Molech' – in traditional
renderings – in fact mean 'give as a sacrifice', and 'lust after
human sacrifice'.[83] The discovery in Ebla of a prototype of
Molech would, however, favour the traditional interpretation.

It might also be interesting to note that if Pettinato is right
and that *beli* can be substituted for Dagan it would shed new
light on perhaps the most familiar of all Canaanite deities,
Baal, also meaning 'lord' which, some believe, was never a
proper name but was a substitute for the name of this or that
god which could be uttered only on chosen occasions. One
is reminded also of the reverence shown by Jews to the divine
name written with the consonants YHWH but pronounced
adonay, which, with remarkable similarity to the Eblaite formula, also apparently means 'my lord ...'

Some evidence on the workings of the Eblaite pantheon can
be drawn, unexpectedly, from one of the great Sumerian-
Eblaite dictionaries. Though it is made up for the most part
of Sumerian words each followed by an Eblaite translation,
we find a few entries consisting of a Mesopotamian deity followed – as if translated – by a Syrian deity.[84] Thus we have
(Sumerian) Nergal = (Syrian) Rasap – both gods of pestilence;
(Sumerian) Utu = (Syrian) Sipish – sun gods; and so on. This
may mean that the Mesopotamian gods were known from
myths current at Ebla but were not familiar objects of worship,
and that their 'translation' into native Syrian gods was intended as a rough explanation of their nature. Alternatively
we could suppose that the Mesopotamian gods were fully assi-
milated and regularly worshipped and that their equation with
native Syrian gods was an attempt to slim down an over-
crowded pantheon.[85]

On the forms of worship, Pettinato reports the mention of
temples of Dagan, Eshtar, Kamish and Rasap.[86] Some variant
names of months refers to festivals of Ashtabi, Adad and Kamish.[87] Bread, libations and animal sacrifices were offered and
one tablet records the offerings made by the royal family over
a whole month, with such entries as: '11 sheep for the god
Adad from the *en* [king] as an offering'.[88] Of cultic personnel,

various kinds of priest are named,[89] as well as the *maḫḫu*, whom Pettinato apparently connects with the ecstatic 'prophet' termed *muḫḫu* who appears at Mari, and the *nabî*, whose most obvious counterpart, philologically at least, is the biblical Hebrew *nābī* 'prophet'.[90] Could Ebla one day shed light on the beginnings of prophecy?

Matthiae was mystified by the discovery of a number of great limestone eyes near the façade of the audience court in the royal palace. Did they signify an all-seeing deity or deities? Were they strategically placed to ward off the evil eye? Were they intended as evil eyes themselves? Matthiae, after some thought, concludes that they 'probably alluded to the acuteness and inflexibility of divine and royal justice regarding the business dealt with in the court'.[91]

Matthiae has also discovered numerous representations of a female figure who subdues lions, protects bulls and is attended by bull-men. Could she have been an Eblaite Diana? Matthiae saw her as the 'mistress of the beasts' and archetypal Nature goddess, the bulls symbolizing fertility and the lions the natural forces hostile thereto.[92]

Another theme to which Matthiae has devoted much attention is a kneeling Atlas who holds over his head a complex symbol composed of two lion heads and two human heads in cross-like opposition.[93] Given the fact that the city of Ebla was divided into four quarters, Matthiae concluded that the Eblaites viewed their city as a model of the universe, that the concept of the world is divided into four quarters derived from Ebla, that the four-part symbol held by the 'Atlas' expressed this visually, and that Naram-Sin took over the title of 'King of the four quarters' (p. 31) upon his conquest of Ebla[94] – a delicate chain of hypotheses.

Professor Pettinato has given some examples of the literary texts he has found in some of the tablets, including a proverb whose first line he once rendered, 'the gift is all, the gift is life'.[95] He now prefers to leave both lines untranslated but their lilting sound transcends the language barrier:[96]

> *ù-šu la kà-la/ù-šu la ti-li*
> *gú-šu la kà-la/gù-šu la ti-li*

The parallelism, or rhyming of thought, displayed in these lines evokes the poetry of Mesopotamia:

> When on high the heaven had not been named,
> firm ground below had not been called by name[97]

And of ancient Israel:

> He maketh me lie down in green pastures:
> he leadeth me beside the still waters.

There is also a familiar echo to an Eblaite hymn praising the 'lord of heaven and earth',[98] but Professor Pettinato does not offer more than a line.

Professor Pettinato sees the character of Ebla, certainly during the period of the archive as 'peaceable' and 'devoted first and foremost to commerce with the whole of the then known world'[99] and finds proof of this in the fact that it employed mercenaries.[100] But the mercenaries could have served as stiffening to a native conscript army, and Enna-Dagan's report from Mari with its claims of heaped-up corpses suggests more than a passing bellicosity. Moreover, wood carvings have been discovered with scenes of warriors impaling one another on swords, which Professor Matthiae believes are derived not from myths, but from reality.[101] Few empires, even commercial empires, are built up or maintained through peaceful persuasion, and it is unlikely that Ebla was an exception, but if its character was not perhaps as peaceable as Pettinato suggests, one does get the impression that it had no martial traditions to speak of – or at least they are not spoken of. The tablets published or summarized to date (though hardly a representative sample, if only because economic texts are least difficult to decipher) speak of kings and queens and judges and priests and scribes and tax-masters, but one rarely finds mention of a general, and Ebla's first concern was not for military glory but to keep intact her prosperity and her widespread interests.

How widespread were those interests? In 1976 Matthiae and Pettinato, still a trifle intoxicated with the extent of their discoveries, spoke of 'a great empire of which all memory has been lost in the historical tradition of the Near East',[102] an empire which encompassed the whole of Syria, Anatolia and Upper

Mesopotamia,[103] and extracted tribute from cities as far apart as Kanesh to the north-west and Akkad[104] to the south-east, the heart of the first – or what hitherto had been thought of as the first – empire in history. Her 'sphere of influence', said Pettinato, reached even to Sinai and to Cyprus.[105] Although some cities, even in Syria itself, were admitted to have maintained their independence,[106] Pettinato declared that Ebla was 'the greatest power in the ancient Near East during the third millennium',[107] which meant in effect that it was the greatest power in the world. He has since had second thoughts and feels that the evidence does not after all justify talk of an empire. It is now clear that in this, as in later periods, Syria was a patchwork of city-states, of which Ebla was but one. Ebla was no doubt greater and mightier than any of her neighbours; she did not however annex them, but, as Pettinato put it, merely 'brought them into her own commercial orbit'.[108] The resulting picture is in fact not very different from that anticipated by the scholar van Liere, who wrote in 1963,[109] a year before the Ebla expedition was launched, that what one would expect to find in Syria was a system of city-states not unlike those of Greece and Sumer. It is possible then that the importance of Ebla to historians may lie, not so much in what it was itself, as the light which its archive may shed on others.

CHAPTER 8

Who Killed Ebla?

Until the Tell Mardikh excavations, Ebla was spoken of, but did not speak. The haul of potsherds and sculptured fragments helped Matthiae to put a tentative date to the different levels of the site, and the statue of Ibbit-Lim enabled him to identify the site itself, but all through an intricate process of induction and deduction. To get his chronology right, Matthiae had not only to establish the design patterns on the pottery, but the incidence of the different types of pottery, and then to compare the finds at other sites (notably in the Amuq) where the chronology of the different strata had been worked out. Thus, for example, he found a prevalence of corrugated 'Simple' ware, a considerable incidence of 'Orange' and 'Reserved-Slip' ware and an almost complete absence of 'Painted Simple' and 'Smeared-Wash' ware in the palace area – a distribution which tallied best with Phase I in the Amuq, which in turn is often assigned to the period of the Akkad dynasty. Hence he dated the palace to the third quarter of the third millennium.[1] Evidence thus amassed is not the sort on which one can hang a man, or, indeed, build a convincing thesis, and it was not till the discovery of the palace archive with its stacks of tablets that Ebla began to speak for itself. Yet though the tablets had much to say on other matters, they were reticent, or rather ambiguous, on the matter of chronology, and if they offered strong indications of period Matthiae had to turn to external sources for confirmation.

The crucial event in the history of Ebla is the destruction of the royal palace, at which point the archive stops dead like a clock in an earthquake. Who did it and when was it done? To answer the first question is to answer the second.

A lot depends on who ruled when in Ebla. Pettinato found

six kings mentioned in the tablets, and drew up a provisional order of succession: Igrish-Halam; Ar-Ennum; Ebrum; Ibbi-Sipish; Dubuhu-Ada and Irkab-Damu.[2] This line had been carefully pieced together. Ibbi-Sipish is explicitly called Ebrum's son. Ebrum in turn appears as a high official during the reign of Ar-Ennum. Furthermore, many officials are common to the reigns of Igrish-Halam and Ar-Ennum, and many to the reigns of Ar-Ennum and Ebrum, but there is no such overlap between Ebrum and Igrish-Halam, who must therefore have preceded Ar-Ennum. The position of the two other kings, however, was less clear, and later had to be revised.[3]

One tablet dating from Irkab-Damu's reign seemed to Pettinato to be a desperate plea for help before the final onslaught. It is addressed to the king of Hamazi (a city probably located in the mountainous region near Sulaimaniya, close to the present Iraqi–Iranian border):

Thus saith Ibubu, overseer of the king's palace, unto the messenger: Hearken. Thou art my brother and I thy brother. To thee, my brother, whatever desire comes forth from thy mouth I grant, and every desire that comes forth from my mouth thou dost grant. Send me, pray, good soldiers – thou, my brother and I thy brother. Ten pieces of wooden furniture, two wooden ornaments, I, Ibubu, have given to the messenger. Irkab-Damu, king of Ebla, is brother unto Zizi, king of Hamazi; Zizi, king of Hamazi, is brother unto Irkab-Damu, king of Ebla. And thus Tirail the scribe wrote, and gave it to the messenger of Zizi.[4]

That Irkab-Damu should have looked to Hamazi for aid in such a crisis was surprising; Hamazi was over five hundred miles from Ebla and any troops dispatched would have been slow in coming over the difficult terrain, and would have had to pass through Akkad, who was no doubt the aggressor, or territory controlled by Akkad. The difficulty vanished, however, when Pettinato re-examined the texts, and concluded that Irkab-Damu was not the last king of Ebla, but the second. The revised king-list now reads: Igrish-Halam; Irkab-Damu; Ar-Ennum; Ebrum and Ibbi-Sipish (Dubuhu-Ada is dropped altogether, and now seems not to have been a king after all).[5] And so the letter becomes a relatively humdrum barter agreement – but on an international level.

The archive, then, covered the reigns of five kings, or say

one hundred and fifty years, but the Italians were still not sure just when that period began and ended. A helpful lead, however, was found in two inscriptions of Naram-Sin, cited more fully on pp. 40f. One calls him 'King of the four regions, conqueror of Arman and Ebla', while the other begins:

In all time, (since) the creation of men, no king among kings had ravaged the land of Armanum and Ibla. Henceforth (?) the god Nergal, having opened the way for the valiant Naram-Sin, has delivered Armanum and Ibla into his hands ...

All of which suggested in fairly emphatic terms that Matthiae's interpretation of the ceramic evidence had been correct and that Naram-Sin had sacked the palace and that the sacking must therefore have taken place at about 2275 BC.

Did the tablets confirm this? Pettinato was uncertain. Sargon the Great, Naram-Sin's illustrious grandfather, also claimed to have vanquished Ebla, as described on p. 40; and the Ebla tablets were found to display many features – in spelling, and in the formation of the cuneiform signs – that were similar to those found in Mesopotamian documents before and during Sargon's reign, but *not* after. Perhaps, then, it was Sargon who conquered Ebla. One should add that evidence of the pottery on which Pettinato and Matthiae based so many of their calculations, was in fact equivocal. Amuq I pottery, thought by Matthiae and others to belong to about the period of Naram-Sin, is ascribed by some scholars[6] to the period 2500–2400 BC which must further undermine the belief that it was Naram-Sin who sacked Ebla.

One could possibly argue that Sargon began the job, that he, so to speak, singed Ebla while his grandson sacked it. Pettinato also felt that the fact that the type of cuneiform in use in Ebla belonged to the time of Sargon was not particularly conclusive. The 'known phenomenon of the slow cultural development of provincial areas'[7] could, he argued, have meant that Ebla used a cuneiform style which had been abandoned elsewhere, much as one can find dialects in rural areas which are extinct elsewhere, and he therefore – for a time at least – came round to Matthiae's view that Ebla fell silent at the time of Naram-Sin. Further discoveries seemed to confirm this view. The name of Sargon appears in the tablets as a buyer of Eblaite goods at the time of King Ebrum.[8] Since further kings are mentioned in the tablets after Ebrum, it suggests that Ebla outlived Sargon, and that Naram-Sin must therefore have put it to the torch.

Another possible time indicator was supplied by a document which named the ruler of the vanquished kingdom of Mari as Iblul-Il. A king of that name had been known since 1952, when a number of statuettes bearing his name were excavated from a temple in Mari.[9] The most striking portrayed a 'great singer' called Ur-Nanshe,[10] who had dedicated this statuette of himself to the temple's presiding goddess, 'for the life of Iblul-Il'. But the date of Iblul-Il was itself disputed, with different suggestions ranging from 'the period immediately before Sargon's time'[11] about 2400 BC, right back to 'between 2900 and 2685 BC'[12] Matthiae and Pettinato opted for the later date. From there they were able to work forward and felt satisfied that the kingdom of Ebla endured from about 2400 to 2250[13] and flourished most brilliantly during the period of weakness to which Akkad succumbed between the death of Sargon and the accession of Naram-Sin. If so, one may presume that Naram-Sin took drastic steps to restore Akkadian hegemony, and if the decline of Akkad had seen the rise of Ebla, its recovery spelt its doom.

But difficulties remained. Everything in the archive – indeed the very existence of the archive – pointed to Ebla as a flourishing centre, to which (according to one tablet) even Akkad paid tribute. What then of Sargon's victory? Mere legend, said Matthiae,[14] or if not, his victory was indecisive, so that even if Ebrum began as a vassal of Akkad he turned the tables and became master.[15]

A further problem was the wording of Naram-Sin's report of his triumph. He couples 'Arman and Ebla' as if the latter was less significant than the former, though Arman was known merely as the capital of a small state. He also mentions how he captured the king of Arman and had him bound to his city gate, but says nothing of the king of Ebla, as if he was a person of no importance. To this Matthiae also had an answer, but it was less than straightforward. Arman, he said, was in fact subject to Ebla, but Ebla must have been suffering from some sort of crisis at the time and Naram-Sin found the place in disarray, but so impressed was he by the exalted bearing of the governor of Arman that he took him to be king of the entire region, and thus mistook the monkey for the organ-grinder. This is perhaps a classical instance of a presupposition without any visible, or, indeed invisible means of support, and the Professor may not have found it totally convincing himself, for he tucked it away in a footnote which, out of charity, one should perhaps have left unread.[16]

The most insurmountable obstacle to the Matthiae-Pettinato chronology, however, lay not in the contents of the tablets but the way they were written. In November 1976 the two participated in a gruelling series of conferences at the Oriental Institute in Chicago, whose presiding genius Professor I.J. Gelb, possibly the world's foremost authority on cuneiform, argued that the narrow columns into which the texts were divided, the formation of the signs, the very spelling, pointed to a period before or during the reign of Sargon, but not after[17] and they could not be explained away, as Pettinato had tried to do, by the time-lag between provinces and the main centres of civilization (especially if it was claimed that Ebla was in fact a metropolis itself). In the face of such argument, Pettinato revised his chronology and concluded that the archive dated about 2500 BC and that it was Sargon who had destroyed Ebla.[18]

But that too brought contradictions. Pettinato had argued that Sargon was a contemporary of Ebrum, which would have made Ebrum the last king of Ebla, or the last king but one, but he had three successors. Pettinato then went back to his tablets for a further reading and concluded that he had misread the name of Sargon for a nonentity called Shariginu, and that the place called A.EN.GA.DU which he had taken to be Akkad was in all probability to be read Arugadu,[19] a town of no particular importance, near Ebla, and that Akkad itself does not appear in the tablets at all.[20] All of which upset Matthiae's calculations and much else, and the two have agreed to differ.

One of the strongest arguments in favour of Matthiae's chronology is Naram-Sin's claim that he was the first king to have vanquished Ebla, but kings are often prone to such claims and this may have been mere bombast. Matthiae also points to certain Eblaite artistic work and traits, such as the representation of bulls on cylinder seals and a wood-carving of a king wielding an axe[21], which seem closely related to the art of Mesopotamia during or shortly after the Sargon epoch. If Ebla was destroyed by Sargon, Matthiae argues, these common features must have arisen first at Ebla, and then spread to Mesopotamia, in which case one has to postulate a degree of Eblaite influence on Mesopotamian art which strikes one as surprising and, indeed, implausible.[22] It should not, however, have appeared as either implausible or surprising to Professor Matthiae who adheres strongly to the belief that Ebla saw the efflorescence of an indigenous Syrian culture which was certainly independent of Mesopotamia and could well have influenced it.

Recently the names of two Egyptian pharaohs were encountered at Ebla – Chephren and Pepi I, commonly but somewhat tentatively dated c. 2550 BC and c. 2300 BC respectively.[23] However, in the absence of details of their archaeological context, they do little to decide the issue.

If there is debate as to which king of Akkad destroyed Ebla, it is accepted that Akkad was the destroyer and her motives seem fairly obvious. She needed the timbers which Syria produced and the metals which passed through Syria. Ebla itself, even at its zenith, was not, as we have seen, in a position to challenge the might of Akkad. But supposing she joined in league with another power, say Ashur? Or perhaps even with the king of Hamazi, who could have threatened Akkad's eastern flank. But it is equally possible that the wealth and the markets of Ebla were in themselves the attraction.

Ancient cities were easily destroyed and easily rebuilt (the building material was ready to hand in the very ruins), and an Ebla of sorts did rise from the ashes; whether it was destroyed by Sargon c. 2350 BC or Naram-Sin c. 2250 BC, it continued as a sizeable entity occupying the entire area now bounded by the walls for a further five or six hundred years. Professor Matthiae believes that it was reoccupied immediately, and suffered no break in cultural development; the pottery continues to be 'refined and perfected along lines already attested' before the destruction of the palace.[24] But it was no longer the centre of a conurbation or the capital of an empire, and if its traditions of literacy persisted, no evidence of them has as yet come to light.

The old royal palace was never restored. It was buried in ruins and a stone stairway built over it leading to a newly-erected temple. The new palace was probably situated on the northern edge of the acropolis, but no traces have been found. By the middle of the twenty-first century, Ebla was probably a dependency of the Ur empire; but the references (pp. 41 f.) to Ebla's exports of wood and textiles, and to the many 'men of Ebla', presumably merchants throughout the Near East dealing in articles as varied as 'asses trained for riding', 'pigs for pasturing' and copper and lead, do suggest that whatever else Ebla may have lost in the course of its travails, its entrepreneurial instincts were fairly intact.

But at about 2000 BC, Ebla was again destroyed. The aggressors, according to Professor Matthiae, were the Amorites, who had been migrating into the area steadily since c. 2200 BC until their sheer numbers caused a 'breakdown of the economic foundations', culminating in the destruction not only of Ebla but also of other Syrian cities.[25] Once again, the city seems to have been immediately rebuilt, but yields pottery of a very different sort – thicker, less varied, and of inferior quality, and Matthiae infers that the Amorite conquerors imposed their own culture on Ebla.[26] One of their first acts was to set up the great earthen rampart that surrounds the city. Ibbit-Lim probably lived not more than a century later, and his position as King shows that Ebla was then politically independent. References to Ebla tail off, however, and by c. 1800 BC it was absorbed in the kingdom of Yamhad. About 1650 BC the city was subjected to a further invasion, probably from the Hittites, whose onslaught must have been pressed with particular vigour, for Ebla was now slow to recover if, indeed, it recovered at all. Yet something of Ebla's literary traditions may have lived on among the Hittites themselves, who seem to have learnt the art of writing at precisely this point. Although many Hittitologists maintain that the Hittites learnt writing from the Hurrians, Professor O.R. Gurney, of Oxford, believes that the Hittites took Syrian scribes back with them, and puts forward the possibility that these scribes came from Ebla.[27] Thereafter, small settlements might grow up sporadically on the acropolis, and died out after perhaps a century; from one such occupation, *c.* 450 BC, a country lodge survives, and the most recent seems to have consisted of a small community of stylite monks some time between the third and seventh centuries AD.[28]

The tablets have now rescued Ebla from oblivion, which is yet another proof that the pen is mightier than the sword, for when the history of the ancient Near East comes to be – as it must be – retold, we shall be hearing less of the Akkadian, Amorite or Hittite warriors than of the clerks of Ebla.

CHAPTER 9

The Connection

The number of tablets discovered at Ebla runs into five figures; the number published has yet to run into two. The limitations of any attempt at this stage to assess the significance of the find are obvious. One can only try to suggest on what lines research might proceed, and, what may be more important in view of all the speculation hitherto, on what lines it is highly unlikely to proceed.

It is of course the 'biblical connection' that has won the lion's share of public attention ever since the discovery of the Ebla archive was announced. The blurb on the very first report by Pettinato to be published in English[1] introduced Ebla thus: 'It spoke a language close to Hebrew. Its greatest king bore a name cognate with Eber, the ancestor of the Hebrews (Genesis 10:21). It worshipped a god named *Ya* ...'[2] Is this where the primary significance of Ebla lies?

The extraordinary interest in the report of a god called Ya, or (as sometimes stated) Yaw stems of course from the occurrence of a divine name Yah in the Hebrew Bible – fifty times altogether, of which twenty-four are in the phrase Hallelu*jah* – 'Praise ye *the Lord*.' Much more often[3] we find a related name, translated 'the Lord' in most English versions. Jewish tradition has handed down its four consonants – YHWH – but not the vowels, and so its pronunciation is uncertain. The Jews so revered this name that they never pronounced it, but read in its place another name, Adonay.[4] In their manuscripts they retained the consonants YHWH but, when they added vowels, the vowels were those of Adonay (ə-o-a).[5] Christian scholars unaware that the consonants and vowels did not correspond erroneously supposed, at least from 1381 onward, that the name was to be pronounced Jehovah.[6] Although nothing more seemed to survive in Jewish tradition,[7] some of the Church Fathers did claim knowledge of the pronunciation of the name. Usually their occasion for bringing up the subject was the doctrine of various heretics that the different divine names of the Old Testament referred to different divine – or rather demonic – beings who ruled over the world;[8] in order to refute it the Fathers offered a translation – and a transliteration – of each Hebrew name. The principal forms[9] they hand down are Iaoue,[10] Iave[11] and Iavai.[12] Hence (and for other reasons),[13] the pronunciation generally agreed today is Yahweh. It seems to have been first suggested[14] in 1567, but it was slow to gain currency. Eissfeldt relates how Heinrich Ewald (1803–75) used to preface his lectures: 'Great Yahweh, whom Gesenius in Halle still calls Jehovah, come to our help.'[15] As to the meaning of the name Yahweh, an enormous number of suggestions have been made, such as:[16] He who is, *or* causes to be, *or* causes to fall (rain? foes?) *or* speaks *or* commands. On all these views, Yah is a later contraction. Theories on which Yah was the original form and Yahweh a secondary expansion enjoyed some popularity about fifty years ago. For example, G. R. Driver suggested[17] that Ya was originally an inarticulate cry which in moments of ecstasy was prolonged to *ya(h)wa(h)* or the like, which in turn by folk etymology came to be connected with the Hebrew root *hwh* 'be' and fixed in pronunciation as Yahweh. Such theories, however, have few adherents today.[18] Perhaps we should also take the opportunity to dismiss the bizarre but much publicized theory of Dr J. Allegro[19] – though it may be indelicate to mention Driver and Allegro in the same breath – who derives the name from the Sumerian (!) words IÀ (which he renders 'juice, strong water' and in fact means 'oil, fat') and U$_5$ (which can mean 'ruttish'), and translates it 'juice of fecundity, seed of life' – an etymology which tells us something about Allegro but nothing about Yahweh.

At all events it is reported that both the biblical names – in the forms Ya and Yaw – have turned up in third-millennium Ebla. Regarding the shorter form Ya, Pettinato bases his claim on the presence of an element -*ia* in several names, e.g. Mi-kà-ià, which he translates 'Who is like Ya?', or Ì-ṣa-ià 'Ya has gone forth'. The occurrence of several other names, each identical with one of the -ià names except that it instead ends in -Il,[20] 'amply demonstrates' in Pettinato's opinion 'that at Ebla at least Ya had the same value as Il and points to a *specific deity*'.[21] As evidence of the longer form Yaw, Pettinato adduced just one name, *viz* Shumiyau (Šu-mi-a-ù), but has not ventured to translate it. He added that 'while till the reign of Ebrum all personal names contained the theophorous element *Il*, from Ebrum on *Il* was substituted for by *Ya*', and deduced that 'under Ebrum a new development in West Semitic religious concepts took place that permitted the rise of Ya' – an observation which, if it seemed valid then, can hardly be so now, after Pettinato's re-shuffle which, for example, changed the third successor of Ebrum (namely Irkab-Damu) into his predecessor.

Now the appearance of the name YHWH (or of Yah) at such an early date, and outside Israel, should not come as an utter shock, since the Bible states that it became known as early as the days of Adam's grandson Enosh (Genesis 4:26) or even of Eve herself (Genesis 4:1).[22] Many pre-biblical sightings of Yahweh have been claimed, but none has won general acceptance, and the list of those that enjoy even minority support is brief.[23] Friedrich Delitzsch came upon the names *Ia-wi-ilu* and *Ia-ú-um-ilu*, which he dated to the period of Hammurapi and translated 'Yahweh is God',[24] but most now prefer to render them 'God causes to be (or live)'[25] and '(the child is) mine, O God'[26] respectively. In an Ugaritic text the chief god El declares: *šm bny yw* 'the name of my son is Yw', and this Yw has been connected with Yahweh; but the connection and even the reading Yw have been disputed. An Edomite place name *Yhw*, appears in an Egyptian list around 1400 BC[27] but the resemblance to Yahweh might be mere coincidence (in rather the same way as car number plates sometimes yield real words). Ya (w) at Ebla could therefore be the first convincing discovery of the name Yahweh before the Bible.

But the assertion is far from secure. First, the polyphony (explained on p. 99 above) of the cuneiform signs means that the names might not have been correctly read; in particular, the sign which Pettinato reads *ià*, can also be pronounced otherwise (e.g. *ì*, *li* or *ni*). Thus Gelb cites a number of the

17 Professor Giovanni Pettinato, epigrapher of the expedition, who first discovered the Eblaite language in the Ebla inscriptions, surrounded by some of the tablets from the palace archive

18 Part of the royal archive as found where it had lain since the palace was sacked in the third millennium BC

19 The 'Audience Court', with podium in the foreground

20 Grand stairway built
on the ruins of the third
millennium royal palace

21 Detail of the
ceremonial stairway with
imprints of inlay
decorations at the third
millennium royal palace

22 Some of the tablets and other finds dug up at Ebla in 1976. Each is marked, numbered and accompanied by identification papers stating exactly where, when and at what level it was found. In the foreground is one of the most exciting discoveries of the 1976 season – a small, 4 inch-long figurine, carved out of steatite and covered with gold

23 Bulla with imprint from cylinder seal

24 Arab labourers cleaning one of the surrounding walls of the royal archive

25 An Arab carefully clearing the sand from one of the walls in the royal palace

26 A young Italian technician reconstructing a piece of pottery

27 An Italian technician at work in her laboratory at the Tell Mardikh base camp

28 Entrance to one of the inner chambers at the royal palace

29 The south-west gate, one of the four entrances to the city (early second millennium)

30 The remains of private dwellings at Ebla

31 Early second millennium temple

THE CONNECTION 181

names wherein Pettinato found *ià*, but he reads and interprets them all differently:[28]

	PETTINATO
En-na-ni-ià	'Ya has mercy on me'
Ip-ḫur-ià	'Ya has gathered'
Ip-ṭur-ià	'Ya has redeemed'
Eb-du-ià	'Servant of Ya'

	GELB
En-na-ì-lí	'Please, O my god'
Ip-ḫur-ni	'He has gathered me/us'
Ip-ṭur-ni	'He has redeemed me/us'
Ib-du-ni	'Our slave'

Of course, neither Gelb nor anyone else would categorically deny that Pettinato's readings of names in which he detects the *ià* element *might* eventually be adopted. As for the one name alleged to contain Yaw, viz. Šu-mi-a-ù, a curious form with no obvious interpretation, the reading cannot be verified until scholars have had the chance of examining it in its full context. The problem of polyphony, then, casts no little doubt, at Ebla as elsewhere (see p. 107 above), on the reading of the names.

Secondly, even if Pettinato's readings are agreed, *ià* (or less formally, *ya*) need not be a divine name. It is well known that the ending -*ya* was often used in Akkadian, Amorite and elsewhere to form pet names (technically termed *hypocoristic* names). Rather as with the English -*y*, the full name to which it was added was usually but not always abbreviated (compare our 'Johnny, Tommy, Vicky, Monty' from 'John, Thomas, Victoria, Montgomery'). Thus we find Immeriya 'little lamb' from *immeru* 'sheep',[29] Ishmiya side-by-side with Ishme-Adad ('Adad hath heard'),[30] Zimriya alongside names like Zimri-Dagan ('my protection is Dagan')[31] and many others. There may even be some instances in biblical Hebrew.[32] Thus the name Ahijah (cf. *aḥ* 'brother') is sometimes analysed as 'my brother is Yah' (or 'brother of Yah'), which hardly fits what is otherwise known of Israelite ideas of God's relationship with man, and 'little brother' seems likelier. Again, for Bakbukiah at Nehemiah 11:17 (cf. *baqbuq* 'bottle'),[33] 'dear little bottle' is a somewhat less improbable rendering than 'bottle

of Yah'. Thus the -ya termination at Ebla could well be hypocoristic, and, as is shown by such examples as Ishmiya and
Zimriya above, the fact that -ya alternates with a known divine
name (Il, according to Pettinato) is no guarantee that ya is
likewise the name of a god. Nor does the -yaw or -yau which
he has read establish his argument; an ending -u[34] was often
added to names, so that -yau could simply be hypocoristic
-ya plus -u. It is true that the first reaction of many scholars
in the early days of Assyriology was to equate the -ya element
in names with biblical Yah or Yahweh[35] but as the supposed
deity ya was found only in proper names,[36] the idea that all
the -ya names refer to a deity who was acclaimed abundantly
in personal names but never elsewhere came to be abandoned.[37] Altogether, then, the evidence so far adduced for the
worship at Ebla of a god Ya is quite unconvincing. It is not
unreasonable to ask for a form which can confidently be read
as Yah (or preferably as Yahweh, which is surely earlier), is
not merely a component of another name, and is shown by
the context or by a divine determinative (see pp. 90 ff.) to denote
a god, before one is invited to believe that the Israelite divine
name was current in Ebla, centuries before it was current
among the Israelites.

Another possible biblical link is seen in the language of
Ebla, which Pettinato first termed 'Palaeo-Canaanite' because
it showed 'such strict affinities with Ugaritic and even more
with Phoenician and Hebrew'.[38] Since both Eblaite and
Hebrew belong to the Semitic family of languages – which has
other members, such as Akkadian and Arabic – they are certainly related, but it is not easy to maintain that there is a
special bond between the two. Gelb's comparison of Eblaite
with other Semitic languages shows that, as least as far as
grammar (the overriding criterion) is concerned, it is with
Akkadian that Eblaite has most in common, far more than
with Hebrew.[39] Again, the Semitic languages are commonly
divided into three branches – North-East (Akkadian), North-
West (languages of Syria and Palestine, including Hebrew)
and South-West (languages of Arabia and Ethiopia) – and
both Matthiae and Pettinato have stressed (or did until
1977)[40] that Eblaite and Hebrew belong to the same branch,
viz. the North-Western, within the Semitic family. In the

strictly geographical sense that both were spoken in the area of Syria–Palestine their statement cannot be challenged; but if it implies a special resemblance which justifies their being grouped together as North-Western as contrasted with, say, Akkadian as North-Eastern, then Gelb's work has shown that it cannot be upheld, and indeed that the whole idea of neat division of the Semitic languages into three distinct groups may have outlived its usefulness.[41] In a further attempt to prove a special relationship, C.H. Gordon has argued[42] that the root *d-b-r* 'speak' is common to Hebrew (where it is very frequent) and Eblaite (in the word *tá-da-bi-ru* 'translator') and to no other Semitic language. He might also have adduced the interrogative *mi* 'who?', common to Eblaite and Hebrew (as well as Phoenician and Ugaritic) but not to the other languages. The fact is, however, that isolated common features of this sort could be picked out between almost any pair of languages within the Semitic family; for example the word *npr/nfr* 'bird'/'to fly' is shared exclusively by two languages at opposite ends of the spectrum in both time and space – Ugaritic in Syria, second millennium BC, and Tigrinya in Ethiopia, second millennium AD.[43]

We can in any case rule out the possibility that Hebrew is derived from Eblaite. The argument, which is necessarily technical, is better explained if one first considers another language family, the Romance. Imagine scholars a few thousand years hence, who have no written material at their disposal from any period prior to 2000 AD. A succession of archaeological finds bring to light a host of documents in present-day French, Italian, Portuguese and Romanian, all of which are successfully deciphered. From the similarities, they infer the existence of a common ancestor. Unlike us, they have no written records of that language (Latin), but they set about reconstructing some of its features. A few years later, a first edition of the Spanish classic *Don Quixote*, bearing the date of 1605 AD, is discovered and deciphered. Somebody suggests that the French of the twentieth century is simply a later form of the Spanish of the early seventeenth. Others will not find it difficult to refute this theory, by pointing to certain features of the overall parent language (as reconstructed) which survive in the French but not in the Spanish.

For example, the scholars will have drawn up lists of words such as:

FRENCH	ITALIAN	PORTUGUESE	ROMANIAN	MEANING
faim	fame	fome	foame	hunger
farine	farina	farinha	făină	flour
fer	ferro	ferro	fier	iron
fil	filo	fio	fir	thread

for which, although they may not reconstruct the parent forms perfectly (Latin *fames, farina, ferrum, filum*), they will surely have the first letter correct (f); yet the corresponding Spanish forms (*hambre, harina, hierro, hilo*) begin in *h*. Here then an original *f* was retained in French but lost in Spanish.[44] Further research would reveal many similar cases.

The same arguments may be applied within the Semitic family. Similarities compel us to suppose that they all derive from one parent language, which we call Proto-Semitic, certain of whose features may be reconstructed from the known Semitic languages, even though the Proto-Semitic language itself must have died out long before the invention of writing. Now even within the little that is as yet available of Eblaite, one can already discern certain features in which it has deviated from Proto-Semitic while Hebrew has not.[45] There are, for example, cases in which an original *ya-* at the beginning of a word survives in Hebrew but degenerated to *i-* in Eblaite,[46] such as:[47]

HEBREW	PROTO-SEMITIC	EBLAITE
yashar (righteous)	*yashar*[48]	*ishar*
yad (hand)	*yad*	*ida*

Such considerations[49] show that Hebrew can no more be descended from Eblaite than present-day French from the Spanish of *Don Quixote*.

Some of the personal names which have been reported from Ebla have obvious counterparts in the Hebrew Bible, such as Ab-ra-mu, Ish-mà-il, Ish-ra-il, Da-u-dum, Mi-kà-il, Mi-kà-yà. These parallels suggested to Pettinato in 1976 'a certain interdependence between the culture of Ebla and that of the Old Testament';[50] but in 1977 he declared, in circumstances already noted, that since Ebla and the Old Testament both represented North-West Semitic cultures the parallels were 'a fact so natural as not to arouse any surprise'.[51] The latter view does seem the safer, especially if one considers how many of the Eblaite names so far reported are quite *un*like anything in the Old Testament (e.g. Ana-Malik 'I am Malik', Besu-pihir 'he has united his house').[52] Since the Ebla texts ante-date even Abraham,[53] it has never been suggested – with one or two exceptions – that the Eblaite and biblical names referred to the same person. Indeed, the occurrence of the names here is rather less relevant to the historicity of the biblical figures than is some of the evidence which we already have from later ages in which they could conceivably have lived, e.g. *Abamrama* from seventeenth-century Babylonia, or *Abrm* and *Y-sh-r-i-l* from Ugarit *c.* 1400 BC.[54] It is, however, interesting that these names should have been in use as far back as the third millennium BC, especially in the case of David, to which name no convincing parallel had yet been found.

One of the exceptions just mentioned is the king whom Pettinato calls Ebrium or Ebrum, suggesting analogues in Hebrew for both.[55] He compares 'Ebrium' with the gentilic name *'ibri* 'Hebrew' and 'Ebrum' with the name of Eber (Genesis 10:21) from whom the Hebrews (including Abraham, who was Eber's great-great-great-great-grandson) traced their descent.

Now Ebrium, if that form is preferred, is a *personal* name, perhaps derived from Hurrian *ewri* (of which *ebri* is one written variant), meaning 'lord',[56] while the biblical *'ibri* is the name of a *people* (or perhaps originally of a social class).[57] The likeness between the two is superficial, and it is not easy to see why – or how – they should be connected. As for the alternative suggestion to read Ebrum and to compare the Eber of Genesis 10:21, one's reaction will depend on whether one is a fundamentalist or not. The non-fundamentalist may be attracted by Matthiae's idea that the name of Ebrum 'remained in the tradition of the Syro-Palestinian area' and 'probably became Eber in biblical tradition and *was inserted* in Shem's genealogy'.[58] He will however know that Genesis 10 is full of personal names which are either identical with, or back-formations from, the names of nations, or places, such as Madai, Javan, Cush, Mizraim (with a dual – or local – ending), Sidon, Heth (from 'Hittite') and Sheba, and that modern scholarship sees them not as historical individuals who fathered the Medes and the Greeks and so on single-handed, but as 'eponymous ancestors' imagined by a later age. Eber ('*Eber*) is just the form expected for the 'ancestor' of the Hebrews ('*ibri*), as is Heth (*Het*) for the 'ancestor' of the Hittites (*ḥitti*). Now to trace the name Eber back to a real person instead, while content to regard the other figures in the same chapter as imaginary or eponymous, is less than consistent. Moreover, Pettinato's recent statement that Ebla was not an empire after all[59] lessens the likelihood that the fame of Ebrum should have so resounded in the Bible. The fundamentalist, who does believe in the historicity of the individuals of Genesis 10, will encounter difficulties of a different sort in equating Eber with Ebrum. The former lived for 464 years, and had two sons – Peleg, in whose days the earth 'was divided' and who lived 239 years, and Joktan, who begat thirteen sons.[60] To identify this figure with the Ebrum who was succeeded on the throne of Ebla by Ibbi-Sipish, is not easy. There may be a crumb of comfort for the fundamentalist in the new evidence that Eber is 'a *real* personal name, not just a legendary invention,'[61] but even that modest conclusion is precarious.[62]

What with all the parallels which Pettinato claimed to have discovered between Ebla and Israel, public speculation that Ebrum actually was Eber and that the Eblaites were the ancestors of the Israelites would have been only natural. Pettinato, of course, has since dismissed any attempt to trace the origin of Israel back to Ebla as nonsense, which it is, whether one holds to the literal truth of the Bible or to any of the critical reconstructions current today.[63] Of course, in the sense that every human being has two parents, four grandparents, and over a million ancestors at twenty generations' remove,[64] there is every likelihood that a dash of Eblaite blood found its way into the veins of many Israelites (and many others too), but this yields no meaningful relationship between two peoples. All the criteria, of which language is the most important, [65] fail to suggest that the Israelites were the descendants – or, perish the thought, the direct successors and rightful heirs – of the people of Ebla.

This tracing of parallels in religion, language and so on between Ebla and Israel has been only one aspect of the 'biblical connection'. Another is the search for references to biblical events. To some this may seem unpromising, in that the range of dates entertained for the Ebla tablets is 2550–2250 BC, a period which if the biblical chronology is taken at face value, includes or even pre-dates the Flood.[66] One point of contact has however been seen in the five cities mentioned in Genesis 14:2 – Sodom, Gomorrah, Admah, Zeboim and 'Bela which is Zoar' – which have never been identified by archaeology. Some accepted Albright's suggestion that they once lay at the south-eastern end of the Dead Sea, which has however since encroached steadily on its shores, so that they have long been submerged;[67] some considered them mythical. Pettinato has now discovered references to all five by name in the Ebla tablets.[68] Professor Freedman has further stated[69] that they are all listed on a single tablet in precisely the same order as in Genesis 14:2; and that Damascus occurs in the same tablet, suggesting that the cities should be sought to the north-east (as opposed to Albright's suggestion of the south-east) of the Dead Sea. At a public meeting in London,[70] he disclosed that the cities were named as destinations of various consignments from Ebla, and that the name of one of the cities was accompanied by that of its king, which was identical with the name borne by the king of that city in Genesis 14 – though he declined to add which it was. All these revelations have generated some excitement, and there have been insistent calls for the excavation of Sodom.[71] Perhaps the brimstone which rained down from heaven upon that city, rather like the lava which engulfed Pompeii, has caught and preserved the inhabitants in their everyday positions – surely a spectacle to beggar the imagination.

The claim that these names at Ebla 'literally shatter the whole liberal-modernist approach to the Scriptures'[72] is of course unjustified. The fact that the five cities really existed, is no proof that the events with which they are connected in the Bible are true, any more than the historicity of King Ahasuerus and the city of Shushan proves that the events narrated in the book of Esther actually took place. But these names have aroused great interest even outside fundamentalist circles, because they relate to what has been aptly described as 'the most tantalizing historic problem of the Bible',[73] namely the fourteenth chapter of Genesis.

Of all the patriarchal narratives in the Bible, Genesis 14 is unique in being set in a context of world history. A coalition of four kings – called Amraphel of Shinar, Arioch of Ellasar, Chedorlaomer of Elam and Tidal of Goyim – attack and defeat Sodom and the other four cities, and carry off Lot, who has made his home in Sodom. Abraham thereupon musters his own force of 318 men, pursues the four kings, smites them, and rescues his nephew Lot. If these four kings could be identified, Abraham would be firmly anchored in history and, given the mass of cuneiform records available, this might seem no hard task. The paradox is that our historical knowledge of Babylonia (which is what Shinar denotes elsewhere)[74], Elam and Anatolia (for Goyim, since Tidal is a Hittite name), which is indeed considerable, does not merely fail to pinpoint an occasion when these three powers combined in a coalition, but it reveals a picture of incessant enmity between all three, and renders such an alliance – regardless of the vexed question of the identity of its remaining member, Ellasar – virtually unthinkable. The attempts to establish some link with Scripture by identifying at least one king, have been many and futile. When Hammurapi became known to history towards the end of the nineteenth century, he was widely identified with Amraphel. In 1896, amid great excitement, a letter of Hammurapi was published[75] which was said to contain the name of Chedorlaomer in a line interpreted to read: 'the day of (the defeat of) Ku-dur-nu-uḫ-ga-mar'. Closer examination showed that four of the cuneiform signs in that line had been misread, partly because of a later scratch on the tablet, and that the line in fact ran: 'the troops under the command of I-nu-uḫ-sa-mar', who was known from elsewhere as a high officer under Hammurapi.[76] Latterly even the identification of Amraphel as Hammurapi (which name could probably be more accurately transcribed as 'Ammurapi) has been all but universally discarded because of the final -el; and no identification of Arioch or Tidal has ever won much popularity.

But Freedman believes that a new approach has now been opened up to Genesis 14. Even if the four great kings cannot be located in history, he argues, the five cities can – now that they have been found in the Ebla texts. At the time of these references, they are still flourishing and their destruction, by which Abraham's life can be dated, must therefore be placed later. But Freedman argues – and he admits that this is the weakest link in his argument – that such a configuration of precisely five cities could not have remained unchanged for many centuries, so that the destruction of the five cities must be dated not long after the heyday of Ebla. This he dates to the twenty-seventh century BC,[77] and so he would place Abraham in or about the twenty-fifth century BC – a clean break with the generally accepted dating of Abraham (accepted, that is, among the many scholars who consider Abraham historical) to the second millennium BC, whether towards the very beginning (Albright and many others) or the middle (C.H. Gordon).[78]

It is only natural, on hearing of a theory which is based on the readings of the names of Sodom and the other cities in a tablet still unpublished, to recall the 'day of the defeat of Chedorlaomer', but such misgivings may be groundless. The step taken by Freedman of separating the patriarchs from the Exodus by nearly a thousand years is certainly novel. It starkly contradicts the biblical traditions which put the Israelites' sojourn in Egypt at 430 years, or, worse still, at two or three generations[79] – though few critics would consider that a fatal objection. On the other hand this theory can claim better than any other to allow enough time for Israel to develop from a family into a nation.[80] In order to sustain the theory it will of course be necessary to offer a new historical interpretation which pays due regard to contemporary (especially Egyptian) records, of the descent into Egypt, the bondage, and so on, and it might be unfair to pass judgement on the theory before it has been properly developed. Even now, however, it is clear that Israel would be condemned to a 'dark age' which is inordinately long and inordinately dark, and one can but marvel at the prospect of thirty-odd generations who preserved so faithfully the traditions of the patriarchs – even down to the proper (geographical?) order of the five cities with which Abraham was briefly connected – and yet left virtually no memory of themselves.

Another point of biblical interest is the occurrence, noted by Pettinato,[81] of a city called Ur in the territory of Haran. Now the fact that Paddan-Aram – i.e. the area around Haran, situated today a few miles beyond the point where the Balikh crosses from Syria into Turkey – is called Abraham's birthplace (compare Genesis 24:4, 10; 27:43), and the reference to Abraham's first home (Joshua 24:2) as 'beyond [i.e. northeast of] the River [Euphrates]', have long been felt to conflict with the statement (Genesis 11:31) that Abraham came from Ur of the Chaldees, which was generally identified with the Ur excavated by Woolley in the south-east of present-day Iraq. Usually it was said that the Pentateuchal sources preserved different traditions of Abraham's birthplace.[82] It has often been suggested, however, notably by C. H. Gordon,[83] that 'Ur of the Chaldees' in fact lay to the north-east of Canaan, in the general area of Haran, and the mention at Ebla of an Ur in just that area should revive interest in that suggestion.

Such theories, which are bound to spring up, *might* ultimately carry conviction, but the basic objection to them all is that, at a time when knowledge of Ebla itself is so limited, the construction of theories about Ebla and the Bible is putting the cart before the horse. It simply is not sound method to assess the relevance of Ebla to the Bible by plucking out some possibly identical names here or a conceivable (if only barely conceivable) point of direct contact there. The Ebla discoveries must first be studied in depth, in themselves and for themselves. That done, they will no doubt add immensely to our knowledge of the whole ancient Near East, and therefore of the context – in language, history, culture – in which the Bible must be set. But at this stage, to quarry the archive for biblical parallels is merely to explain one unknown through another, *ignotum per ignotius*.

The question has also been raised of an 'Arabian connection', in Dr Bahnasi's declaration[84] that Ebla revealed 'the antiquity of the Arab nation and the deep-rootedness of its civilization', and that it was an 'Arabian kingdom'.

It is hard to be sure what Dr Bahnasi meant by this. Today of course the population of Syria identify themselves as Arabs, but that was not the case before the Arabian conquest of Syria (c. 635–640 AD). The people of ancient Ebla were of course

Semites. True, the Arabs are also Semites (in common with the Akkadians, the Israelites, the Canaanites and others) and have even been said – though such a statement cannot rank as a scientific conclusion but rather reflects its author's preconceptions as to the character and potential of the Semite – to be the most truly Semitic Semites,[85] none of which, however, justifies talk of Ebla as Arabian. It might perhaps be argued that the original home of the Semites, in that remote era when they dwelt as one people speaking a single language, is commonly located in Arabia, in which sense *all* Semites are émigré Arabs. But if that is taken to mean that Ebla was an Arabian kingdom, one might as well argue that because the original home of the peoples whose languages belong to the Indo-European family (which includes English, Russian, Sanskrit, Greek and Latin) is often thought to have been somewhere near the Caucasus mountains or the lower Volga, ancient Rome could fairly be described as a Russian kingdom. Ebla does demonstrate the antiquity of civilization in Syria but it is very doubtful how much cultural continuity can be claimed between the Syria of the twenty-fourth century BC and of the twentieth century AD, after the impact of so many conquerors – not least the Arabs themselves – whose concern was to implant their own civilizations rather than conserve the native traditions. The acid test of language (applied above in relation to Hebrew) shows that Eblaite cannot be considered an ancestor of Arabic. Thus, for example, the Proto-Semitic *ya-* at the beginning of words still survives in Arabic (e.g. *yad* 'hand', *yaktub* 'he will write') but in Eblaite it has degenerated to *yi-* or *i-* (thus (*y*)*ida*, (*y*)*iktub*),[86] and the reconstructed Proto-Semitic form for 'our slave', viz. '*abduna*, preserved virtually unchanged in Arabic, has been modified to '*ebduni* in Eblaite.[87]

Pettinato has also found at Ebla the names of three cities – Shamutu, Ad and Iram – which he identifies with three names in the 89th Sura of the Koran. The relevant passage – though far from straightforward – has been translated:[88] 'Hast thou not seen how thy Lord did with Ad, Iram of the pillars, the like of which was never created in the land, and Thamud, who hollowed the rocks in the valley ...' Of these, Thamud is generally believed to be the name of a tribe first mentioned by Sargon II in the eighth century BC;[89] Iram has been much debated, some considering it a tribe (cf. Aram) and others a place; and Ad, thought to be a tribal name, was dismissed as mythical by that ubiquitous kill-joy Wellhausen.[90] The reported occurrence of such names at Ebla is certainly interesting, especially since the Ebla names denote cities while Ad and Thamud have been generally considered the names of tribes. It should be about as useful in substantiating the 89th Sura of the Koran as the reported occurrence of Sodom and Gomorrah in substantiating the fourteenth chapter of Genesis.

All in all, when one considers how other archaeological discoveries were first reported, public discussion of the Ebla archive so far has run more or less true to form. On the one hand, eagerness for confirmation of the Bible has always been widespread among laymen and scholars alike. Typical of the former is the enthusiastic editorial in the *Daily Telegraph* on 27 November 1872, celebrating the discovery of a cuneiform account of the Flood: 'The date of the Deluge is uncertain enough; yet certain it is that, from an age so remote that not even an approximate century can be assigned to it, news – actual "news" – has today come down to us of the great flood itself ... It is possible, nay even probable, that any moment some Egyptologist may unwrap for us a thin scroll which shall prove to be no less than a copy of the marriage settlement made by Solomon upon the eve of his nuptials with Pharaoh's daughter...'[91] Cuneiformists too have been at risk, ever since Hincks in 1849 mistook Borsippa for Jerusalem, but the best example of biblicism among scholars may be H. Grimme's treatment of the so-called Proto-Sinaitic inscriptions, discovered in the Sinai Peninsula in the winter of 1904/5 and dated by the archaeological context to c. 1500 BC. Grimme supposed that they were written in pure biblical Hebrew, albeit in an unfamiliar alphabet, and succeeded in reading them – to his own satisfaction at least. The very presence of Hebrew documents in Sinai at that date, he argued,[92] confirmed the time and the place at which the Bible states that Israel received the Ten Commandments. He moreover found three instances of a name consisting of the four consonants M N SH H, which, he noted, once (Judges 18:30) serves as a by-name of Moses. In other inscriptions he found a name

meaning 'His name (or manifestation) is the bush' and a line
which he translated 'Thou wast gracious, thou didst draw me
out of the Nile';[93] and he concluded, at least provisionally,
that the Proto-Sinaitic Inscriptions were contemporary
records of Moses himself.[94] That he also found 'clearly
enough' the name of Yahweh – in the form Y H W, which
he pronounced Yahu – goes almost without saying.[95] Subsequent scholarship, though not yet at all certain how these
texts are to be interpreted,[96] has at least agreed to reject these
results of Grimme.[97]

Meanwhile others have used ancient texts as a weapon
against the Bible. Friedrich Delitzsch amassed parallels with
Babylonian literature in an attempt to show that 'the purely
human origin and character of the Israelitish Law is sufficiently obvious', and to sustain his own novel credo: 'I believe
that in the Old Testament we have to deal with a process of
development effected or permitted by God like any other
earthly product, but, for the rest, of a purely human and historical character, in which God has *not* intervened through
"special, supernatural revelation" '.[98] The effect, which lingered
for many years, was to cast suspicion on any attempt to illuminate the Bible through Assyriology. Meanwhile Heinrich Zimmern argued from parallels that the history of Christ as told
in the New Testament was almost wholly mythical, and that
not only his birth, death and resurrection but even the episode
in which he was mocked as 'King of the Jews' were mere reflec-
tions of Babylonian lore.[99] Thus the statement from Dr Bahnasi that 'scholars were certain that the events of the Old
Testament were taken from the stories current in Mesopotamia, Syria and the coast, and now the writings of Ebla have
come to confirm that fact'[100] has not an unfamiliar ring. All
in all, the controversial treatments to which the Ebla tablets
have already been subjected, whatever they might or might
not do for Genesis 14, do at least confirm the truth of Ecclesiastes 1:9, that 'there is nothing new under the sun'.

Where then does the real significance of Ebla lie? At this stage
it would be folly to venture an answer, but one can consider
in what areas that significance may be sought.

First, while the Ebla tablets are not the oldest writings yet known,[101] they constitute by far the oldest great archive, outnumbering by about four to one all the third-millennium (or earlier) tablets that were previously known from all sites put together.[102] The beginnings of human accomplishment in whatever areas of life are represented in the tablets, such as law and religion, science and mathematics, can now be traced further back than ever before. For the first time a detailed picture can be reconstructed of the economic life of a community in the third millennium BC, and some of the mysteries which now shroud the origins of urban settlement should receive their explanation at Ebla.

The impact of Ebla on the history of the Near East has already been dramatic and will long continue. A new people with an established and flourishing culture has been identified in northern Syria in the middle of the third millennium BC, and must have arrived there centuries earlier. Their newly-discovered language shows them to have been Semites, but quite distinct from the people previously thought to have been the first Semitic inhabitants of Syria, namely the Amorites,[103] whose arrival in Syria is to be dated later in,[104] or even at the very end of,[105] the third millennium. This raises a new question: what population movements in remote antiquity must we now suppose in order to account for the presence of this new people? One possibility is that the prehistoric expansion of the Semites (from a starting-point generally located in the Syrian Desert, near the point at which the present-day borders of Jordan, Iraq and Saudi Arabia meet) which brought the Akkadians to Mesopotamia may also have branched out to Syria and established a Semitic presence there too, of which the Ebla discoveries are just our first indication. One could thus explain both the close affinity of the Eblaite language with Akkadian (both being traced back to the same wave of emigration) and its lesser affinity with the later 'North-West' Semitic languages (which would bear marks of its influence). No doubt many other possibilities will be canvassed, and lively debate can now be expected on the vast prehistoric movements out of which the various peoples of the Near East eventually emerged. Coming down to the time of the archive itself, political and other relations within a huge area will be brilliantly illuminated. For example, the involvement of Mari

with the cities to the east had long been known, but at Ebla
we now learn, unexpectedly, of her relations with a power to
the west. Again, the thousands of place names now recovered
will help to reconstruct in detail the geography of the Near
East during the third millennium. As for places already well
known from later ages – such as Hazor, Lachish and Salem
– the mention of them at Ebla affords at least an intriguing
glimpse of their earlier relations with the outside world. A precise chronology will be worked out, enabling us to date events
at Ebla and elsewhere, in figures, rather than having to speak,
as Matthiae has done, of 'Ebla in the Late Early Syrian
Period',[106] and our whole chronological framework for the
ancient world should become somewhat sounder.

A further question is how far the culture represented by the
tablets may extend, both in time and in space. From Mari a
group of administrative texts[107] of a period somewhat later
than the Ebla archive – perhaps the twentieth century BC –
exist which were, naturally enough, first thought to be in
Akkadian but turned out to present certain features without
parallel elsewhere, and have on that account intrigued scholars
for decades. But now, Gelb discovers, these peculiar features
are paralleled after all – at Ebla. Gelb has also studied the
texts yielded by Mari which are contemporary (as the mention
in them of Iblul-Il demonstrates) with the Ebla archive, and
there too has found striking links – in the writing system, in
the language, in the month names and general dating system,
and possibly even among the deities worshipped – with Ebla.
In particular, the features common to the language of Ebla
and Mari include grammatical particles - such as *i-na* 'for',
iš 'to' and perhaps *mi* 'who?' – which would not have been
borrowed from one language into another, and which betoken
close relationship. Gelb is in fact inclined to suppose, on the
evidence available, that what had previously been thought to
be the aberrant Akkadian of these Mari texts was in fact
Eblaite, so that[108] 'the so-called "Iblaic" language was spoken
not only at Ibla but also around Mari along the Euphrates,
and ... its attested lifespan extended from the pre-Sargonic
period to post-Ur III times',[109] which is to say about
2000 BC.[110] The language of Ebla thus appears at Mari also,
where it may have survived longer than at Ebla itself, and it

may well have been current elsewhere in Syria. Whether that
is so, and whether other cultural features of Ebla were more
or less widespread in Syria, will have to be determined by
excavation at other sites, perhaps at Qatna or Carchemish.
Much that has been ascribed primarily to Ebla may prove to
have been widely diffused over Syria and merely happened to
be first brought to light at Ebla. Even Matthiae's statement
that 'Ebla was the major centre of late Early Syrian culture'[111]
might conceivably come to be challenged, because the correla-
tion between the cultural importance of a site and the volume
and even the worth of what is discovered there is notoriously
imperfect. At all events, Ebla has certainly made it impossible
to maintain any longer that the lands which separate Egypt
and Mesopotamia, the two poles of ancient civilization, were
a cultural desert; as so often elsewhere, the 'native barbarians'
turn out to have been badly underestimated.[112]

More will be learnt from the revisions which Ebla will
bring about in our picture of the ceaseless process of the development and blending of cultural traditions in which our
present-day culture is ultimately rooted. A deep-seated connection between Ebla and Mesopotamia is immediately
obvious, from the use at Ebla of cuneiform, which was invented by (or at least borrowed from) the Sumerians. One can
go further and link Ebla with specific currents within the
stream of Mesopotamian tradition. At Abu Salabikh, the
external form of the tablets and the writing system are 'either
identical or very similar';[113] the same dating system and the
same month names that appear in the earlier texts from
Ebla[114] are found also at Abu Salabikh (and, as just noted, at
Mari). Some of the scholastic texts from Abu Salabikh, e.g. the
lists of professions and of geographical names, are now dupli-
cated at Ebla.[115] Again, certain features of writing found at
Ebla – notably the use of Sumerian logograms for verbs – but
not standard in Akkadian are paralleled at Mari and in some
inscriptions of Sargon and his son Rimush.[116]

Detailed study of such parallels is one thing. It is quite
another to decide who influenced whom. Not unexpectedly,
Pettinato has stated that Mesopotamia owes an enormous cultural debt to Ebla. First and foremost, writing at Ebla pre-
dated – so Pettinato evidently believes – any demonstrably

Akkadian text ever found,[117] and he has inferred that it was
Ebla that first devised the adaptation of Sumerian cuneiform
to another language, which was then passed on to Mesopotamia.[118] He supposes many other borrowings from Ebla,
though none could be quite so momentous. Regarding the geographical list common to Ebla and Abu Salabikh, in which
the location of the places had seemed wholly uncertain,[119] Pettinato announces that he has 'evidence that it was drawn up
in Syria – more precisely at Ebla – and then transmitted to
Mesopotamia'[120] – but declines to say what the evidence is.
In further explanation of the Ebla–Abu Salabikh parallels, he
suggests that many of the scribes of Abu Salabikh were in fact
imported from Ebla.[121] He would not, of course, deny that
Ebla was profoundly influenced by Mesopotamia; the knowledge of Sumerian cuneiform and the mention of visiting
scholars from Kish and Mari, are sufficient proof. But
he also supposes considerable influence in the opposite direction – though he stops well short of the statement in the Syrian
newspaper *Tishrin*, that the Ebla discoveries have added to
ancient Egypt and Mesopotamia 'a third flourishing civilization, not less important than they'.[122]

Not all may take so positive a view of the influence of Ebla
on Mesopotamia. That Eblaite preceded Akkadian cuneiform
writing is quite uncertain. Grave doubts beset the dating not
only of the Ebla archive but also of the earliest Akkadian inscriptions; there is at present no knowing which came first, and
the likelihood that, both on the Eblaite and on the Akkadian
side, an interval of unknown length separates our earliest sur-
viving material from the earliest attempts to adapt Sumerian
cuneiform, aggravates the uncertainty.[123] Beyond that, the
only evidence so far published of Ebla's priority consists of
the geographical list. The bilingual dictionaries at Ebla and
the lists in pure Eblaite do betoken great originality, but it
has not been suggested that they were taken up in Mesopotamia. At this stage, then, there is room (though after the
revelations yet to come there might not be) for the view that
Ebla was a distant provincial outpost of Mesopotamian civilization, and that the impact of its undoubted creativity, in
using cuneiform for its own language and in inventing peda-
gogic aids, was local and short-lived.

In his *Thoughts about Ibla*, Gelb comes within sight of such
an opinion. From perhaps 2800 BC he would distinguish in
Mesopotamia two separate civilizations, corresponding to the
two languages attested there, namely Sumerian and Akkadian.
Adopting as his criterion the regular use of the language, he
concludes that the Sumerian civilization was confined to
Sumer proper, and could be thought of as centred on Nippur
(though not extending many miles north of it). Again on the
basis of language, and also certain distinctive features (which
can be traced down to *c.* 2280 BC) in the writing system, he
finds that the Akkadian civilization dominated everywhere
outside Sumer, extending northwards to Mari and beyond,
and he suggests Kish as its centre. He alighted on Kish partly
because the distribution of the Akkadian culture over so wide
an area suggests that it had once been united politically, and
native tradition – e.g. in the fact that the title 'King of Kish'
came ultimately to signify dominion of the whole known world
– indicates that at an early stage, perhaps between 2900 and
2700 BC, much if not all of Mesopotamia was united under
the control of Kish.[124] Although the Akkadians were indebted
to the Sumerians for the art of writing, Gelb maintains – contrary to prevailing opinions – that they produced a civilization
of, on the whole, equal standing, from which the Sumerians
borrowed as much as they gave. Now the special features of
writing noted above as linking Ebla with Abu Salabikh and
pre-Sargonic Mari are characteristic, in Gelb's opinion, of this
northern, or Kish, tradition. He therefore suggests that the
empire of Kish may once have reached as far as Ebla. Since
Sargon, and Lugalzagesi before him, claim to have extended
their conquests to the Mediterranean, the kings of Kish may
have done the same.[125] Thus was scholarship first brought to
Ebla, and Gelb is convinced that Ebla received rather than
gave. The writing tradition of Kish derived ultimately from
Sumer, its rise long pre-dated the heyday of Ebla, and, in short,
'there is no way to even think of the cultural influence radiating
from Ibla towards Kish and the Kish tradition'. Thus also was
Ebla put into contact with so many other centres near and
far, which goes some way towards explaining the broad
outreach of her political and other relations in the period of
the archive. The renewal of excavations at Kish now seems

to Gelb to have become one of scholarship's most urgent tasks.[126]

The questions which Ebla raises about cultural radiation will long be debated. Their consequences can be important. To take a familiar instance, one of the arguments adduced in support of the biblical tradition that Israel's ancestors migrated from Mesopotamia is that the material in Genesis 1–11 exhibits countless striking resemblances to Mesopotamian tradition but finds few echoes in the early literature of Syria–Palestine.[127] Should it now transpire that Mesopotamian lore was implanted in the region as early as the mid-third millennium BC, the whole question would have to be reconsidered.

Even areas of research which are not primarily connected with Ebla at all will be illuminated by the tablets. Their sheer number raises the hope that copies of some of the compositions in pure Sumerian which are known to have existed,[128] but have never yet been discovered, may have been preserved at Ebla. The new addition to the family of Semitic languages will contribute (and would have contributed far more were it not for the profusion of Sumerian logograms) to the understanding of the other members. In view however of some of the very dubious results that have been drawn prematurely from Ugaritic,[129] we would plead that no Eblaite text whose interpretation is itself disputed be used to elucidate another Semitic language.

So much for the past, but Ebla may yet hold a lesson for the future. Here, out of the confluence of traditions of three very different peoples – Sumerians, Semites and Hurrians – there flourished a vital and creative culture, enriched by all three. The tablets should have something to tell us of how this harmony was achieved, and it is here that the world today may have most to learn from Ebla.

CHRONOLOGICAL TABLE

Any chronological table must be subject to the reservations expressed on pp. 14ff, and the earliest dates are to be treated with particular caution. The chronology adopted in the *Cambridge Ancient History* (3rd ed.) is, in the main, followed here.

BC	MESOPOTAMIA	EGYPT	EBLA
3100	Development of Sumerian city-states	Foundation of First Dynasty	Acropolis and adjacent areas occupied (perhaps since as early as 3500)
2700	Rulers of city-states include: Mebaragesi (Kish), *c.* 2700 Gilgamesh (Uruk), *c.* 2680 Aka (Kish), *c.* 2680	Old Kingdom founded 2686	
2600	Shub-Ad¶ (queen of Ur), *c.* 2600 Ur-Nanshe (Lagash), *c.* 2540	Pharaohs include: Chephren (*c.* 2550)	Range of dates proposed for Ibul-II, King of Mari, vanquished by Ebla (2685–2400)
2500	Eannatum (Lagash), *c.* 2500 Urukagina (Lagash), 2378–2371 Lugalzagesi (Umma), 2371–2347 Dynasty of Agade: Sargon (2371–2316) Rimush (2315–2307)		Destroyed by Sargon?

BC	MESOPOTAMIA	EGYPT	EBLA	BIBLICAL EVENTS
2300	Manishtushu (2306–2292) Naram-Sin (2291–2255) Shar-kali-sharri 2254–2230)	Pepi I (c. 2300)	Destroyed by Naram-Sin?	
2200	Kaku (Lagash), c. 2200 Gudea (Lagash), c. 2175	End of Old Kingdom (2181) (Middle Kingdom begins (2133)		
2100	Utuhengal (Uruk), 2120–2114 Third Dynasty of Ur: Ur-Nammu (2113–2096) Shulgi (2095–2048) Amar-Sin (2047–2039) Shu-Sin (2038–2030) Ibbi-Sin (2029–2006)			
2000	Ishbi-Erra (Isin), 2017–1985		Destruction (by Amorites?), c. 2000	Range of dates proposed for Abraham (c. 2000–1400)
1800	Hammurapi (Babylon), 1792–1750	End of Middle Kingdom (1786)		
1700	Rise of Kassite Dynasty (c. 1700)			
1600	Babylon destroyed by Hittites under Murshilis I (1590)	Hyksos Rulers (c. 1684–1567)	Destruction (by Hittites?), c. 1650–1600	
1500		New Kingdom begins 1567 Pharaohs include: Hatshepsut (1503–1482) Tuthmosis III (1504–1450¶)		
1400		Akhenaten (1379–1362)		

¶ Note co-regency.

BC	MESOPOTAMIA	EGYPT	EBLA	BIBLICAL EVENTS
1300		Ramses II (1304–1237)		Exodus (c. 1280?) Conquest (c. 1250–1200)
1200 1100	Assyria: Tiglath-Pileser I (1115–1077)	New Kingdom ends 1085	Villages founded on site of Ebla, c. 1200	Judges (1200–1020)
1000	Ashurnasirpal (1050–1032)			Saul (c. 1020–1000) David (c. 1000–960) Solomon (c. 960–922) Divided monarchy Kings of Israel / Kings of Judah
800	Shalmaneser III (859–825) Tiglath-Pileser III (745–727) Sargon II (721–705)			Ahab (869–850) Jehu (842–815) Menahem (745–738) Fall of Samaria (722/1)
700	Sennacherib (704–681) Esarhaddon (680–669) Ashurbanipal (668–627) Fall of Nineveh (612)			Manasseh (686–642) Josiah (640–609)
600	Babylonia: Nebuchadnezzar II (604–562) Cyrus takes Babylon (539)			Deportation (597) Fall of Jerusalem (587/6)
500	Persia: Cyrus (550–530) Cambyses (530–522) Darius I (son of Hystaspes) 522–486 Xerxes (486–465)	Conquered by Cambyses (525)	Renewed settlement:	Cyrus' edict (538); the Return Temple rebuilt (520–515)

Notes

Abbreviations
MAIS Missione Archeologica Italiana in Siria
JRAS Journal of the Royal Asiatic Society
TRIA Transactions of the Royal Irish Academy

Chapter 1

1 *Los Angeles Times* 7 June 1976.
2 Ibid.
3 *Philadelphia Inquirer* 7 November 1976.
4 *The Times* 26 June 1976.
5 The *Observer* 16 January 1977.
6 Interview with C. Bermant.
7 *The Tell-Mardikh Tablets*, distributed by '20th Century Reformation Hour', (Collingswood, New Jersey, 1977).
8 D.N. Freedman, 'A City Beneath the Sands' in *Science Year* 1976.
9 P. Matthiae in *Missione Archeologica in Siria* (*MAIS*) 1964 (Rome 1965), p. 17.
10 *Biblical Archaeologist*, September 1976, p. 93.
11 The *Observer* 16 January 1977.
12 P. Matthiae in *MAIS* 1964, p. 18.
13 *Biblical Archaeologist* May 1976, p. 50.
14 *Philadelphia Evening Bulletin* 9 July 1977.
15 Ibid.
16 *Tishrin* 20 September 1977.
17 Dr Bahnasi may have been the victim of a printer's error, for the Babylonian exile began in 587 and lasted till 538 BC.
18 Interview with M. Weitzman.
19 *Biblical Archaeologist* May 1976, p. 50.
20 Ibid, p. 44.
21 *The Times* 15 January 1977.
22 *Midstream* February 1977, p. 49.
23 *The Tell-Mardikh Tablets*, p. 14.
24 *Tishrin* 20 September 1977.
25 *Archaeology* (1977) p. 251.

26 *Rivista Biblica* (1977), p. 236.
27 Ibid, p. 236.

Chapter 2

1 K. Kenyon, *Archaeology in the Holy Land*, 3rd ed. (London 1970), pp. 39 ff.
2 J. Mellaart, *The Neolithic of the Near East* (London 1975), pp. 98 ff.
3 See J.-R. Kupper in *Cambridge Ancient History*, 3rd ed., (Cambridge 1970–), vol 2, pt 1, ch. 1.
4 A. Ungnad, in *Reallexikon der Assyriologie*, II, p. 430 (article 'Eponymen').
5 R.A. Parker, *The Calendars of Ancient Egypt* (Chicago 1950), p. 66.
6 This is the Sumerian king-list. A translation is available in *Ancient Near Eastern Texts*, ed. J.B. Pritchard, 2nd ed., (Princeton 1955), pp. 265 f.; the primary study is Th. Jacobsen, *The Sumerian King List* (Chicago 1939).
7 V. Gordon Childe, *Man Makes Himself*, 4th ed. (London 1965), pp. 66 ff.
8 At such early periods one tries to fix one's bearings by radio-carbon dating; see C. Renfrew, *Before Civilization* (London 1976), pp. 280–94.
9 See P.J. Ucko and G.W. Dimbleby (eds), *The Domestication and Exploitation of Plants and Animals* (London 1969).
10 J.E. Dixon, J.R. Cann and C. Renfrew, 'Obsidian and the Origins of Trade', in *Old World Archaeology: Foundations of Civilization* (Readings from *Scientific American*) (San Francisco 1972), pp. 80 ff.
11 On the place of origin of the Halaf culture, see Mellaart, *The Neolithic of the Near East*, pp. 144 ff.
12 H. Helbaek, 'Samarran Irrigation Agriculture at Choga Mami in Iraq', *Iraq* (1972), pp. 35 ff.
13 K. Wittfogel, *Oriental Despotism* (New Haven 1957); against the importance of irrigation as a stimulus for Egyptian civilization, see K.W. Butzer, *Early Hydraulic Civilization in Egypt* (Chicago 1976).
14 See David and Joan Oates, *The Rise of Civilization* (Oxford 1976), pp. 120 ff.
15 R.M. Adams, in C.H. Kraeling and R.M. Adams (eds), *City Invincible* (Chicago 1960), pp. 25 ff.
16 Seton Lloyd and Fuad Safar in *Sumer*, III (1947), pp. 84 ff., IV (1948), pp. 115 ff. and VI (1950), pp. 27 ff.
17 See, for example, H. Frankfort, *Cylinder Seals* (London 1939), p. 124.
18 Such is the main source of income of the Marsh Arabs today; see W. Thesiger, *The Marsh Arabs* (London 1964).
19 See Joan Oates, 'Ur and Eridu: the Prehistory', in M.E.L. Mallowan and D.J. Wiseman (eds), *Ur in Retrospect* (= *Iraq* XXII), (London 1960), pp. 32–50. Some however attribute a foreign origin to the Uruk culture; see H. Frankfort, *Archeology and the Sumerian Problem* (Chicago 1932). The art and architecture of the period are well illustrated by E. Strommenger, *The Art of Mesopotamia*, (London 1964).

20 E. Heinrich, in *Reallexikon der Assyriologie* IV, pp. 27 f.

21 T.B. Jones (ed), *The Sumerian Problem* (New York 1969).

22 B. Landsberger, *Three Essays on the Sumerians* (originally published 1943–5, Eng. tr. by M. de J. Ellis), *Monographs of the Near East* 1/2 (Los Angeles 1974).

23 The tradition is preserved by Berossus (F. Jacoby, *Fragmenta Graec. Hist.*, IIIC [Leyden 1958], no. 680, F 1, Sect. 4); cf. E. Reiner, 'The Etiological Myth of the "Seven Sages"', in *Orientalia* (1961), pp. 1 ff.

24 S.N. Kramer, *The Sumerians* (Chicago 1963), p. 42.

25 Cf. the myth of Enki and Ninhursag in Pritchard, *Ancient Near Eastern Texts* pp. 37 ff.; on the equation of Dilmun with Bahrein see G. Bibby, *Looking for Dilmun* (London 1970).

26 E.A. Speiser, 'The Sumerian Problem Reviewed', *Hebrew Union College Annual* 23/1 (1950–1), pp. 339 ff.

27 See Frankfort, cited in n. 19 above.

28 A. Finet in *S.N. Kramer Anniversary Volume* (ed. B.L. Eichler, Neukirchen 1976), pp. 183 ff.

29 G. Roux, *Ancient Iraq* (London 1966), p. 85.

30 According to the Sumerian king-list, the first king after the Flood had a Semitic name (Mashkakatu 'harrow' – a doubtful reading), as did some of his successors (the seventh king, for example, is named Kalibum 'dog').

31 At this time, before the effective domestication of the camel (p. 58), nomads could not stray far from fertile areas, and their way of life is often called 'semi-nomadic'. Nomadism has been the subject of several studies by M.B. Rowton, the most recent in *Journal of Near Eastern Studies* (1977), pp. 181–98.

32 Roux, *Ancient Iraq*, pp. 138 ff.

33 Kenyon, *Archaeology in the Holy Land*, pp. 101 ff.

34 In favour of Mesopotamian influence, see H. Frankfort, *The Birth of Civilization in the Near East* (London 1951), pp. 100 f.; this view is strenuously opposed by W. Helck, *Die Beziehungen Agyptens zu Vorderasien im 3. und 2. Jahrtausend v. Chr.* (Wiesbaden 1962), ch. 2.

35 See n. 6 above.

36 The section on the antediluvian kings, however, is a later addition, according to the generally accepted view of Jacobsen, *The Sumerian King List*, pp. 55 ff.

37 Kramer, *The Sumerians*, pp. 163 ff.

38 P.R.S. Moorey, 'The "Plano-Convex Building" at Kish and Early Mesopotamian Palaces', *Iraq* (1964), pp. 83 ff.

39 Translation in Pritchard (ed.), *Ancient Near Eastern Texts*, pp. 44 ff.

40 E. Sollberger and J.-R. Kupper, *Inscriptions Royales Sumériennes et Akkadiennes* (Paris 1971), no. IA1.

41 Translation in Pritchard, *Ancient Near Eastern Texts*, pp. 72 ff.; see P. Garelli (ed.), *Gilgameš et sa légende* (= *VIIème Renc. Assyr. Internationale*, Paris 1960).

42 W.W. Hallo, *Early Mesopotamian Royal Titles* (New Haven 1957), pp. 34 ff.

43 Th. Jacobsen, *Journal of Near Eastern Studies* (1953), pp. 180 ff.

44 Th. Jacobsen, *The Treasures of Darkness* (New Haven 1976), pp. 23 ff.; S.N. Kramer, *The Sacred Marriage Rite* (Bloomington 1969).

45 Ezekiel 8:13–14.

46 Kramer, *The Sumerians*, pp. 120 f.

47 Th. Jacobsen, 'Early Political Development in Mesopotamia', *Zeitschrift für Assyriologie* (1957), pp. 91–140; see pp. 104 ff.

48 A. Deimel, *Šumerische Tempelwirtschaft zur Zeit Urukaginas und seiner Vorgänger* (Rome 1931).

49 Sollberger and Kupper, no. I c 5 b.

50 Sollberger and Kupper, no. I c 7 h.

51 Kramer, *The Sumerians*, pp. 79–83.

52 See ibid, p. 323, and Sollberger and Kupper, no. I c 11 m.

53 Hruška, in P. Garelli (ed.), *Le Palais et la Royauté (= Recontre Assyriologique* XIX, Paris 1974), pp. 151–61.

54 Kramer, *The Sumerians*, p. 79.

55 Sollberger and Kupper, no. I h 2 b.

56 The texts have been edited by H. Hirsch, 'Die Inschriften der Könige von Agade', *Archiv für Orientforschung* XX (1963), pp. 1 ff.

57 See the translation of his birth legend in Pritchard, *Ancient Near Eastern Texts*, p. 119.

58 See D.J. Wiseman in *New Bible Dictionary*, ed. J.D. Douglas (London 1962), p. 888.

59 Such, essentially, is the order of events envisaged by Kramer, *The Sumerians*, pp. 60 f., C.J. Gadd in *Cambridge Ancient History*, vol. 1, pt 2, ch. 19, and many others.

60 See W.W. Hallo, in *The Ancient Near East*, ed. J.M. Blum (New York 1971), pp. 55 ff.

61 A portrait of her is shown in ibid, p. 26 (fig. 4).

62 E. Weidner, 'Der Zug Sargons von Akkad nach Kleinasien', *Boghazköi Studien* VI (1922), pp. 57–99, argues that this is a mere historical romance.

63 Kramer, *The Sumerians*, p. 61.

64 U. Moortgat-Correns, in *Reallexikon der Assyriologie* IV, pp. 480–7.

65 Sollberger and Kupper, no. II a 2 e.

66 Ibid, no. II a 3 b; Kramer, *The Sumerians*, pp. 61 f.

67 A.K. Grayson, *Assyrian Royal Inscriptions*, I (Wiesbaden 1972), pp. 2 f, 22 ff.

68 Kramer, *The Sumerians*, p. 62.

69 See Kramer, loc. cit.

70 Jacobsen in *Zeitschrift für Assyriologie* (1957) p. 138, n. 108, suggests that the king's divinization was to show that the 'genius' of the country was embodied in him, rather than to add him to the pantheon.

71 See discussion by Hallo, *Early Mesopotamian Royal Titles* (New Haven 1957), pp. 65 ff.

72 Strommenger, *The Art of Mesopotamia*, plates 122–3.

73 See the diagram of the royal house of Akkad, drawn up by Hallo in *The Ancient Near East*, p. 58.

74 M. Mallowan, *Iraq* (1947), pp. 63 ff.

75 E. Porada, *The Art of Ancient Iran* (London 1965), p. 40 and fig. 15.

76 Kramer, *The Sumerians*, p. 64.

77 See especially W.W. Hallo, in *Reallexikon der Assyriologie* III, pp. 708 ff. (article 'Gutium'), and E. A. Speiser, 'Some Factors in the Collapse of Akkad', *Journal of the American Oriental Society* (1952), pp. 97 ff.

78 I.J. Gelb, *Hurrians and Subarians* (Chicago 1944).

79 Ibid. 'New Light on Hurrians and Subarians', in *Studi Orientalistici in onore di Giorgio Levi della Vida* (Rome 1956) I, pp. 378 ff.

80 Particularly Kenyon, *Archaeology in the Holy Land*, pp. 135 ff.

81 Various officials were acquiring such power as to establish what amounted to local dynasties; see W. Helck, *Geschichte des alten Ägypten*, in *Handbuch der Orientalistik* (ed. B. Spuler) I. 2. iii (Leyden 1968), pp. 71 ff.

82 On the Amorites in general, see M. Liverani in *Peoples of Old Testament Times*, ed. D.J. Wiseman (Oxford 1973), pp. 100–33.

83 E. Sollberger, 'Sur la chronologie des rois d'Ur', *Archiv für Orientforschung* XVII (1954–6), pp. 10 ff.; see n. 8.

84 Th. Jacobsen, in *Zeitschrift für Assyriologie* (1957), p. 138.

85 He also promulgated a law-code. See J.J. Finkelstein, 'The Laws of Ur-Nammu', *Journal of Cuneiform Studies* (1968), pp. 66–82.

86 On the last see H. Frankfort, S. Lloyd and T. Jacobsen, *The Gimilsin Temple and the Palace of the Rulers at Tell Asmar* (Chicago 1940).

87 Kramer, *The Sumerians*, p. 254.

88 G. Buccellati, *The Amorites of the Ur III Period* (Naples 1966).

89 See Gelb, *Hurrians and Subarians*.

90 On the last days of the Ur Empire see Jacobsen in *Journal of Cuneiform Studies* (1953), pp. 36 ff.

91 P. Garelli, *Les Assyriens en Cappadoce* (Paris 1963).

92 See Pritchard (ed.), *Ancient Near Eastern Texts*, pp. 163 ff. for a translation of the code of Hammurapi.

93 In 1962 D.J. Wiseman suggested 'at a conservative estimate, almost a quarter of a million' as the number of cuneiform texts recovered. See *The Expansion of Assyrian Studies* (London 1962), p. 8.

94 For detailed lists see G. Pettinato in *MAIS* 1967–8 (Estratto), ed. P. Matthiae (Rome 1972); M. Heltzer, in *Annali dell' Istituto Orientale di Napoli* (1975), pp. 298 ff.; Pettinato in *Reallexikon der Assyriologie* (1976) V, pp. 9 ff.

95 Pettinato in *MAIS* claims that one reference (3.4) predates Sargon, but others assign it to the period of Gutian domination. See I.J.Gelb, *Old Akkadian Writing and Grammar*, 2nd ed., (Chicago 1961), p. 11.

96 Translation by A.L. Oppenheim, in *Ancient Near Eastern Texts* (ed. Pritchard), p. 268.

97 On this title, see p. 22.

98 E. Weidner, 'Das Reich Sargons von Akkad', *Archiv für Orientforschung*, 16 (1952–3), pp. 1–24; see especially p. 4.

99 M. Lambert, 'Masse d'armes de pierre au nom de Naramsin', in *Orientalia* (1968), pp. 85 f. Various duplicates survive.

100 Akkadian had just three primary vowels *a i u* (or rather six, in that each can be either short or long), and *e* seems to have functioned merely as

a shade of sound which an original *a* or *i* might on occasion assume, but without the meaning ever being affected. (Contrast the situation in English, where, for example, *pan pen pin* are all distinct in sense.) One therefore hesitates to prefer the claims of *e* rather than *i* without cogent proof. Now two texts of the *second* millennium spell the name of the city with the E sign added at the beginning, showing that the pronunciation 'Ebla' (not 'Ibla') was then current; many are thus satisfied that Ebla is correct. It remains possible, however, that the pronunciation in the *third* millennium and earlier was in fact 'Ibla'. See P. Fronzaroli, in *Journal of Semitic Studies* (1977), p. 153, and references there cited.

101 Translated by J. Bottéro, *Cambridge Ancient History*, I, pt 2 (1971), pp. 325 f.

102 Pettinato, *MAIS* 2.1.1 and 2.2.1 (whence the foregoing translation).

103 Ibid, 3.3.5.

104 Ibid, under heading (3), notably 3.1.3 (pigs), 3.2.1 (beer).

105 Ibid, p. 33, n. 74.

106 See T.B. Jones and J.W. Snyder, *Neo-Sumerian Economic Texts* ... (University of Minnesota 1961), p. 212; Buccellati, *The Amorites of the Ur III Period*, p. 302.

107 Pettinato in *MAIS*, 3.3.8; 3.1.2; 3.1.1.

108 *Journal of Cuneiform Studies* (1961), p. 35.

109 Following the chronology adopted in the *Cambridge Ancient History*, 3rd ed.

110 'Empfang von Hölzern (zum Aufwickeln der Wolle?)' suggested by A. Pohl, *Rechts- und Verwaltungsurkunden der III Dynastie von Ur* (Leipzig 1937), p. 15.

111 'Wurfhölzer', according to B. Landsberger, *Türk Tarih Kurumu: Belleten* (1939), p. 223.

112 Pettinato in *MAIS* 3.3.1, 2,16.

113 Ibid, 3.0.1.

114 A.J. Ferrara, *Nanna-Suen's Journey to Nippur* (Rome 1973), p. 87.

115 E. Sollberger, *Journal of Cuneiform Studies* (1965), p. 26; all references in Pettinato in *MAIS* under 3.4.

116 B. Kienast, *Altassyrische Texte* (Berlin 1960), p. 47. The tablets were bought from dealers, but almost certainly from Kültepe (Kanesh), level II (p. v).

117 The rate varied ordinarily between 1:46 and 1:180, but the Eblaites offered 1:25.7. What follows is a free paraphrase.

118 Pettinato in *MAIS*, 7.1.1,2,4,5; 7.2.1.

119 M. Astour, *Journal of Near Eastern Studies*, (1963) p. 232.

120 Pettinato in *Reallexikon der Assyriologie* V, p. 11.

121 For references, see Pettinato in *MAIS*, pp. 36 f.

122 W.F. Albright, *Bulletin of the American Schools of Oriental Research* (1939), pp. 28 f.

123 C.J. Gadd (ed.), *Ur Excavations: Texts I* (London 1928), p. 80.

124 *Journal of Cuneiform Studies* (1953), p. 103, n. 4.

Chapter 3

1 The best-known book in this category must be W. Keller, *The Bible as History* (London 1956). One of the best informed of recent works is K.A. Kitchen, *The Bible in its World* (Exeter 1977).

2 J.H. Hertz, *Affirmations of Judaism* (London 1927), p. 49.

3 M. Magnusson, *BC: The Archaeology of the Bible Lands* (London 1977), p. 113. See also p. 23 ('obviously a legend, and a borrowed and garbled one at that'); p. 49 ('confused and rambling material'); p. 58 ('quite obviously a folk-tale'); p. 80 ('those areas that the Israelites mastered and then rationalized as having been the "Promised Land"'); p. 120 ('we are dealing with saga, not history'); p. 161 ('the prejudiced accounts in the Bible'); p. 207 '(the Book of Daniel is known to be a very late composition ... and it has no historical value whatsoever'). Despite the title, these pronouncements proceed not from the 'concrete evidence' of archaeology but from the intangibilities of literary criticism. Compare the rejoinder by A.R. Millard, *The Bible BC: What can Archaeology Prove?* (Leicester 1977).

4 J.B. Pritchard, in foreword to Magnusson, op. cit.

5 Kitchen, *The Bible in its World*, p. 7.

6 R.E. Clements, *A Century of Old Testament Study* (Guildford and London 1976) provides a useful point of entry for the reader who wishes to go further.

7 See Exodus 17:14, 24:4, 34:27, Numbers 32:2, Deuteronomy 1:1, 31:9, 22.

8 Among those that have no portion in the World to Come is he that denies that the Pentateuch is from Heaven (*Mishnah* Sanhedrin 11:1), even if he declared that all but one verse was from Heaven but that that one verse was not uttered by God but was Moses' own (*Talmud* Sanhedrin 99a).

9 For this date, see J.J. Slotki, *Index Volume to the Soncino Talmud*, (London 1952), pp. 681b, 694b, 724a.

10 *Talmud* Baba Bathra 15a.

11 He was born towards the end of the first century; see G. Quispel's edition of his *Letter to Flora* (Paris 1949), p. 5.

12 For an English translation, see R. M. Grant (ed.), *Gnosticism: An Anthology* (London 1961), pp. 184–90.

13 The unknown author is troubled by the account of Moses' death, and also by passages which to him seem to deny the perfection of God (e.g. his omniscience, at Genesis 18:21).

14 A convenient English edition is *Ante-Nicene Christian Library* (Edinburgh 1870), vol. 17.

15 Commentary on Genesis 36:31.

16 Exodus 24:4, Numbers 33:2, and (especially) Deuteronomy 31:9.

17 A. Geiger, *Nachgelassene Schriften*, ed. L. Geiger, (Berlin 1875), II, p. 165.

18 Compare also Leviticus 18:24–30, which seems to look back on the conquest.

19 Joseph was at least seventeen (Genesis 37:2) when he was sold to Egypt, and thirty (41:46) when first summoned before Pharaoh; there

immediately followed seven years of plenty (41:52), and Joseph's brothers arrived in Egypt after a further two years (45:6).

20 The episodes described could not have begun before Joseph's sale, since Genesis 38:1 explicitly states 'And it came to pass *at that time*'.

21 Contrast Genesis 1:1–2:4 (where animals are created before man), and Genesis 2:5 ff. (where man – though not woman – is created before animals).

22 Genesis 21:22 ff. and 26:36 ff.

23 Genesis 32:29 and 35:10.

24 *Conjectures sur les mémoires originaux dont il paroit que Moyse s'est servi pour composer le Livre de la Genèse* (Brussels 1753). On the state of biblical criticism up to Astruc's time, see A. Lods, *Jean Astruc et la critique biblique au XVIIIᵉ siècle* (Paris 1924).

25 W.M.L. de Wette, *Dissertatio ... Deuteronomium a prioribus Pentateuchi libris diversum ... esse. ...* Deuteronomy's characteristic style can be appreciated even in translation. Certain expressions (e.g. 'the land which the Lord will give thee', 'with all thy heart and with all thy soul') are repeated time and again. The verses tend to be somewhat longer (average: 15.0 words) than in the rest of the Pentateuch (average: 13.7 words).

26 H. Hupfeld, *Die Quellen der Genesis und die Art ihrer Zusammensetzung* (Berlin 1853).

27 E.g. Genesis 1, with set phrases 'And God said', 'and it was so', 'and it was evening and it was morning'.

28 E.g. Genesis 20:1–17.

29 Genesis 28:10–22 and 35:9–15.

30 Genesis 32:28 and 35:9–15.

31 A.T. Chapman, *An Introduction to the Pentateuch* (Cambridge 1911), p. 68. This phenomenon is attributed to a belief, on the part of both E and P, that the name Yhwh was first revealed to mankind when Moses received the divine call to bring Israel out of Egypt; see Exodus 3:13 f. (E) and Exodus 6:2 f. (P).

32 See, e.g., J.E. Carpenter and G. Harford, *The Composition of the Hexateuch* (London 1902).

33 But the separation of J and E is particularly difficult after Exodus 3; the term JE is sometimes used of material which may come from either or mix the two in unknown proportions.

34 Deuteronomy 4:19, 17:3.

35 See especially his *Prolegomena to the History of Israel* (Eng. tr., Edinburgh 1885).

36 We have refrained from adducing here the 'Jehovistic laws' (e.g. Exodus 20:24, 22:30) suggesting a multiplicity of sanctuaries, since we could not argue at this point that they belong to (and can therefore be used to date) *both* J *and* E.

37 For example, the angel speaks to Hagar on earth (Genesis 16:7) in J, but from heaven (Genesis 21:17) in E. Jacob amassed wealth while in Laban's employment through his own sheer cunning according to J (Genesis 30:29 ff.), but through God's intervention against Laban's attempts to cheat him according to E (Genesis 31:9 ff.).

38 See e.g. Numbers chaps. 1–3, 31.

39 *Prolegomena to the History of Israel*, pp. 348, 405.

40 A suggestion aired, for example, in S.R. Driver's *Commentary on Exodus* (Cambridge 1911), p. 349.

41 We find a (somewhat larger than life) reflection of this shift in Ezekiel (44:10 ff.), who restricts the priesthood to the sons of Zadok, who were just one branch of the family of Aaron.

42 Wellhausen, *Prolegomena to the History of Israel*, pp. 318–19.

43 First we hear of Judith, Basemath (Genesis 26:34) and Mahalath (28:9); of these, 36:1 mentions Basemath alone, but adds Adah and Oholibamah.

44 This is accepted in O. Eissfeldt, *The Old Testament: An Introduction* (Eng. tr. Oxford 1965), who calls his two Yahwistic sources L and J, and R.H. Pfeiffer, *Introduction to the Old Testament* (New York 1941) – S and J.

45 B. Baentsch, *Exodus-Leviticus-Numeri, übersetzt und erklärt* (Göttingen 1903).

46 Note that Psalms 105, 106 present history in a cultic context. The nature of the festival(s) concerned is debated: Passover, New Year, an annual renewal of the covenant between the twelve tribes? Law – as the revelation of God's will – as well as history would have been communicated to the people at such festivals, and so this approach in particular promises to explain the continual juxtaposition of narrative and law in the Pentateuch.

47 Many of the alternative schemes once advanced in preference to Wellhausen's – e.g. to date D soon after Solomon, or later than the exile, or to make P the earliest source – thus came to look misconceived.

48 Thus, most think J predominantly early, but would see Abraham's plea for Sodom (Genesis 18:23 ff.) as a late element; P is thought mainly post-exilic, but the duties of the next-of-kin (Leviticus 25:25 ff.) seem pre-exilic.

49 *Critical Essays on the Old Testament* (London 1970), pp. 50–67.

50 H. Gunkel, *What Remains of the Old Testament* (London 1928), pp. 180 ff.

51 Ibid, p. 160.

52 Such as W.F. Albright, *The Archaeology of Palestine and the Bible* (New York, 1933), pp. 146 ff. and E.A. Speiser, *Genesis* (New York 1964), p. 38.

53 T.L. Thompson, *The Historicity of the Patriarchal Narratives* (Berlin 1974); J. van Seters, *Abraham in History and Tradition* (New Haven 1975).

54 Van Seters does however admit that J. incorporated the work of two earlier authors (including, for example, the promise of the land to Abraham, in Genesis 12:7) into his own.

55 More examples appear in A. Cohen (ed.), *The Soncino Chumash* (London 1956).

56 Cf. J.H. Hertz, *The Pentateuch and Haftorahs* (London 1963), p. 493.

57 Thus R.K. Harrison, *Introduction to the Old Testament* (London 1970), who is committed to the infallibility of scripture (p. 475), admits several scribal glosses (p. 524).

58 Apart from the last few verses of Deuteronomy (see p. 45).

59 *Midrash Rabbah* Numbers XVII.2, – citing Ecclesiastes 9:7.

60 For references, see L. Ginzberg, *The Legends of the Jews* (Philadelphia 1928), VI pp. 316 f.

61 Talmud Yebamoth 90b; Maimonides, *Hilekoth Yesode Hatorah* 9.3.

62 Talmud Menaḥoth 45a. The root underlying the Hebrew word for 'month' (ḥodesh) means 'new'.

63 See Menaḥoth 45a.

64 *Introduction to the Old Testament* (London 1970), p. 525.

65 Critics may retort that it is the presence of duplicates *which show no awareness of one another* that suggests that the Pentateuch is composite: why, for example, are Abraham and Sarah in Genesis 20 oblivious of their experience in Genesis 12:10 ff?

66 *Sifrei* on Numbers 10:33.

67 J. Barr, *Fundamentalism* (London 1977), pp. 56 ff., discusses similar harmonizations, involving multiple events, in the interpretation of the Gospels.

68 In what follows, the words underlined are extracted from the text.

69 *New Bible Dictionary*, ed. J.D. Douglas (London 1962), p. 657. Kitchen supplied the Egyptian original for all three terms used to denote the 'one general foe'.

70 E.g. in David's census Israel was found to number 800,000 men and Judah 500,000 according to 2 Samuel 24:9, while 1 Chronicles 21:5 gives the figures as 1,100,000 and 470,000.

71 R.K. Harrison, *Introduction to the Old Testament* (London 1970), pp. 1163, 633. The Rabbis avoided this source of embarrassment by declaring that Chronicles was written for homiletic rather than historical purposes (*Midrash Rabbah* Leviticus, I.3).

72 *New Bible Dictionary*, p. 478.

73 *Midrash Rabbah* Genesis, XXXIII:4.

74 H.M. Wiener, *The Origin of the Pentateuch* (London 1910), p. 118.

75 E.A. Speiser, *Genesis* (New York 1964), p. XXIX.

76 J.D. Purvis, *The Samaritan Pentateuch and the Origin of the Samaritan Sect* (Harvard 1968); R.J. Coggins, *Samaritans and Jews* (Oxford 1975), esp. pp. 148 ff.

77 See discussion by J. van Seters, *Abraham in History and Tradition*, p. 17.

78 W.F. Albright, *From the Stone Age to Christianity* (Baltimore 1957), p. 165; J. Bright, *A History of Israel* (London 1972), p. 80; J. van Seters, op. cit., p. 17.

79 Various dates within the second millennium are suggested for the Patriarchs; see Thompson, *Historicity of Patriarchal Narratives*, pp. 315 ff.

80 See J. A. Thompson in *Interpreter's Dictionary of the Bible* (New York 1962) 'camel'; E.A. Speiser, *Genesis*, p. 90.

81 Following T.C. Mitchell in *New Bible Dictionary*, p. 990 and Harrison, *Introduction to the Old Testament*, pp. 311 f.

82 Speiser, *Genesis*, p. 80.

83 John Garstang and J.B.E. Garstang, *The Story of Jericho* (London 1940); see esp. pp. 129 ff.

84 Kathleen M. Kenyon, *Digging Up Jericho* (London 1957), Ch. 7.

85 Ibid, p. 262.

86 A date *c.* 1400 is suggested by the Bible itself; 1 Kings 6:1 places the Exodus 480 years before (so that the settlement, after 40 years in the wil-

derness, would be 440 years before) the foundation of the Temple in or about 967 BC (a date reached by working backwards from a reference to Ahab in the Assyrian records for 853 BC; see J. Gray in M. Black (ed), *Peake's Commentary on the Bible* (London 1962), pp. 70 ff.). But breaks in occupation datable to the thirteenth century at Lachish, Hazor and elsewhere support a later date (see further J. Bright, *History of Israel*, pp. 121 ff.); then 480 is merely schematic ($= 12 \times 40$).

87 Kenyon, *Digging Up Jericho*, pp. 262 f.

88 Kitchen, *The Bible in its World*, p. 89.

89 See J.A. Callaway in *Encyclopedia of Archaeological Excavations in the Holy Land*, ed. M. Avi-Yonah (London 1975–), article 'Ai'.

90 Harrison, *Introduction to the Old Testament*, pp. 327 f.

91 Kitchen, *The Bible in its World*, pp. 89 f.

92 See the discussion by J.M. Miller, 'Archaeology and the Israelite Conquest of Canaan: Some Methodological Observations' in *Palestine Exploration Quarterly* (1977), pp. 87–93.

93 D.J. Wiseman, *New Bible Dictionary*, p. 889.

94 *Ancient Mesopotamia* (Chicago 1964), p. 116; similarly Wiseman.

95 Babylon fell in 539 BC. The historical Darius I (a Persian, not a Mede) began his reign in 521 BC.

96 D.J. Wiseman et al., *Notes on Some Problems in the Book of Daniel* (London 1965).

97 Taking the *waw*, usually 'and', as explicative: cf. 1 Chronicles 5:26 ('the spirit of Pul king of Assyria *even* the spirit of Tiglath–Pileser king of Assyria').

98 Herodotus 1:107, though Ctesias (*Persica*, ed. F. W. König [Graz 1972], p. 2) disagrees.

99 For another attempt to defend the historicity of Darius the Mede, see J.C. Whitcomb, *Darius the Mede* (Grand Rapids 1959).

100 See discussion by R. de Vaux, *The Early History of Israel* (London 1978), I, pp. 291 ff.

101 Kitchen, *Bible in its World*, pp. 11 ff. has a useful discussion of the problems here.

102 See W.G. Dever in *Encyclopedia of Excavations in the Holy Land*, p. 492.

103 Statement in *Challenge*, ed. A. Carmell and C. Domb (London 1976), pp. 143–9. But even among orthodox Jews, his is by no means the general view; others are described on pp. 123–285.

104 The figures in Genesis 5 and Genesis 7:6 place it in the year 1656 after the creation, yielding a date 2349 BC according to James Ussher, archbishop of Armagh (*Annales Veteris Testamenti*, London 1650), and 2106 BC according to the conventional Jewish reckoning. Compare the dates involved in the debate as to who destroyed Ebla – Sargon (2371–2316) or Naram-Sin (2291–2255) – following the chronology of the *Cambridge Ancient History* (3rd ed.).

105 Editorial insertion by G.E. Wright in John Bright's article 'Has archaeology found evidence of the Flood?' *Biblical Archaeologist* (1942), pp. 55–62.

106 J. Bright, *Biblical Archaeologist* (1942), p. 58.

107 Reports that parts of Noah's ark have been found (see W. Keller, *The Bible as History*, (1974), p. 58) do perhaps deserve a footnote, to give us the opportunity of stating that they are without any confirmation and belong to gossip rather than scholarship.

108 See Sir James G. Frazer, *Folklore in the Old Testament* (London 1918), I, pp. 104–332.

109 J. Bright, *Biblical Archaeologist* (1942), p. 60.

110 T.C. Mitchell in *New Bible Dictionary*, p. 429, mentions theories which associate the Flood with the last glaciation (*c.* 10,000 BC).

111 The statement in *Midrash Rabbah* Genesis XXXIII.9 that the Flood did not cover the land of Israel is reminiscent of this view but only superficially.

112 Despite the valiant attempt of Mitchell in *New Bible Dictionary*, p. 427b.

113 See J. Barr, *Fundamentalism*, (London 1977), pp. 94 ff.

114 Justin, *Dialogue* 67:1. We cite the English translation of A. Lukyn Williams (London 1930).

115 1 Samuel 17:34 f.

116 *Babel and Bible* ed. C.H.W. Johns (New York 1903), p. 22.

117 The title of an article by S. Sandmel in *Journal of Biblical Literature* (1962), pp. 1–13.

118 *Dialogue*, 69:1 ff.

119 'Berosus the Chaldean ... recorded some of the most ancient inscriptions, in which are described the Flood and the Tower of Babel, among other relevant facts. These are all intermingled with the fantasies and stupidities of the ancient idol-worshippers', from A. Miller, *Rejoice, O Youth* (New York 1962), p. 65.

120 *The Archaeology of Palestine and the Bible*, (New York 1933), p. 127.

121 *New York Times*, 28 October 1956, Section VII. Not that Glueck approved of the book whole-heartedly; he warns the reader to 'sprinkle not only grains but even barrels of salt on some of its contents'.

122 C. Renfrew, *Before Civilization* (London 1976), p. 108.

123 A.G. Lie, *The Inscriptions of Sargon II* (Paris 1929), p. 7.

124 A.K. Grayson, *Assyrian and Babylonian Chronicles* (New York 1975), pp. 73 ff.

125 C.J. Gadd, 'Inscribed Barrel Cylinder of Marduk-Apla-Iddina II', *Iraq* (1953), pp. 123–34 (esp. p. 128).

126 But the position of A. Miller (*Rejoice O Youth*, p. 56) that 'every archaeologist reads as he pleases' is offensive.

127 See S.M. Paul and W.G. Dever (eds.), *Biblical Archaeology* (Jerusalem 1973), p. 97.

128 See references in Paul and Dever.

129 L.B. Patton, *A Critical and Exegetical Commentary on the Book of Esther* (Edinburgh 1908), p. 205. He adds that the total annual income of the Persian empire, on the basis of Herodotus' testimony, amounted to 17,000 Babylonian talents.

130 There is also the evidence of classical writers, which confirm some points (e.g. that there was a council of state consisting of seven viziers – 1:14) and contradict others (notably, Herodotus' statement that Xerxes' queen was

Amestris, daughter of a Persian general); but as we are dealing with the bearing of *archaeology* on the Bible, we leave the classical evidence aside.

131 Indeed the first decipherer of the name in its Old Persian form tells us how he found confirmation in the biblical name; G.F. Grotefend, in A.H.L. Heeren, *Historical Researches* ... (Eng. tr., London 1846), II, p. 335.

132 R.G. Kent, *Old Persian* (New Haven 1953), p. 151.

133 The Akkadian form is *pūru*, which could well have been borrowed into contemporary Persian.

134 M. Dieulafoy, 'Le livre d'Esther et le palais d'Assuérus', in *Revue des Etudes Juives* (1888), pp. CCLXV–CCXCI; see p. CCLXVIII.

135 Ibid, p. CCLXXVII *et seq.* We cite Dieulafoy's results uncritically; some present-day archaeologists have little faith in his findings, based on relatively primitive methods of excavation.

136 So L.E. Browne in *Peake's Commentary on the Bible*, ed. Black, p. 382a; this is just one out of a host of opinions.

137 The Bible separates the patriarchal age from the Exodus by 430 years at Exodus 12:41, but by only three generations (suggesting a shorter period) in Exodus 6:16 f., Numbers 16:1. Given such dates for the Exodus as those mentioned in n. 86, the patriarchs must be dated to the fourteenth century BC at the very latest.

138 Bright, *A History of Israel*, p. 77 f. See also Albright, *The Archaeology of Palestine and the Bible*, p. 133.

139 See Paul and Dever, *Biblical Archaeology*, pp. VII–XI.

140 A topic about which the Bible has little to say, not out of general misanthropy (as is sometimes alleged) but because the Bible's first concerns lie elsewhere. Similarly the political manoeuvres of Hezekiah in relation to the Assyrians are not mentioned, even though Hezekiah receives warm approbation in the Bible.

Chapter 4

1 P. Fr. Antonio de Gouvea, *Relaçam em que se tratam das guerras* ..., (Lisbon 1611), p. 32.

2 *De emendatione temporum* (Leyden 1583).

3 *Calendar of State Papers* (*Domestic Series*), *1698*, ed. E. Bateson (London 1933), p. 389.

4 *Historia Religionis Veterum Persarum* (Oxford 1700), p. 526, where he speaks of 'ductuli pyramidales seu cuneiformes'.

5 Carsten Niebuhr, *Voyage en Arabie* (Amsterdam 1780), II, p. 117 n.

6 Ibid., p. 112.

7 He drew up an 'alphabet' reproduced in ibid, facing p. 106.

8 The main movement is usually said to have begun about 775 AD, but the true date may well be over a century later; see S.H. Hodivala, *Studies in Parsi History* (Bombay 1920), pp. 1–17.

9 R. Schwab, *Vie d'Anquetil-Duperron* (Paris 1934).

10 See most recently A.S. Shahbazi in *Bulletin of the School of Oriental and African Studies* (1977), pp. 34 f.

11 A term used for written Middle Persian, i.e. the Persian language between about 300 BC and 900 AD.

12 A. I. Silvestre de Sacy, *Mémoires sur diverses antiquités de la Perse* (Paris 1793).

13 Vol. II, Tab. xxvii.

14 Now known as Middle Persian (Pahlavi) and Parthian.

15 To the Persians this term (which *may* by etymology mean 'noble') simply meant 'Iranian', whence also the name Iran. The extension of the term to the whole Indo-European family to which the languages of Iran belong (as do also Sanskrit, Latin, Greek, English, Russian, etc.) and thence to the 'race' supposed to consist of speakers of those languages, dates only from the last century or two.

16 O.G. Tychsen, *De Cuneatis Inscriptionibus Persepolitanis* (Rostock 1798), p. 24. He says that the stroke 'ante et post monosyllabas et disyllabas haud raro *vel* ommittitur ... *vel* abundat'.

17 Frederik Münter, *Versuch über die keilförmigen Inschriften* (Copenhagen 1802), p. 113.

18 The name Takht-e-Jamshid seems to have gained the ascendant only during the most recent centuries; the earliest European travellers (fifteenth to seventeenth centuries) report the name Chehel Minar ('Forty Columns').

19 *Histoire de l'astronomie ancienne* (2nd ed., 1781), pp. 129 f., 354 f.

20 Garcia de Sylva y Figueroa, *De Rebus Persarum Epistola* (Antwerp 1620), p. 6.

21 Cf. Diodorus Siculus 1:46, 17:72.

22 Sir John Chardin visited Takht-e-Jamshid between 1666 and 1674, and an account of his travels appeared (in French) in 1711.

23 Münter pointed to Herodotus 7:70.

24 Münter, *Versuch über die keilförmigen Inschriften*, pp. 100 ff.

25 Ibid., p. 107 n. where Münter offers examples like *Keoue* and *opeste*.

26 He is often credited with having discovered the *a* sign; in fact he explained it as '*e* to include bright *a*', and the sign which he took as straightforward *a* is actually *m(a)*.

27 Münter, *Versuch über die keilförmigen Inschriften*, pp. 87 ff.

28 Ibid. Compare pp. 123 ff. with p. 89.

29 In his original paper (published by W. Meyer, *Nachrichten von der Königl. Gesellschaft der Wissenschaften zu Göttingen* (1893), pp. 571 ff.) he does not mention de Sacy's work, but in a later account (accessible in English in A.H.L. Heeren, *Historical Researches* (London 1846), II, pp. 319 ff.) he acknowledges its aid.

30 The extra ending on the second occurrence must be equivalent to the *of ... s* in 'king *of* king*s*'; in grammatical terminology it must be the case-ending of the genitive plural.

31 i.e. Darius I (521–486 BC) and Xerxes I (486–465 BC).

32 As his original paper puts it, 'quadrare videretur' (p. 581); this seems more authentic than the complex and somewhat obscure reasoning (or, we suspect, rationalization) in his later account (Heeren, p. 332). In the latter his own memory of the decipherment may have faded; certainly his recol-

lection of de Sacy's inscriptions as 'N.N. REX MAGNUS(?) REX REGUM . . .'
is badly defective.

33 Meyer, p. 581 (Hebrew only); Heeren, p. 333 (citing also the accusative
Dareiauēn from Strabo 16.4.27, implying *Dareiauēs* as nominative; the
common reading *Dariēkēn* was considered corrupt).

34 Heeren, pp. 333–5; *kh* is to be pronounced rather like *ch* in Scots 'loch'
or German 'nach'. Grotefend thought that the same character could
express either A or Ê – an open *e*, distinct from the closed vowel which
is denoted E.

35 Heeren, p. 334. Grotefend does not say how he decided that the errors
were in Xerxes' rather than Darius' name.

36 Meyer, pp. 581 f.; Heeren, p. 340.

37 There is no need to dwell on Grotefend's unsuccessful attempts at this
point to pronounce the third word (which he rightly took as an adjective
going with 'king' and meaning 'valiant' or the like) in either inscription
and the endings added to 'king'; see Meyer, p. 582.

38 Grotefend does not tell us how he answered this question; what follows
is conjectural.

39 On the third word in either inscription see n. 37.

40 Meyer, p. 583; Heeren, p. 333. The last three characters were discarded
as the case-ending.

41 Meyer, p. 583 (whence it is clear that Grotefend was *not* guided by this
factor to his initial choice of royal names); Heeren, p. 342.

42 R. G. Kent, *Old Persian: Grammar, Texts, Lexicon* (New Haven 1953),
p. 135.

43 Grotefend found his improbable Moro in Duperron's Avesta (II,
p. 349) as one of the twenty-eight 'male' constellations; see Meyer,
p. 583.

44 See Meyer. The first paper had been read on 4 September 1802, and this
later paper on 20 May 1803.

45 For details see S.A. Pallis, *The Antiquity of Iraq*, (Copenhagen 1956), pp.
105 ff.

46 See Kent, *Old Persian Grammar*, p. 136 (DPe).

47 C. Lassen, *Die Altpersischen Keil-Inschriften von Persepolis* (Bonn 1836),
p. 146.

48 See Pallis, pp. 89 f.

49 Rawlinson, *Journal of the Royal Asiatic Society* (1847), p. 187.

50 Diodorus of Sicily called it Bagistan (2:18 – *to Bagistanon oros*). Behistun
(for which Bahistun might be more correct) was derived from the Arabic
geographer Yaqut by Rawlinson; see L.W. King and R.C. Thompson,
*The Sculptures and Inscriptions of Darius the Great on the Rock of Behistun
in Persia* (London 1907), p. xi.

51 A. J. Booth, *The Discovery and Decipherment of the Trilingual Cuneiform
Inscriptions* (London 1902), p. 106.

52 See *JRAS* (1847), p. 5. The matter is further discussed by Pallis, *Antiquity
of Iraq* (pp. 110 f.), who points out that Rawlinson in 1839 was under the
misapprehension that the inscriptions studied by Grotefend were not from
Persepolis but were the very ones that Rawlinson himself had copied at

Mt Elvend (*JRAS*, p. 5); he must therefore have known next to nothing of Grotefend's work.

53 *JRAS* (1847), pp. 5 f.

54 *Archaeologia* (1852), p. 74.

55 *JRAS* (1847), p. 15.

56 See n. 54.

57 *JRAS* (1847), p. 6.

58 Ibid, p. 6, n. 2.

59 *Athenaeum* (1884), II, p. 593. He refers to his residence at Baghdad between 1843 and 1855, during which years all three versions of the Behistun inscription were published in the *JRAS*.

60 *JRAS* (1847), p. 6.

61 *The Rise and Progress of Assyriology* (London 1925), pp. 48 f.

62 More literally: 'May I not be begotten of Darius the (son) of Hystaspes the (son) of ...'

63 *JRAS* (1847), pp. 8 f.

64 British Museum, Add. 47619, 47620.

65 A preliminary report was published in the London *Athenaeum* (1840), p. 79.

66 See pp. 135 f. of his biography, *A Memoir of Major-General Sir Henry Creswicke Rawlinson*, by his brother, Canon George Rawlinson (London 1898).

67 The whole work was published as *JRAS* (1847).

68 Transactions of the Royal Irish Academy (1848), 'Polite Literature', pp. 116ff.

69 W. Hinz, *The Lost World of Elam* (London 1972), p. 38.

70 Münter, *Versuch über die keilförmigen Inschriften*, pp. 84 f.

71 As well as other important words; see his *Neue Beiträge zur Erläuterung der persepolitanischen Keilschrift* (Hannover 1837), p. 21.

72 'On the Deciphering of the Second Achaemenian or Median Species of Arrowhead Writing', in *Mémoires de la Société Royale des Antiquaires du Nord* (1840–44), pp. 271–439 (with figures).

73 Pallis, *Antiquity of Iraq*, p. 127.

74 Ibid, pp. 123–6, lists no less than eleven names.

75 *Mém. de la Soc. Royale des Antiq. du Nord* (1840–44).

76 *TRIA* (1848), pp. 125 ff.

77 *Archaeologia* (1852), pp. 74 f.

78 *JRAS* (1847), p. 228 (on the last paragraph in the second column). His worst mistake was that he wrote 'Hystaspes, who was my father, the Parthian forces rose in rebellion against him', instead of 'My father Hystaspes was then in Parthia, and the people forsook him and revolted.'

79 In *JRAS* (1855), pp. 7–46, he explains how almost every character was found as a constituent of one or more names; his other results fill pp. 1–213.

80 Voiced consonants involve resonance of the vocal cords. Examples are *b g d v z*; their unvoiced counterparts are *p k t f s*.

81 See E. Reiner in *Handbuch der Orientalistik*, ed. B. Spuler (Leyden 1969), I.2. i–ii.2 p. 64n and p. 112.

82 Ibid. pp. 54–68.

83 Hinz, *The Lost World of Elam*, pp. 31 ff.

84 For details, see Pallis, *Antiquity of Iraq*, p. 132.

85 Ibid, pp. 133 f.

86 We follow I.J. Gelb *A Study of Writing*, 2nd ed. (Chicago 1963), pp. 65, 107 in preferring this term to 'ideogram'.

87 See I Löwenstern, *Essai de déchiffrement de l'écriture assyrienne* (Paris 1845), p. 12.

88 Ibid, p. 13.

89 This is intriguing. Confusion may have occurred between Cush (which ordinarily denotes Ethiopia), the son of Ham, who is called Nimrod's father, and the Kassites (usually spelt Kaššû but occasionally Kuššû) who ruled Babylonia between the 16th and 13th centuries BC. See Speiser, *Genesis*, p. 20.

90 Detailed accounts in chronological order are offered by A.J. Booth, *The Discovery and Decipherment of the Trilingual Cuneiform Inscriptions* (London 1902), ch. 6; Pallis, *Antiquity of Iraq*, pp. 140–59.

91 *TRIA* (1848), p. 243 n.

92 Long enough for the apparent identity not to be attributable to mere chance; often a single word is enough.

93 *TRIA* (1848), p. 131.

94 This principle has since been fully accepted; a few signs, however, have been found to stand for two syllables, such as *rama, garak*.

95 *TRIA* (1850), pp. 56 ff.

96 Pallis, *Antiquity of Iraq*, p. 151.

97 *TRIA* (1850), p. 11.

98 Ibid (1848), p. 130.

99 Ibid (1848), p. 247.

100 It is now read *libbu* or *libbi*, the -*u* and -*i* being different case-endings. Some might protest that the spelling is syllabic, but see W. von Soden, *Das akkadische Syllabar*, 2nd ed. (Rome 1967), p. xxvii.

101 *TRIA* (1850), pp. 24–30.

102 In that 'I' may express the sound *i*, or a word such as 'first'; ibid, pp. 18 ff.

103 Ibid, pp. 26 f.

104 *TRIA* (1848), p. 247.

105 Ibid, p. 245.

106 P.E. Botta, *Mémoire sur l'écriture cunéiforme* (Paris 1848).

107 Ibid, p. 22.

108 *Revue Archéologique* (1847–8), IV, 2, pp. 501–7.

109 Longpérier ignored (with impunity, as it turned out) the fact that in Hebrew the two words begin with different letters, *śin* and *samek*.

110 *JRAS* (1847), pp. 29, 24.

111 *Archaeologia* (1852), pp. 75 f.

112 *JRAS* (1850), p. 403.

113 British Museum, Add. 47627.

114 *JRAS* (1850), p. 403.

115 These are the forms in his final sign-list in *JRAS* 1851 (see nos. 18, 46);

in the former case he probably first noticed that the same sign cropped up in both his *kh* and *d* collections.

116 *JRAS* (1850), p. 409 f.

117 For example, the Babylonian month-names (such as *Iyyar*, *Sivan*) were quite unlike their Old Persian and Elamite counterparts.

118 Only the Babylonian text mentions the numbers slain and captured in Darius' battles.

119 British Museum, Add. 47622, fols. 39 f.

120 *JRAS* 1851.

121 But not the rest of *JRAS* (1851), in which instances abound of cuneiform characters transcribed by single consonants.

122 For details see Pallis, pp. 143, 146 ff.

123 *TRIA* (1850–5), pp. 305 ff. Rawlinson's claims to priority are exhaustively discussed by Booth (see n. 90), ch. 6.

124 *JRAS* (1855), p. 6.

125 *JRAS* (1850), pp. 430 ff.

126 Ibid p. 408.

127 See p. 207, n. 93.

128 See W. von Soden and W. Röllig, *Das akkadische Syllabar* (Rome 1967).

129 Ritual texts, for example, may use values unknown in other texts of the same period and locality.

130 Conventionally called KIB.

131 A.L. Oppenheim, *Ancient Mesopotamia* (Chicago 1964), pp. 243 ff.

132 Three signs receive the value *qal* in von Soden's index (pp. 65 ff.), but the last is labelled qal_4; of four original values, one has since been abandoned (von Soden, *Syllabar*, 1st ed., p. 107), but the numbering of the others has been left unchanged. The present calculation is based on an overall count of such gaps.

133 Though scanty pre-Sargonic writings exist (see Gelb, *Old Akkadian Writing and Grammar*, pp. 1–6), and the term 'Akkadian' was first coined for quite a different purpose (p. 110).

134 See the *Chicago Assyrian Dictionary* on both words.

135 A.L. Oppenheim in *Journal of the American Oriental Society* (1943), pp. 31 ff.

136 E. Cassin, *La Splendeur Divine* (Paris 1968), p. 14.

137 *Akkadisches Handwörterbuch* (ed. W. von Soden), almost complete; and the *Chicago Assyrian Dictionary*, under the auspices of the Oriental Institute.

138 *Ephemerides Theologicae Lovanienses* (1950), p. 348.

139 James Barr, in *Heythrop Journal* (1974), p. 387. Authorized Version offers: 'I am a husbandman; for *man taught me to keep cattle* from my youth.'

140 In 1857, W.H. Fox Talbot, a mathematician and the inventor of talbotype photography, persuaded the Royal Asiatic Society to conduct an experiment which is said to have won over public opinion. He submitted under sealed cover a translation of an as yet unpublished inscription, and Rawlinson, Hincks and Oppert, who all happened to be in London, were then given copies of the same inscription and requested to submit, also under sealed cover, their independent translations. A committee was appointed

to open all four simultaneously, and reported that 'the coincidences between the translations, both as to the general sense and verbal rendering, were very remarkable'; see the full report in *JRAS* (1861), pp. 150–219.

141 Von Soden and Röllig list about 1400 values, for about 330 signs, an average of more than four values per sign.

142 See E. Leichty, 'The Colophon', in *Studies Presented to A.L. Oppenheim* (Chicago 1964), pp. 147–54.

143 G.R. Driver, *Semitic Writing*, 3rd ed. (London 1976), p. 61, n. 3; A.L. Oppenheim, in *Glass and Glassmaking in Ancient Mesopotamia* (New York 1970), pp. 59 ff.

144 *Babylonian Wisdom Literature* (Oxford 1960), p. 27.

145 Job 19:25; see Lambert, pp. 23, 46.

146 Suggested orally by B. Landsberger and cited by Lambert, p. 295.

147 Lambert, *Babylonian Wisdom Literature*, p. 344. Whether Lambert's interpretation of *irīm* is correct is a separate question; see J.S. Cooper in *Journal of Cuneiform Studies* (1975), pp. 248 ff.

148 Moreover, some fifty signs (including some of these fifty-odd) can be used as (or enter into composite) logograms, as well as represent syllables.

149 F. de Saulcy in *Revue Orientale et Algérienne* 2 (1852), p. 162.

150 *Daily Telegraph*, 4 December 1872, p. 6.

151 *Cambridge Ancient History* (3rd ed.), I, pt 2, pp. 244, 283 ff.

152 W.G. Lambert in *Orientalia* (1970), p. 419.

153 On the nature of emphasis, see S. Moscati et al., *An Introduction to the Comparative Grammar of the Semitic Languages* (Wiesbaden 1964), pp. 23 f.

154 Though they have been variously modified (e.g. many Arabic dialects pronounce *g* like English *j*, and most speakers of Hebrew pronounce *k* and *q* alike).

155 In Hebrew the former is called *ṭet* and the latter *taw*. We now know, however, that in certain periods and areas special signs were allocated to some (never all) of the syllables containing emphatic consonants; see von Soden and Röllig, *Das akkadische Syllabar*, p. xx.

156 *TRIA* (1850), p. 57. He thought it likely that the inventors were under Egyptian influence (see Pallis, *Antiquity of Iraq*, p. 189).

157 *TRIA* (1850), p. 19 n.

158 Cited by T.B. Jones, *The Sumerian Problem* (New York 1969), p. 14; the date is 1857. Note that the Irish example (*ts'* for *takt*) goes further than the English (only in a puzzle could *im£* express 'impound').

159 Hincks declined to draw what might seem the natural conclusion, that *an* was the word for 'god' in that language; and his caution was justified. In fact, the character is used for more than one word, and may denote either 'god' (for which the word is *dingir*) or 'heaven' (pronounced *an*).

160 *JRAS* (1850), p. 404.

161 J.S. Cooper in *Orientalia* (1973), pp. 239–46.

162 *Athenaeum* (1855), p. 1438.

163 According to Oppert (cited by Jones in *The Sumerian Problem*, p. 23), it was invented by Hincks in 1855.

164 Transcribed by C. Bezold in *Zeitschrift für Assyriologie* (1889), pp. 434 ff.

165 See Pallis, *Antiquity of Iraq*, p. 233, whose translation has been followed, but is disputed.

166 There the *n* is followed by the guttural sound '*ain*, which was audible in antiquity.

167 S.N. Kramer, *The Sumerians* (Chicago 1963), pp. 297 f., citing A. Poebel. It is a regular feature of Sumerian to drop the final sound, whether consonant or vowel, of each word.

168 *The Rise and Progress of Assyriology* (London 1925), pp. 269 f.

169 Pallis, op. cit. (tentatively), p. 180; P.E. Cleator, *Lost Languages* (London 1959), p. 102.

170 *Die grosse Täuschung* (Stuttgart 1920–21).

171 Though G. Roux (*Ancient Iraq*, London 1966, p. 83) argues that these features – 'the big, fleshy nose, the enormous eyes, the thick neck ...' betoken differences not of race but of artistic convention.

172 'On an Accadian Seal' in *Journal of Philology* (1871), pp. 1–50.

173 See Pallis, *Antiquity of Iraq*, p. 240.

174 A remarkable number and variety of languages have been tried, e.g. Bantu languages, Chinese, Polynesian, Basque; see Pallis, p. 232.

175 Fifteen were published by E. Sollberger in *Iraq* (1962), pp. 63–72. Extensive formal proof of the decipherment of Akkadian was supplied by the discovery in 1907/8 at Elephantine (near Aswan, Egypt) of portions of an Aramaic version made from the Akkadian text of the Behistun Inscription. See E. Sachau, *Aramäische Papyrus und Ostraka aus einer jüdischen Militär-Kolonie zu Elephantine*, (Leipzig 1911), p. 185.

176 Pallis, *Antiquity of Iraq*, p. 235.

177 S.N. Kramer, *Sumerian Mythology*, 2nd ed. (New York 1961), p. 52; Th. Jacobsen, *Towards the Image of Tammuz* (University of Harvard 1970), p. 114.

178 Discrepancies between the extant copies are an added factor; see G. Pettinato, *Die altorientalische Menschenbild*, (Heidelberg 1971), pp. 82 ff.

179 J. N. Postgate in *Journal of Cuneiform Studies* (1972), p. 161.

180 M.E. Cohen in *Journal of Cuneiform Studies* (1976), p. 92.

181 See the pioneering work of W.G. Lambert in *Bulletin of the School of Oriental and African Studies* (London 1976), pp. 428 ff.

182 For details of the most ancient texts see G.R. Driver, *Semitic Writing*, 3rd ed., (London 1976), pp. 3–8.

183 See *Peredneaziatskiy Sbornik*, (Moscow, 1966), pp. 3–15 (Russian text), pp. 161–5 (English summary). The Uruk texts were published by A. Falkenstein (Berlin 1936), and those from Jamdat Nasr by S. Langdon (London 1928); Vaiman found about 1090 *prima facie* different signs in the two combined.

184 Vaiman stated that 'about 70 to 100 [of these archaic] texts have become translateable', and hoped to prepare 'a complete edition of the Proto-Sumerian pictographic texts'.

185 According to Kramer, *The Sumerians*, p. 107, the GAR is 20 ft, the IKU 37600 sq ft, and the BÙR equals 18 IKU. The area would then be about six per cent less than the product of the length and breadth.

186 Driver, *Semitic Writing*, p. 2.

187 Gelb (*A Study of Writing*, pp. 217 ff.) argues that all other systems of writing, as he defines that term, were inspired ultimately by Mesopotamian writing.

188 See discussion by Gelb, p. 63; many, however, argue for a rather earlier date.

189 Oppenheim, *Ancient Mesopotamia*, p. 238, appeals to polyphony – which could however be due to the Sumerians themselves. Gelb (*IXe Renc. Assyr. Internationale*, Geneva 1960, pp. 262 f.) adduces signs bearing syllabic values which do not, however, go back to any Sumerian word.

190 That cuneiform had a pictorial origin was the conclusion of Oppert as early as 1859 (*Expédition Scientifique en Mésopotamie* (Paris 1858–63), II, p. 63.

191 In his *Study of Writing*, p. 12 ff.

192 This example is borrowed from L. Cottrell, *Reading the Past* (London 1972), p. 20.

193 Gelb, *A Study of Writing*, p. 66.

194 The Sumerian for 'life' if *til*, but the final *l* is silent; see n. 167.

195 Driver, *Semitic Writing*, pp. 60 f.

196 Only a small minority cannot be thus explained; see von Soden and Röllig, *Das akkadische Syllabar*.

197 And others besides; see von Soden and Röllig, op. cit., p. 4.

198 For example, signs of the type 'consonant + vowel + consonant' (CVC) are almost a luxury, because one can instead use two signs, of type CV and VC; thus the syllable *ral* never had a sign of its own, but was always *ra* + *al*. Now down to the end of the Third Dynasty of Ur, many CVC signs occur; they then become comparatively rare, in the time of the First Babylonian Dynasty; thereafter they steadily increase (von Soden and Röllig, op. cit., pp. xxix ff.).

199 On writing implements and materials, see Driver, *Semitic Writing*.

200 This is very much a simplification; see Driver, op. cit., pp. 39 ff. for details on the arrangement of the text.

201 In economic texts circular marks often occur; these were used to indicate numerals, and were formed with the round head of the stylus, which was of course inverted.

202 Driver, op. cit., p. 62.

203 Its rival was the alphabetic system which was used for writing Aramaic (but never adapted to Akkadian); numerous Aramaic inscriptions from the 9th century onward in Mesopotamia show that the people were becoming bilingual.

204 Driver, op. cit., p. 234, gives references to dated tablets.

205 Gelb, *A Study of Writing*, p. 196.

206 R.T. Hallock, in *Journal of Near Eastern Studies* (1970), pp. 52 ff., dates the invention to Cyrus' time.

207 I.M. Diakonoff, 'The Origin of the "Old Persian" Writing System', in *W.B. Henning Memorial Volume* (London 1970), pp. 98–124.

Chapter 5

1 Professor Matthiae in an interview with C. Bermant.
2 *Tishrin*, 20 September 1977.
3 In communication to C. Bermant.
4. K.M. Kenyon, *Digging up Jericho* (London 1957), pp. 34 ff.

Chapter 6

1. H. Butler, F.A. Norris and E.R. Stoever, *Syria: Publications of the Princeton University Archaeological Expedition to Syria in 1904–5 and 1909* (Leyden 1930).
2 G. Tchalenko, *Villages antiques de la Syrie du Nord* (Paris 1953–8).
3 *Annales Archéologiques de Syrie* (1965), II, p. 91.
4 Ibid, pp. 84 ff.
5 Pritchard (ed.), *Ancient Near Eastern Texts* (3rd ed., 1969), pp. 655 f.
6 *Ann. Arch. de Syrie* (1965), II, pp. 91 ff.
7 Ibid, p. 93 f.
8 Ibid, p. 96.
9 E.D. Van Buren, *Clay Figurines of Babylonia and Assyria* (New Haven 1930), pp. xlviii ff.
10 *Ann. Arch. de Syrie* (1965), II, p. 100.
11 Ibid.
12 *Archaeology* (1971), p. 58.
13 Ibid., p. 56.
14 *MAIS* 1965 (Rome 1966), pp. 104 ff.
15 Ibid, p. 112.
16 Ibid, pp. 104 f.
17 Ibid, pp. 52 f., 209 f.
18 *Archéologia* (April 1974), p. 23 f.
19 *Archaeology* (1967), p. 132.
20 *Archaeology* (1971), p. 60.
21 Matthiae, *Ebla: Un Impero Ritrovato* (Turin 1977), p. 132.
22 *MAIS*, 1967–8 (Rome 1972), pp. 11 f.
23 *Rivista Biblica* (1977), pp. 226 f.
24 *MAIS*, 1964, pp. 121 f.
25 *MAIS*, 1967–8, p. 37; *Archaeology* (1971), p. 61.
26 *Ugarit-Forschungen* (1971), pp. 14 f.
27 *Les Annales Archéologiques de Syrie* (1963), pp. 110 f.
28 A. de Maigret: 'Due punte di lancia iscritte da Tell Mardikh' in *Rivista degli Studi Orientali* (1976), pp. 31 ff., citing Pettinato's tentative interpretations.
29 *Orientalia* (1975), p. 362.
30 I.J. Gelb, 'The Early History of the West Semitic Peoples' in *Journal of Cuneiform Studies* (1961), pp. 27–47; see pp. 38 and 41.
31 Conversation with Professor Pettinato, 23 April 1977.
32 Pettinato, in *Rivista Biblica* (1977), p. 240.
33 See pp. 90 ff. above.

34 *The Times*, 15 January 1977.
35 *Biblical Archaeologist* (September 1976), p. 93.
36 *Archaeology* (1977), p. 251.
37 As he reports in *Orientalia* (1975), p. 374 n.
38 Matthiae, *Ebla: Un Impero Ritrovato* (Turin 1977).

Chapter 7

1 Pettinato, in *Biblical Archaeologist* (1976), p. 47a.
2 *Journal of World History*, IV, 1, 1957, p. 246.
3 Matthiae, in *Bibl. Arch.* (1976), p. 107b.
4 *Rivista degli Studi Orientali* (1976), pp. 10 ff.
5 *Annales Archéologiques de Syrie* (1965), II, p. 91.
6 *Annales Archéologiques Arabes Syriennes* (1970), p. 63; *Archaeology* (1971), p. 58.
7 This was far less well preserved; *Riv. d. Stud.* (1976), p. 18.
8 Ibid, p. 17.
9 Ibid, p. 11.
10 I.J. Gelb, *Old Akkadian Writing and Grammar* (Chicago, 1961), p. 35.
11 Arabic *dağn* 'abundant rain'.
12 Hebrew *dāgān* 'corn'.
13 *Riv. d. Stud.* (1976), p. 11, n. 17.
14 Ibid, p. 16.
15 *Rivista Biblica* (1977), p. 229.
16 *Riv. d. Stud.* (1976), p. 25.
17 *Bibl. Arch.* (1976), p. 47a.
18 And perhaps among the Hittites also. See Pettinato, *Riv. Bibl.* (1977), p. 235.
19 D.N. Freedman in *Science Year* (1976), p. 188.
20 Pettinato in *Bibl. Arch.* (1976), p. 47a.
21 Matthiae in *Akkadica* (1977), no. 2, p. 12.
22 *Bibl. Arch.* (1976), p. 47a.
23 R. Harris, *Journal of the Economic and Social History of the Orient* 9 (1966), p. 309; J. Bottéro, in P. Grimal (ed.), *Histoire Mondiale de la Femme* (Paris 1965), pp. 203 ff.
24 Despite the claim of P. Clough, *The Times*, 15 January 1977.
25 Our information is drawn largely from Professor Pettinato's article, 'I testi cuneiformi della Biblioteca reale di Tell Mardikh. Notizia preliminare sulla scuola di Ebla' in *Rendiconti della Pontificia Accademia Romana di Archeologia* 48, 1976. We are grateful to Professor Pettinato for sight of his manuscript. We have not seen the article in print.
26 Cf. Matthiae, *Comptes Rendus de l'Académie des Inscriptions*, 1976, p. 209, n. 52.
27 J.S. Cooper in *Orientalia* (1973), pp. 239–46.
28 R.D. Biggs, *Inscriptions from Tell Abū Ṣalābīkh* (Chicago 1974), ch. 3.
29 S.N. Kramer, *The Sumerians* (Chicago 1963), p. 229.
30 A.L. Oppenheim, *Ancient Mesopotamia* (Chicago 1964), pp. 248 ff.
31 *Riv. Bibl.* (1977), p. 237.

32 *Oriens Antiquus* (1976), pp. 169–78 (with plate).

33 R. D. Biggs, *Inscriptions from Tell Abū Salābīkh* (Chicago 1974), p. 71, 'in the vicinity of Kullaba'.

34 *Bibl. Arch.* (1976), p. 52 (though his grounds are not stated).

35 In article cited in n. 25.

36 *Riv. Bibl.* (1977), p. 232.

37 Ibid.

38 *Riv. Bibl.* (1977), p. 231.

39 *Bibl. Arch.* (1976), p. 45b.

40 *Akkadica* (1977), 2, p. 22.

41 Called *ugula* in Sumerian and *nase* (cf. Hebrew *nasi*) in Eblaite.

42 *Archiv für Orientforschung*, 1977, pp. 1–36.

43 Diri v 242: see T.G. Pinches, *JRAS* (1905), p. 827.

44 Matthiae in *Akkadica* (1977), no. 2, p. 12.

45 *Riv. Bibl.* (1977), p. 230.

46 *Los Angeles Times*, 7 June 1976.

47 Deuteronomy 22:29.

48 Pettinato in *Akkadica* (1977), no. 2, pp. 24 ff.

49 Matthiae, *Comptes Rendus* (1976), p. 209, n. 51.

50 See p. 173.

51 Pettinato supposes (*Akkadica* (1977), 2, p. 27) as a further cause that Mari had been a tributary to Ebla but had witheld its tribute. The available evidence, however, notably the statement (ibid, p. 26) that 'Iblul-Il fled, bringing to the town of Nema the tribute due to Ebla', does not seem enough to justify this.

52 Our English equivalents are based on 1 mina=60 shekels=approx. 500 gm (S.N. Kramer, *The Sumerians*, p. 107). Pettinato, however, gives the far higher figures of '11,000 lbs of silver and 880 lbs of gold' (*Bibl. Arch.* (1976), p. 47b).

53 Matthiae, *Ebla* (Turin 1977), pp. 188 f.

54 *Bibl. Arch.* (1976), p. 48a; *Oriens Antiquus* (1976), p. 14.

55 I.J. Gelb, *Journal of Near Eastern Studies* XIII, 1954, pp. 209–26.

56 J.J. Finklestein, *Journal of Cuneiform Studies*, 1966, p. 117.

57 *Bibl. Arch.* (1976), p. 48a, which includes the quoted extract.

58 *Cambridge Ancient History*, 3rd ed., I, pt. 2, p. 708.

59 *Oriens Antiquus* (1976), pp. 13 f.

60 *Riv. Bibl.* (1977), p. 230.

61 *Bibl. Arch.* (1976), p. 106b.

62 The text has the NI sign twice; these could be read *i-li*, literally 'of god', or as a sort of superlative ('wonderful, precious garment') just as a lady today might call a garment 'divine' (*Oriens Antiquus* (1976), pp. 12 f.).

63 M.S. Drower, *Cambridge Ancient History*, 3rd ed., I, pt. 2, p. 334.

64 *Bibl. Arch.* (1976), p. 48b.

65 Matthiae, *Ebla*, pp. 62 ff.

66 Code of Hammurapi §15, after the translation by G.R. Driver & J.C Miles, *The Babylonian Laws* (Oxford 1955), II.

67 So too, incidentally, were the scribes of Mesopotamia; the priests, as a

rule, were illiterate. See B. Landsberger in C.H. Kraeling and R.M. Adams (eds), *City Invincible* (Chicago 1960), pp. 94 ff.

68 The gods tend to be complex individuals and they are studied at length in H. W. Haussig (ed.), *Wörterbuch der Mythologie* (Stuttgart 1965–).

69 *Bibl. Arch.* (1976), p. 45b.

70 Ibid, p. 110b.

71 *Riv. Bibl.* (1977), p. 232.

72 *Philadelphia Inquirer*, 11 July 1976.

73 *Archiv für Orientforschung* (1977), p. 33.

74 Ibid, pp. 28 ff, 35.

75 *Riv. Bibl.* (1977), p. 229.

76 The sex of this deity is problematic. Pettinato (*Bibl. Arch.* (1976), p. 48b) is quite convinced that Aštar (= Eshtar) was masculine in Ebla, but one text equates 'him' (ibid p. 49b) with the Sumerian Inanna, who was definitely a goddess, and Eshtar in Ibbit-Lim's inscription (being there referred to as 'his lady') was likewise feminine.

77 *Archiv für Or.* (1977), pp. 28, 29, 35.

78 I.J. Gelb, *Hurrians and Subarians* (Chicago 1944), p. 57.

79 Ibid, p. 89. But note their limited presence at Urkish *c.* 2200 BC (p. 32 above).

80 We find evidence of this also in the time of Ibbit-Lim whose name incorporates the Semitic (Amorite) Lim, while that of his father Igrish-Hepa is derived from Hebat the chief Hurrian goddess.

81 *Archiv für Or.* (1977), p. 29b.

82 Ibid, p. 30a.

83 W. Röllig in *Wörterbuch der Mythologie*, pp. 299 f.; cf. New English Bible.

84 *Bibl. Arch.* (1976), p. 49.

85 The Babylonians later adopted this method of equating deities. See W. von Soden, *Zweisprachigkeit in der geistigen Kultur Babyloniens* (Vienna 1960), pp. 13 ff.

86 *Bibl. Arch.* (1976), p. 49a.

87 *Archiv für Or.* (1977), p. 35.

88 *Bibl. Arch.* (1976), p. 49a.

89 *Oriens Antiquus* (1976), pp. 170 ff.

90 *Akkadica* (1977), 2, p. 21.

91 *Archaeology* (1977), p. 249.

92 Matthiae, *Ebla*, pp. 83 ff.

93 *Archaeology* (1977), p. 248. For illustration see Matthiae, *Ebla*, fig. 14 (p. 84).

94 Matthiae, *Ebla*, pp. 247 ff.

95 A. Shuster, *New York Times*, 25 October 1976.

96 *Riv. Bib.* (1977), p. 232.

97 Opening lines of *Enuma Elish* in E.A. Speiser's translation. See *Ancient Near Eastern Texts Relating to the Old Testament*, ed. J.B. Pritchard (Princeton 1955), pp. 60 ff.

98 *Riv. Bibl.* (1977), p. 231.

99 Ibid, p. 242.

100 *Bibl. Arch.* (1976), p. 48a.

101 *Orientalia* (1975), p. 353.
102 Matthiae, *Bibl. Arch.* (1976), p. 92.
103 Pettinato, *Reallexikon der Assyriologie*, V, pp. 9b, 12b.
104 *Bibl. Arch.*, (1976), p. 109.
105 Ibid, p. 46.
106 *Reallexikon der Assyriologie*, V, pp. 12 f.; *Bibl. Arch.* (1976), p. 109a.
107 *Bibl. Arch* (1976). p. 46.
108 *Riv. Bibl.* (1977), p. 235. Yet on p. 242 of the same article he curiously reverts for a moment to his former position and speaks of Ebla in 2500 BC as 'the centre of an immense empire'.
109 *Les Annales Archéologiques de Syrie* (1963), p. 112.

Chapter 8

1 Matthiae, *Biblical Archaeloogist* (1976), p. 97.
2 Pettinato, *Bibl. Arch.* (1976), p. 47a.
3 Matthiae, *Ebla*, pp. 178 f.
4 *Rivista Biblica* (1977), pp. 239 f.
5 Ibid, pp. 234 f.
6 R. W. Ehrich (ed.) *Chronologies in Old World Archaeology* (London 1965), pp. 78, 178 f.
7 *Orientalia* (1975), p. 364, n. 15.
8 Matthiae, *Comptes Rendus de l'Académie des Inscriptions*, 1976, p. 210.
9 A. Parrot, *Syria* (1953), p. 209.
10 E. Strommenger, *The Art of Mesopotamia* (London 1964), Plates 92–3.
11 J. Bottéro, *Cambridge Ancient History* (3rd ed.), I, pt 2, p. 323.
12 Strommenger, *The Art of Mesopotamia*, p. 474 ('Fara phase').
13 Matthiae, *Bibl. Arch.* (1976), p. 99a.
14 *Comptes Rendus* (1976), p. 203, n. 33.
15 Pettinato, *Bibl. Arch.* (1976), p. 47b.
16 *Comptes Rendus* (1976), pp. 212 f., n. 70.
17 *Thoughts about Ibla: A Preliminary Evaluation, March 1977* (Syro-Mesopotamian Studies, 1/1, May 1977, pp. 5–8).
18 *Riv. Bib.* (1977), p. 233.
19 Matthiae in *Akkadica* (1977), 2, pp. 13, 18.
20 *Riv. Bibl.* (1977), p. 234.
21 *Orientalia* (1975), p. 354 and plate xxxvii.
22 *Archaeology* (1977), p. 253.
23 Reported by Professor Matthiae at a public lecture in London, 28 February 1978.
24 Matthiae, *Ebla*, p. 113.
25 Ibid., pp. 113, 234.
26 Ibid, pp. 114 f.
27 BBC radio broadcast, 16 April 1978.
28 Matthiae, *Ebla*, p. 51.

Chapter 9

1 Pettinato in *Biblical Archaeologist* (May 1976), pp. 44–52.
2 *Bibl. Arch.* (1976), p. 41. The editor responsible is D.N. Freedman.
3 'About 6823 times', according to A. Murtonen, *A Philological and Literary Treatise on the Old Testament Divine Names* (Helsinki 1952) (*Studia Orientalia* 18:1), p. 43.
4 On this name, see O. Eissfeldt, *Adonis und Adonaj* (Berlin 1970).
5 The first vowel in Adonay is a very brief *a* (the technical term is *ḥateph pathaḥ*) which cannot follow (and would therefore look odd together with) the consonant Y, and was replaced by a short vowel like that in English 'the' or 'abide', here denoted ə, and technically termed *shewa*.
6 The earliest instance is the occurrence of the form Yehova in a manuscript, dated 1381, of Raymundus Martini's *Pugio Fidei*; see G.F. Moore, 'Notes on the Name YHWH' in *Old Testament and Semitic Studies in Memory of W.R. Harper* (Chicago 1908), pp. 145 ff.
7 In the *Mishnah* (Succah 4:5), *ani waho* (or *wahu*) seems intended to hint at the pronunciation of the phrase *ana* ('we beseech thee') YHWH, but if so, it may have been deliberately distorted beyond recognition.
8 Cf. H. Jonas, *The Gnostic Religion* (Boston 1958), esp. p. 43.
9 Besides those mentioned here, a form *Iao* enjoys some support in classical, patristic and gnostic sources, but seems to have been inferred from the contracted form *Yeho* – found in names like Jehoshaphat, and may therefore be disregarded; see W.W.G. Baudissin, *Studien zur semitischen Religionsgeschichte* I (Leipzig 1876), pp. 182 ff. *Ia* also occurs (e.g. Origen, *Contra Celsum* VI, 32), but no doubt refers to Yah, not YHWH.
10 Clement of Alexandria (*c.* 150–215 AD), *Stromata* V, 6, 34.
11 The third letter is in fact *beta* in Greek, which was pronounced then (as in modern Greek) as *v*. For this form see Epiphanius, *Panarion* 40, 5, 8–10, and Theodoret in *Patrologia Graeca* 80, 244 (where *Iave* is said to be the Samaritan pronunciation, while the Jews say *Aia*). Epiphanius wrote in the fourth century AD, Theodoret in the fifth.
12 Theodoret *Patrologia Graeca*, 83, 460 (but again *Aia* is ascribed to the Jews).
13 Such as: (1) the forms *yo* and *yahu* which are frequent components in names (e.g. *Yoel* 'Joel', *Eliyahu* 'Elijah', both meaning 'YHWH is God') are readily explained as contractions of *Yahweh*; (2) Exodus 3:14 suggests a resemblance between the pronunciation of YHWH and that of the Hebrew for 'I am', viz. *ehyeh*. See Murtonen, *Old Testament Divine Names*, pp. 55 f.
14 G.F. Moore in *American Journal of Semitic Languages and Literatures* 25 (1908–9), p. 316.
15 Eissfeldt, *Adonis und Adonaj*, p. 8 ('Grosser Jahwe, den Gesenius in Halle immer noch Jehowah nennt, steht uns bei!').
16 See discussion in Murtonen, *Old Testament Divine Names*, pp. 61 ff. and 89 f.
17 'The original form of the name "Yahweh"', *Zeitschrift für die alttestamentliche Wissenschaft* (1928), pp. 7–25.

18 A complex and ingenious (but to us unconvincing) theory, according to which Yaho or the like is the original form and Yahweh a later development, is expounded by L. Delekat in *Tradition und Glaube*, ed. G. Jeremias (Göttingen 1971), pp. 23–75.

19 J.M. Allegro, *The Sacred Mushroom and the Cross* (London 1970), pp. 20, 215 f.

20 Pettinato seems inclined to regard *Il* as the name of a specific deity (as at Ugarit). According to Murtonen (*Old Testament Divine Names*, pp. 27–30), common Semitic *Il* was originally a proper name rather than indicating 'god' in general.

21 *Bibl. Arch.* (1976), p. 48b; italics ours.

22 On prevailing critical theories, these passages stem from J, while P held (Exodus 6:3) that the name was first revealed to Moses. K.A. Kitchen (*The Bible in its World*, Exeter 1977, p. 47) states that were Pettinato's view upheld, 'then of course the common misconception about Exodus 6:3, that the name YHWH was unknown before Moses, would be eliminated at a stroke, together with much of the "critical" theories based in part upon such misconceptions'; on the contrary, it would merely show that J was better informed than P.

23 For fuller discussion see Murtonen (who regards all but the last of the following as valid parallels) and other works cited in L. Koehler and H. Baumgartner, *Hebräisches und Aramäisches Lexikon* (3rd ed., Leyden 1967–), II, pp. 377 f.

24 *Babel and Bible*, tr. C.H.W. Johns (New York 1903), p. 71.

25 H.B. Huffmon, *Amorite Personal Names in the Mari Texts* (Baltimore 1965), pp. 159 f.

26 Or, 'God is mine'; see G. Buccellati, *The Amorites of the Ur III Period* (Naples 1966), p. 150.

27 R. Giveon in *Vetus Testamentum* (1964), p. 244. The symbol ꜣ denotes a glottal stop (a sort of catch in the throat) like Hebrew (or Arabic) *aleph*.

28 The four names are found in Pettinato: (1) *Bibl. Arch.* (1976), p. 50b; (2) *Riv. d. Stud. Orient.* (1976), p. 5; (3) Ibid, p. 7; (4) Ibid, and in Gelb, *Thoughts about Ibla* (1977): (1) p. 18, (2–4), p. 20. For other examples of names ending in *-ni* meaning 'our' or 'us', see Gelb, *Old Akkadian Writing and Grammar*, p. 129 (n. 14) and p. 131 (n. 3).

29 J.J. Stamm, *Die akkadische Namengebung* (Leipzig 1939), p. 113 etc.

30 I.J. Gelb et al., *Nuzi Personal Names* (Chicago 1943), p. 74.

31 H.B. Huffmon, *Amorite Personal Names in the Mari Texts*, pp. 134 f.

32 See M. Jastrow, 'Hebrew Proper Names compounded with *yh* and *yhw*' in *Journal of Biblical Literature* (1894), pp. 101–27.

33 Cf. the name Bakbuk in Nehemiah 7:53 etc.

34 The nominative case-ending; see Gelb, *Old Akkadian Writing*, pp. 145 f.

35 See, for example, T.G. Pinches, 'Yâ and Yâwa (Jah and Jahweh) in Assyro-Babylonian Inscriptions', *Proceedings of the Society of Biblical Archaeology* XV (1893), pp. 13–15, and sporadically later (e.g. P.S. Landersdorfer, 'Die Gottesname *yhwh* in den Keilinschriften', *Biblische Zeitschrift* (1912), pp. 24–35).

36 Friedrich Delitzsch put this silence down to mere chance, but that was in 1881; see his *Wo lag das Paradies?* (Leipzig 1881), p. 164.

37 In a few names, Murtonen (p. 53) does think of *-iaum* as a divine element, but few seem to agree.

38 *Bibl. Arch.* (1976), p. 50a.

39 *Thoughts about Ibla*, pp. 24 ff. He is however satisfied that Eblaite is not merely a dialect of Akkadian (p. 26).

40 See e.g., *Bibl. Arch.* (1976), pp. 50a, 112b.

41 'North-West Semitic' ceases to be a meaningful term if it cannot be defined. The only way to define it formally is to specify some linguistic feature – or preferably a list of features – common to all the languages it denotes and to no others; and such features one would now be hard pressed to find. Scholars in the field of Indo-European linguistics gave up the idea of neat division into branches over a century ago.

42 '1000 Years Before Abraham', *Midstream* (February 1977), pp. 45–52; esp. p. 49.

43 E. Ullendorff, *Orientalia* (1951), pp. 273 f.

44 Some of our sixth millennium linguists might argue that the usual reconstruction of all these words was wrong, and that they originally began in *h* which survived in Spanish alone but was corrupted to *f* elsewhere; but others would retort that a change from *h* to *f* was far less likely than the reverse.

45 Conversely, there are some (probably more) features in which Eblaite is more conservative than Hebrew, but this is beside the point.

46 Or *yi-* according to Gelb, *Thoughts about Ibla*, p. 18; even so, the Hebrew stands closer to the original.

47 For references see Gelb as above.

48 Cf. Amorite *Yasharum*, Arabic *yasar* 'submissive'.

49 Again, after '*ain* the vowel *a* may change to *e* in Eblaite but not in Hebrew. Thus Eblaite has (according to Gelb, p. 18) '*ebduni* for 'our slave'; compare Arabic (and Proto-Semitic) '*abduna*, Hebrew '*abdenu*.

50 *Bibl. Arch.* (1976), p. 50b.

51 *Riv. Bibl.* (1977), p. 242.

52 *Bibl. Arch.* (1976), p. 50b.

53 Except on the new theory of D.N. Freedman (p. 188).

54 T.L. Thompson, *The Historicity of the Patriarchal Narratives* (Berlin 1974), ch. 2.

55 One has to remove the ending *-um*, which has not survived into Hebrew.

56 A. Kammenhuber, *Die Arier im Vorderen Orient* (Heidelberg 1968), p. 262.

57 If the term is identified with 'Apiru (often called Habiru) – a vexed question, on which H. Cazelles, 'The Hebrews', in *Peoples of Old Testament Times*, ed. D.J. Wiseman (Oxford 1973), pp. 1–28, should be consulted.

58 *Bibl. Arch.* (1976), p. 109b; our italics.

59 *Riv. Bibl.* (1977), pp. 235 f.

60 See Genesis 10:24 ff., 11:16 f.

61 Kitchen, *Bible in its World*, p. 52.

62 Ebrum can plausibly be explained as 'companion'; this is the meaning of Akkadian *i/ebrum*, and the cognate root in Hebrew (*ḥbr*) has supplied

the name Heber, also 'companion'. See M. Noth, *Die israelitischen Personennamen* (Stuttgart 1928), p. 222. The possible equivalents of Ebrum in Hebrew are then either *ḥeber* (etymologizing) or *'eber* (as a phonetic transcription), but hardly the form attested in the Bible (*'eber*, with *'ain*).

63 Such as the very different Histories of Israel by M. Noth (London 1960), and J. Bright (London 1972).

64 The figure is on the high side, since one and the same person will sometimes occupy more than one position in the genealogy.

65 See herein the remarks of Gelb, *Hurrians and Subarians* (Chicago 1944), pp. iv ff; he defines the main traits of a people as 'community of tradition, customs, religion, culture, language and geographic position'.

66 The first is the view of Archbishop Ussher, the second is that of Jewish tradition (see p. 213). Christian fundamentalists sometimes seek to put back the date of the Flood and of earlier events by supposing that an indefinite number of generations were omitted in the genealogies of Genesis 5, 11; see *New Bible Dictionary*, ed. J.D. Douglas (London 1962), pp. 213, 457.

67 W.F. Albright, *The Archaeology of Palestine and the Bible* (New York 1933), pp. 134 f.

68 *Riv. Bibl.* (1977), p. 236.

69 *Science Year* (1976), pp. 191 ff.; similarly C.H. Gordon, *Midstream* (February 1977), p. 49.

70 At the Geological Society in Piccadilly on 5 January 1978.

71 *The Tell Mardikh Tablets*, distributed by '20th Century Reformation Hour' (Collingswood, New Jersey), pp. 2, 4.

72 Ibid, p. 3.

73 C.H. Gordon, *The World of the Old Testament* (New York 1958), p. 87.

74 See especially Genesis 10:10 and Daniel 1:2.

75 See discussion in L.W. King, *The Letters and Inscriptions of Hammurabi*, I (London 1898), pp. xxvi ff.

76 On the other hand, the discovery by T.G. Pinches, also discussed (and dismissed) by King (pp. xlix ff.), of the names of Chedorlaomer, Arioch and Tidal on three Babylonian tablets not earlier than the fourth century BC has been essentially approved in the ingenious treatment by M.C. Astour, 'Political and Cosmic Symbolism in Genesis 14 and in Its Babylonian Sources', in *Biblical Motifs*, ed. A. Altman (Harvard 1966), pp. 65–112, who uses it for a purpose quite other than the authentication and dating of Abraham.

77 *Science Year* (1976), p. 194. This is a surprisingly early dating – even earlier than that of Pettinato, who dated the archive 'about 2500 BC' (*Riv. Bibl.* (1977), p. 233).

78 *World of the Old Testament*, ch. 8.

79 Cf. Exodus 12:40 (for 430 years), and Exodus 6:16ff. (Levi–Kohath–Amram–Moses; Levi–Jochebed–Moses), and Numbers 16:1.

80 Even the biblical figures begin to look credible. If we date the destruction of Sodom and the birth of Isaac around 2500 BC, then Jacob arrived in Egypt around 2310 BC (cf. Genesis 25:26; 47:9). Dating the Exodus in 1250 BC, we have an interval of 1060 years, or say forty generations, over which a population of 70 (Genesis 46:27) could reach about 1,500,000

(cf. Exodus 12:37) by a steady increase of about twenty-eight per cent per generation.

81 *Riv. Bibl.* (1977), p. 236.

82 For details see J. Skinner, *A Critical and Exegetical Commentary on Genesis,* (Edinburgh 1910), p. 239.

83 'Abraham and the Merchants of Ura' in *Journal of Near Eastern Studies* (1958), pp. 28–31, which should be read in the light of the crushing reply of H.W.F. Saggs, 'Ur of the Chaldees', *Iraq* (1960), pp. 200–9. Many similar suggestions have been made; see R. Kittel, *A History of the Hebrews,* I (London 1895), pp. 180 ff.

84 Quoted in *Tishrin,* 20 September 1977.

85 For example, A.H. Sayce, *Assyrian Grammar* (London 1872), p. 13 lists the 'racial characteristics' of the Semite as 'intensity of faith, ferocity, exclusiveness, imagination', and calls Arabia 'the only part of the world which has remained exclusively Semite'.

86 See pp. 149, 183. The uncertainties which still cloud the workings of the 'tenses' in Eblaite and indeed in Semitic generally, do not affect this purely phonetic observation.

87 See n. 49 above.

88 A.J. Arberry, *The Koran Interpreted* (London 1955).

89 *Ta-mu-di,* preceded by the determinative *lú*; see A.G. Lie, *The Inscriptions of Sargon II,* (Paris 1929), p. 20.

90 J. Wellhausen, *Muhammed in Medina* (Berlin 1882), p. 24. As if to avoid any charge of partiality, Wellhausen did a fair job in dismembering the New Testament as well.

91 Whether one approves of this biblical emphasis or not, it did induce the *Telegraph* in 1873 to finance an expedition (which succeeded almost immediately) in search of a tablet which had hitherto been missing from the account of the Deluge, and thereby to earn the lasting gratitude of scholarship.

92 H. Grimme, *Althebräische Inschriften vom Sinai,* (Darmstadt 1923), p. 91.

93 Ibid, p. 58 (SNHSHMH, with the same word for 'brush' as at Exodus 3:2) and p. 69 (MSHWTN for 'thou didst draw me', using the same root for 'draw' as at Exodus 2:10).

94 Ibid, pp. 92 ff.

95 Ibid, pp. 65 f., 85 ff.

96 See, however, W.F. Albright, *The Proto-Sinaitic Inscriptions and their Decipherment* (Harvard 1966) for what is widely thought to be a useful starting-point.

97 J. Friedrich, *Entzifferung verschollener Schriften und Sprachen,* 2nd ed. (Berlin 1966), pp. 140 ff.

98 *Babel and Bible,* ed. C.H.W. Johns (New York 1903), pp. 188, 219.

99 H. Zimmern, *Zum Streit um die 'Christusmythe'* (Berlin 1910), pp. 5 f., 38 ff.

100 Cited in *Tishrin,* 20 September 1977.

101 The oldest Sumerian records may well go back to the fourth millennium; see G.R. Driver, *Semitic Writing,* 3rd ed. (London 1976), p. 7.

102 See Pettinato, in *Riv. Bibl.* (1977), pp. 225 f., who gives the number of Ebla tablets as 20,000 (though how many are mere fragments is not yet clear).

103 The Amorites were however by no means confined to Syria; see, for example, M. Liverani in *Peoples of Old Testament Times*, ed. D.J. Wiseman (Oxford 1973), pp. 100–33.

104 M.S. Drower in *Cambridge Ancient History*, 3rd ed., vol. 1, pt 2, p. 321.

105 I.J. Gelb in *Journal of Cuneiform Studies* (1961), pp. 38b, 40b.

106 *Bibl. Arch.* (1976), p. 94.

107 For the following discussion see Gelb, *Thoughts about Ibla*, pp. 9 ff.

108 Gelb speaks of Ibla and Iblaic, for our Ebla and Eblaite; see p. 40.

109 Gelb, *Thoughts about Ibla*, p. 12.

110 The third dynasty of Ur (abbreviated to Ur III) ended *c.* 2006 BC, according to the chronology adopted in the *Cambridge Ancient History* (3rd ed.).

111 *Bibl. Arch.* (1976), p. 109b.

112 For other examples see C. Renfrew, *Before Civilization* (London 1976).

113 Gelb, *Thoughts about Ibla*, pp. 8 ff.

114 Pettinato, *Riv. Bibl.* (1977), p. 234; this is not the calendar introduced by Ibbi-Sipish (pp. 164 ff.).

115 For the former, see Pettinato in *Oriens Antiquus* (1976), pp. 169–78; for the latter, R.D. Biggs, *Inscriptions from Tell Abū Salābīkh* (Chicago 1974), pp. 71 ff.

116 Gelb, *Thoughts about Ibla*, pp. 11, 13.

117 Of some of the earliest texts one cannot be sure whether they were written (a) in Sumerian or (b) in Akkadian but with Sumerian logograms. Probably the oldest royal (and therefore roughly datable) inscription that is demonstrably Akkadian has been published by E. Sollberger, *Ur Excavations: Texts* VIII (London 1965), p. 1; it bore the name of Mes-kiaǧanuna, of the first dynasty of Ur (*c.* 2550 BC).

118 *Orientalia* (1975), p. 364, n. 17 (tentatively); *Rendiconti della Pontificia Accademia Romana di Archeologia* (1976), pp. 47 ff. Matthiae, however, suggests 'a parallelism of experience' between the East and West Semites (*Bibl. Arch.*, 1976, p. 110a).

119 Biggs had thought tentatively of southern Iraq; see p. 157.

120 *Bibl. Arch.* (1976), p. 52a.

121 *Rendiconti della Pontificia Accademia Romana di Archeologia* (1976).

122 Edition of 20 September 1977.

123 Similarly the fact that the first known inscription in a West Semitic alphabet was found at Byblos need not imply that the alphabet was invented there, rather than anywhere else in the west Semitic area extending from Sinai to northern Syria (Gelb, *A Study of Writing*, p. 136).

124 See W.W. Hallo in *The Ancient Near East*, ed. J.M. Blum (New York 1971), pp. 39 ff.

125 Cf. Hallo, above, especially his remark that Kish lies within the 'capital district' noticed by D. Oates. The fact that Kish is mentioned at Ebla more frequently than any other Mesopotamian city may possibly be significant (*Riv. Bibl.*, 1977, p. 234).

126 For the foregoing, see Gelb, *Thoughts about Ibla*, pp. 13 ff.
127 See, for example, J. Bright, *A History of Israel* (London 1972), p. 87.
128 In that a catalogue listing them is extant; see S.N. Kramer in *Bibl. Arch.*, (1976), p. 83.
129 For example in 1952 the rendering 'let my right hand *wither*' (Hebrew *tishkah*) for Psalm 137:5b appeared in the Revised Standard Version, on the basis of a newly identified Ugaritic root *t k h* 'wither'; yet in 1965 the standard *Ugaritic Textbook* of C.H. Gordon had no trace of that meaning for the Ugaritic root, which is rendered, in the relevant passages, 'shine'.

Index